SHAKESPEARE IN PRODUCTION

MACBETH

This is a detailed account of the theatre history of Shakespeare's *Macbeth* from 1607 to the present day. The shortest of the tragedies, *Macbeth* is compressed, complex, and ambiguous and has been variously interpreted. The introduction describes major productions and performers including David Garrick, Sarah Siddons, Henry Irving, Ellen Terry, and Laurence Olivier. Sarah Siddons, the greatest Lady Macbeth, portrayed her as a ruthlessly ambitious woman who dominated her husband. Irving, on the other hand, saw Macbeth as 'a bloody-minded villain', unlike his wife, played by Ellen Terry, who was gentle and devoted. Ian McKellen and Judi Dench, in the most successful production of the last century, were united in their ambition and pursuit of evil. A detailed commentary alongside the New Cambridge Shakespeare text of the play describes how specific episodes and passages have been interpreted in the theatre.

D1194337

SHAKESPEARE IN PRODUCTION

SERIES EDITORS: J. S. BRATTON AND JULIE HANKEY

This series offers students and researchers the fullest possible staging of individual Shakespearean texts. In each volume a substantial introduction presents a conceptual overview of the play, marking out the major stages of its representation and reception. The commentary, presented alongside the New Cambridge Shakespeare edition of the text itself, offers detailed, line-by-line evidence for the overview presented in the introduction, making the volume a flexible tool for further research. The editors have selected interesting and vivid evocations of settings, acting, and stage presentation, and range widely in time and space.

MACBETH

EDITED BY
JOHN WILDERS

Emeritus Fellow
Worcester College, Oxford

CAMBRIDGE
UNIVERSITY PRESS

CAMBRIDGE UNIVERSITY PRESS
Cambridge, New York, Melbourne, Madrid, Cape Town,
Singapore, São Paulo, Delhi, Mexico City

Cambridge University Press
The Edinburgh Building, Cambridge CB2 8RU, UK

Published in the United States of America by Cambridge University Press, New York

www.cambridge.org
Information on this title: www.cambridge.org/9780521534826

First published 2004

A catalogue record for this publication is available from the British Library

ISBN 978-0-521-49562-2 Hardback
ISBN 978-0-521-53482-6 Paperback

CONTENTS

ILLUSTRATIONS

SERIES EDITORS' PREFACE

It is no longer necessary to stress that the text of a play is only its starting-point, and that only in production is its potential realised and capable of being appreciated fully. Since the coming-of-age of Theatre Studies as an academic discipline, we now understand that even Shakespeare is only one collaborator in the creation and infinite recreation of his play upon the stage. And just as we now agree that no play is complete until it is produced, so we have become interested in the way in which plays often produced – and pre-eminently the plays of the national Bard, William Shakespeare – acquire a life history of their own, after they leave the hands of their first maker.

Since the eighteenth century Shakespeare has become a cultural construct: sometimes the guarantor of nationhood, heritage, and the status quo, sometimes seized and transformed to be its critic and antidote. This latter role has been particularly evident in countries where Shakespeare has to be translated. The irony is that while his status as national icon grows in the English-speaking world, his language is both lost and renewed, so that for good or ill, Shakespeare can be made to seem more urgently 'relevant' than in England or America, and may become the one dissenting voice that the censors mistake as harmless.

'Shakespeare in Production' gives the reader, the student, and the scholar a comprehensive dossier of materials – eye-witness accounts, contemporary criticism, promptbook marginalia, stage business, cuts, additions, and rewritings – from which to construct an understanding of the many meanings that the plays have carried down the ages and across the world. These materials are organised alongside the New Cambridge Shakespeare text of the play, line by line and scene by scene, while a substantial introduction in each volume offers a guide to their interpretation. One may trace an argument about, for example, the many ways of playing Queen Gertrude, or the political transmutations of the text of *Henry V*; or take a scene, an act, or a whole play, and work out how it has succeeded or failed in presentation over four hundred years.

For, despite our insistence that the plays are endlessly made and remade by history, Shakespeare is not a blank, scribbled upon by the age. Theatre history charts changes, but also registers something in spite of those changes. Some productions work and others do not. Two interpretations may be entirely

different, and yet both will bring the play to life. Why? Without setting out
to give absolute answers, the history of a play in the theatre can often show
where the energy and shape of it lie, what has made it tick, through many
permutations. In this way theatre history can find common ground with
literary criticism. Both will find suggestive directions in the introductions
to these volumes, while the commentaries provide raw material for readers to
recreate the living experience of theatre, and become their own eye-witness.

J. S. Bratton
Julie Hankey

This series was originated by Jeremy Treglown and published by Junction
Books, and later by Bristol Classical Press, as 'Plays in Performance'. Four
titles were published; all are now out of print.

ACKNOWLEDGEMENTS

Two studies of the theatrical history of *Macbeth* have been invaluable in the preparation of this book. They are Dennis Bartholomeusz, *Macbeth and the Players* (Cambridge, 1969) and Marvin Rosenberg, *The Masks of Macbeth* (Newark, DE, 1978). No doubt I have been influenced by both books in ways of which I am unaware, but when I have been conscious of their influence, I have acknowledged it. I am grateful for the assistance I have received from the librarians of the Bodleian Library, the British Library, the London Theatre Museum, the Harvard Theater Collection, the Shakespeare Centre at Stratford-upon-Avon, and the library of Middlebury College, Vermont. I should also like to thank the series editors, Professor J. S. Bratton and Julie Hankey, for the care with which they read my typescript and the valuable criticisms and suggestions they made.

PRODUCTIONS

This is a selective list of productions of *Macbeth* mentioned in the text together with the year of first performance and the names of the players of the two principal roles. The name of the director is given when he is not also the principal actor. The following sources were consulted: the collection of playbills and newspaper cuttings in the Theatre Museum in London and the Harvard Theater Collection; John Genest, *Some Account of the English Stage from the Restoration to 1830*, 10 vols., Bath, 1832; *The London Stage 1660–1800*, edited by William Van Lennep and others, 11 vols., Carbondale, IL, 1963–8; Charles Beecher Hogan, *Shakespeare in the Theatre*, 2 vols., Oxford, 1951, and Dennis Bartholomeusz, *Shakespeare and the Players*, Cambridge, 1969.

YEAR	PLAYERS	THEATRES
pre-1642	Burbage?	Globe?
1664	Betterton and Mrs Betterton	Lincoln's Inn Fields
1673	Betterton and Mrs Betterton	Dorset Garden
1707	Betterton and Mrs Barry	Queen's, Haymarket
1708	Powell and Mrs Knight	Drury Lane
1710	Mills and Mrs Knight	Queen's, Haymarket
1713	Mills and Mrs Porter	Drury Lane
1718	Quin and Mrs Knight	Lincoln's Inn Fields
1719	Quin and Mrs Bullock	Lincoln's Inn Fields
1720	Mills and Mrs Horton	Drury Lane
1721	Quin and Mrs Seymour	Lincoln's Inn Fields
1727	Quin and Mrs Berriman	Lincoln's Inn Fields
1733	Delane and Mrs Roberts	Goodman's Fields
1735	Delane and Mrs Hallam	Covent Garden
1733	Quin and Mrs Hallam	Covent Garden
1744	Garrick and Mrs Giffard	Drury Lane

YEAR	PLAYERS	THEATRES
1744	Sheridan and Mrs Pritchard	Covent Garden
1746	Garrick and Mrs Horton	Covent Garden
1748	Garrick and Mrs Pritchard	Drury Lane
1752	Barry and Mrs Cibber	Covent Garden
1754	Mossop and Mrs Pritchard	Drury Lane
1761	Sheridan and Mrs Pritchard	Drury Lane
1762	Garrick and Mrs Pritchard	Drury Lane
1764	Holland and Mrs Pritchard	Drury Lane
1768	Powell and Mrs Yates	Covent Garden
1768	Garrick and Mrs Pritchard	Drury Lane
1769	Smith and Mrs Yates	Covent Garden
1773	Macklin and Mrs Hartley	Covent Garden
1779	Henderson and Mrs Hartley	Covent Garden
1781	Henderson and Mrs Yates	Covent Garden
1785	Smith and Mrs Siddons	Drury Lane
1788	Kemble and Mrs Siddons	Drury Lane
1814	Edmund Kean and Mrs Bartley	Drury Lane
1820	Macready and Mrs Bunn	Covent Garden
1831	Macready and Miss Huddart	Drury Lane
1835	Macready and Ellen Tree	Drury Lane
1836	Macready and Mrs Bartley	Drury Lane
1840	Macready and Mrs Warner	Haymarket
1842	Macready and Helen Faucit	Drury Lane
1842	Charles and Ellen Kean	Haymarket
1843	Macready and Charlotte Cushman	Chestnut, Philadelphia
1844	Phelps and Mrs Warner	Sadler's Wells
1846	Macready and Charlotte Cushman	Princess's
1848	Macready and Fanny Kemble	Princess's
1850	Phelps and Isabella Glyn	Sadler's Wells

YEAR	PLAYERS	THEATRES	
1853	Charles and Ellen Kean	Princess's	
1857	Vitaliani and Ristori	Lyceum	
1875	Irving and Kate Bateman	Lyceum	
1876	Rossi and Glech-Pareti	Drury Lane	
1876	Salvini and Piamonte	Edinburgh	
1884	Salvini and Piamonte	Covent Garden	
1884	Marais and Sarah Bernhardt	Gaiety	
1888	Irving and Ellen Terry	Lyceum	
1898	Forbes-Robertson and Mrs Patrick Campbell	Lyceum	
1909	Hubert Carter and Lillah McCarthy	Grand, Fulham	Poel
1911	Beerbohm Tree and Violet Vanbrugh	His Majesty's	
1926	Henry Ainley and Sybil Thorndyke	Prince's	Casson
1928	Eric Maturin and Mary Merrall	Court	Ayliff
1930	Gielgud and Martita Hunt	Old Vic	Williams
1932	Malcolm Keen and Margaret Webster	Old Vic	Carrick
1933	George Hayes and Fabia Drake	Stratford	Komisarjevsky
1934	Charles Laughton and Flora Robson	Old Vic	Guthrie
1937	Olivier and Judith Anderson	Old Vic	Saint-Denis
1942	Gielgud and Gwen Ffrangcon-Davies	Piccadilly	
1947	Michael Redgrave and Ena Burill	Aldwych	Houghton
1948	Orson Welles and Jeanette Nolan	Film	
1952	Ralph Richardson and Margaret Leighton	Stratford	Gielgud
1954	Paul Rogers and Ann Todd	Edinburgh	Benthall
1955	Olivier and Vivien Leigh	Stratford	Byam Shaw

YEAR	PLAYERS	THEATRES	
1956	Paul Rogers and Coral Browne	Old Vic	Benthall
1957	Toshiro Mifune and Isuzu Yamada	*Throne of Blood* (Film)	Akira Kurosawa
1962	Eric Porter and Irene Worth	Stratford	McWhinnie
1966	Alec Guinness and Simone Signoret	Royal Court	Gaskill
1967	Paul Scofield and Vivien Merchant	Stratford	Hall
1971	Jon Finch and Francesca Annis	Film	Polanski
1974	Nicol Williamson and Helen Mirren	Stratford	Nunn
1976	Ian McKellen and Judi Dench	Other Place, Stratford	Nunn
1986	Jonathan Price and Sinead Cusack	Stratford	Noble
1993	Alan Howard and Anastasia Hille	National	Eyre
1994	Derek Jacobi and Cheryl Campbell	Barbican	Noble
1996	Roger Allam and Brid Brennan	Stratford	Albery
1999	Antony Sher and Harriet Walter	Swan, Stratford	Doran

INTRODUCTION

JACOBEAN 'MACBETH'

Macbeth, like *Julius Caesar*, is a play about a political assassination and a consequent civil war, and in both plays the pivotal episode is the assassination itself. Everything before the murder of Duncan leads up to it and everything after the murder follows as a result of it. In comparison with the earlier tragedy, however, *Macbeth* is predominantly a private, intimate drama. There are no public orations, no turbulent crowds; the murder of Duncan, unlike that of Caesar, takes place off stage and not in a public arena, and Macbeth's prolonged inner disintegration is more significant than his death. The most dramatically tense episodes consist of soliloquies or conversations between two people, especially Macbeth and his wife, and the longest scene, the 'England' scene (4.3), consists largely of a dialogue between Malcolm and Macduff. The focus of attention is consistently on the feelings, the states of mind, of the principal characters, and on the influence of one character on the mind of another.

These predominantly intimate passages are interspersed with more public, visually spectacular episodes such as Duncan's arrival with his retinue at Inverness with 'torches' and to the music of 'hautboys' (1.6.0 SD); the sequence following the discovery of Duncan's murder (2.3.55–110), when the stage rapidly becomes crowded with characters; the mysterious sinking of the witches' cauldron (4.1.104 SD), also to the sound of 'hautboys'; the supernatural vision of the eight kings presented by the witches to Macbeth (4.1.110 SD); and the entry of Malcolm's soldiers under the camouflage of their 'leafy screens' (5.6.0 SD).

Shakespeare also made good use of the limited sound effects at his disposal. The witches always arrive to the sound of thunder; there is a 'drum within' (signifying battle) as Macbeth and Banquo make their first entrance (1.3.27 SD); a bell sounds as the signal for Macbeth to enter Duncan's chamber (2.1.61 SD); an owl shrieks as he commits the murder (2.2.2 SD); there is a prolonged knocking at the castle gate immediately after the murder (2.2.68 SD–76 SD), and a loud 'alarum bell' is rung after it has been discovered (2.3.74 SD). Simple though these sounds are, they are made dramatically expressive and powerful by their timing, the precise moments at which they occur.

I

The intimate tone of the play may indicate that it was originally designed to be performed not at the Globe, a large public auditorium which held several thousand spectators, and where Shakespeare's company regularly acted, but in a smaller, more private setting. It would have been ideally suited for the Blackfriars, a small, indoor theatre, but *Macbeth*, by general consent, was probably written late in 1606 and the company did not begin to use the Blackfriars until three years later. It is possible that it was first performed not in a public theatre but at the court because, as a result of the increasing number of deaths from the plague, public performances were prohibited between June 1606 and early the following year (Barroll, *Politics*, p. 144). A theory has been proposed that it was acted for the first time on 7 August 1606 at Hampton Court where the reigning monarch, James I, entertained his brother-in-law, Christian IV of Denmark (Paul, *Royal Play*, pp. 2; 239). Certainly the company was paid in October of that year for putting on three plays (unnamed) 'before his Ma and the kinge of Denmarke two of them at Grenewich and one at Hampton Courte' (Paul, *Royal Play*, pp. 41, 329). Since the play is not specifically named as *Macbeth*, however, this idea can be no more than a hypothesis. It would, of course, be performed regularly at the Globe, where the astrologer Simon Forman, according to the manuscript 'Bocke of Plaies' attributed to him, saw it in April 1611 (Chambers, *Shakespeare*, vol. II, pp. 337–8). Doubt has been cast, however, on the authenticity of the 'Bocke of Plaies'.[1]

---

1 Forman's 'Bocke of Plaies' is one of a number of documents first published in 1836 by John Payne Collier in his *New Particulars Regarding the Works of Shakespeare*. It purports to contain the earliest extant accounts of the performance of three of Shakespeare's plays on the days when Forman saw them. The account of *Macbeth* at the Globe consists of a synopsis of the plot, parts of which do not appear in the text but have apparently been derived from Shakespeare's source, the *Chronicles* of Holinshed. There are other details which do not correspond to the play and some significant episodes, such as the 'cauldron' scene (4.1), are not mentioned. Collier was a notorious forger and other documents printed or referred to in *New Particulars* are known to be spurious. The authenticity of the 'Bocke of Plaies' was seriously challenged by S. A. Tannenbaum in his *Shakespearian Scraps* (New York, 1933), but its genuineness was reasserted by John Dover Wilson and R. W. Hunt in 'The Authenticity of Simon Forman's *Bocke of Plaies*', *Review of English Studies*, vol. 23, no. 91, July 1947, pp. 193–200. In 'Simon Forman's "Bocke of Plaies" Examined', *Notes and Queries*, new series, vol. 5, no. 1, January 1958, pp. 9–14, Sydney Race concludes that it is a forgery, but the biographer of Forman, Barbara Howard Traister (*Works and Days*, p. 171), believes he was the author and simply confused Shakespeare with Holinshed.

Whereas performances at the Globe, which was open to the sky, had to take place during daylight hours, indoor performances, such as those given at the court and the Blackfriars, were lit artificially by candles and could be given at night, thus allowing the effect of darkness to be created literally. Darkness plays a significant role in *Macbeth*, and several of its episodes take place at night. Such scenes are usually indicated by stage directions calling for torches, as in Duncan's arrival at Inverness (1.6) and the scene (1.7) in which he is feasted off stage. The murders of both Duncan and Banquo take place at night, as does Lady Macbeth's sleep-walking where she enters 'with a taper' (5.1.15 SD). Darkness is invoked by Macbeth who, horrified by the deed he is tempted to commit, calls on it as a means of concealing his own evil impulses:

> Stars, hide your fires,
> Let not light see my black and deep desires,
> The eye wink at the hand. Yet let that be,
> Which the eye fears when it is done to see.
>
> (1.4.50–3)

The darkness which enfolds many of the early scenes is accompanied by repeated verbal references to night and becomes associated with the pervasive impression of evil which is unique to this play:

> Light thickens,
> And the crow makes wing to th'rooky wood;
> Good things of day begin to droop and drowse,
> Whiles night's black agents to their preys do rouse.
>
> (3.2.50–3)

At indoor performances, the stage could be made literally dark, but in the daylight of the Globe its pervasiveness could be vividly imagined as a result of Shakespeare's repeated allusions to it.

In 1606, when *Macbeth* was probably first acted, it had a number of topical associations which are now largely forgotten. Shakespeare's only Scottish play was written shortly after England's only Scottish king came to the throne. James VI of Scotland became James I of England in 1603, and one of his first acts was to take Shakespeare's company, the Lord Chamberlain's Men, under his patronage, and thereby to give them their new title of the King's Men (Chambers, *Elizabethan Stage*, vol. II, p. 208). In the following year they put on *The Tragedy of Gowrie*, a play now lost, but presumably based on an incident which had occurred four years earlier when James narrowly escaped being murdered by the Earl of Gowrie, while a guest at the Earl's castle in Perth (Willson, *James*, pp. 126–30; Kernan, *Playwright*,

p. 60). The event was kept fresh in people's minds because James had instituted an annual day of thanksgiving, Gowrie Day, on 5 August, the anniversary of his miraculous escape from death, and, after he became King of England, the feast was observed there as well as in Scotland (Willson, *James*, p. 172). The play may have been designed as an offering to the company's new patron, and to appeal to popular interest in the monarch. Certainly it attracted large audiences, but after two performances it was stopped by the authorities because it was thought 'unfit that Princes should be played on the stage in their lifetime' (Chambers, *Elizabethan Stage*, vol. I, p. 328). The incident at Gowrie House, moreover, was by no means the only attempt on James's life and he lived in constant fear of assassination. The most recent attempt had taken place less than a year before *Macbeth* was written. In November 1605, a plot was discovered to blow up parliament at the opening of the new session when the King, the Queen, and Prince Henry were to be present. The interception of the plotters is, of course, still celebrated annually in Britain with fireworks and bonfires on the day, 5 November, on which the explosion was to have occurred. *Macbeth* is often linked with or thought to be in some way inspired by the Gunpowder Plot, but the secretive murder of Duncan does not obviously resemble an attempt to blow up the King and parliament. In dramatising the assassination of a Scottish king, Shakespeare could have awoken the memories of similar incidents, and, indeed, two were reported in 1606. The first was rumoured in March when James was on a hunting expedition and the other was supposedly planned in July by a group of English Catholics (Barroll, *Politics*, pp. 139, 142–3). In any case, Englishmen at the time of James's accession seem to have regarded Scottish history as a chronicle of violence. When, in 1606, the House was discussing the union of the two countries, one member, Sir Christopher Piggott, declared of the Scots, 'They have not suffered above two kings to die in their beds these 200 years' (Bullough, *Sources*, vol. VII, pp. 428–9). To Shakespeare's first audiences, the murder of Duncan could have seemed like a characteristic episode from Scottish history.

There are other features of the tragedy which had a particular interest for the King, as several scholars have pointed out. He believed in the diabolical powers of witches, and was the author of a treatise on the subject, the *Daemonologie* (1597), reprinted in the year of his accession to the English throne. In 1590–1 there had been extensive trials for treason by sorcery during which it was alleged that over three hundred witches had gathered to destroy the King (Larner, *Witchcraft*, p. 9), and he himself interrogated many of them. A further connection with James I is the presence in *Macbeth* of Banquo, a legendary Scottish nobleman of the eleventh century, from whom he claimed to be descended. Indeed Holinshed's *Chronicles* (1577; 1587), the principal source on which Shakespeare drew for this play, includes a detailed geneal-ogy of the kings who had descended from Banquo, ending with the then James VI of Scotland. It was from this material that Shakespeare created the 'show' of eight kings presented by the witches to Macbeth (4.1.110 SD). These are the descendants of Banquo and ancestors of James, who, anx-ious to establish his ancient and royal lineage, commissioned the drawing of an elaborate family tree with Banquo at the root (Kernan, *Playwright*, p. 77).

It is beyond dispute, therefore, that a number of central elements in *Mac-beth* (and there are others; see Braunmuller, pp. 5–15) associate the play with the reigning monarch. Had James not recently come to the throne, this play would probably not have been written. What is not clear, however, is the function it may have been designed to serve. Some scholars (Paul, Kernan) believe that *Macbeth* was written as a tribute to the company's patron, but it would be odd if Shakespeare depicted the murder of one Scottish king as a way of complimenting another. The King's Men appear to have learned from their experience with *Gowrie* not to depict the reigning monarch or episodes from his life on the public stage, but in *Macbeth* they avoided this difficulty by depicting some of his major preoccupations. As Kernan observes of *Mea-sure for Measure*, Shakespeare 'construc[ed] a fiction that explored the king's concerns . . . without seeming to go near actual affairs of state' (*Playwright*, p. 79).

What kind of acting did James and his subjects actually see? So few accounts of Jacobean acting have survived that it is impossible to recon-struct it in any detail, but there appears to have been a reaction against the exaggerated, bombastic manner encouraged some twenty years earlier by the popularity of Marlowe's *Tamburlaine*. It was to this style that Ben Jonson referred with contempt in his *Timber or Discoveries* (1640), where he described the '*scenicall* strutting, and furious vociferation' of the '*Tamer-lanes*, and *Tamer-Chams* of the late Age' (*Works*, vol. VIII, p. 587; Armstrong, 'Actors', p. 196), and it is to such mannerisms that Hamlet objects when he speaks of players who have 'so strutted and bellowed that I have thought some of nature's journeymen had made men, and not made them well, they imitated humanity so abominably' (3.2.27–9). The new style, appropriate for the acting of *Hamlet* itself, was much more restrained and naturalistic; the actor did not so much 'perform' a role as appear to transform himself into the character he was playing, 'as if the personator were the thing per-sonated' (Heywood, *Apology*, p. 250). 'Suit the action to the word, the word to the action, with this special observance, that you o'erstep not the modesty of nature', says Hamlet (3.2.15–16), in an informal, relaxed speech which invites this kind of delivery.

The supreme practitioner of this art in Shakespeare's time was Richard Burbage, the first man to speak Hamlet's words on the stage. We do not know for certain that he played Macbeth but we do know that, in addition to Hamlet, he played Lear and Othello, and it is unlikely that the man who undertook these major tragic roles would not also be cast as Macbeth. The intimate quality of the writing, mentioned above, would have suited what we know of Burbage's style very well. He is said to have been able to transform himself totally into the role he was playing, 'putting off himself with his Cloaths, as he never (not so much as in the Tyring-house) assum'd himself again until the play was done' (Flecknoe, *Discourse*, p. 95). He could 'artfully vary and modulate his Voice, even to know[ing] how much breath he is to give to every syllable' and could 'animat[e] his words with speaking and Speech with Action' (*ibid.*) in much the way that Hamlet recommended.

The role of Lady Macbeth was almost certainly played by a boy, as were all women's roles at the time. It is an unusually demanding part in that the actor is required to express a wide range of mature emotions and must, at times, dominate Macbeth. It has been suggested that he was John Rice (Bartholomeusz, *Players*, p. 11), but there is no evidence that Rice was the actor, and some scholars believe that the first Lady Macbeth was not a boy but a young man (Braunmuller, p. 264).

Lady Macbeth is one of a number of powerful Shakespearean women who tend to dominate the men with whom they are associated. These include Queen Margaret in the three parts of *Henry VI*, Cleopatra, Volumnia, and Beatrice in *Much Ado About Nothing*. In his introduction to *Much Ado* in this present series, John D. Cox points out that 'gender issues were particularly prominent in the ideological ferment in late sixteenth- and early seventeenth-century England', and that 'assertive, independent, loquacious and insubordinate women were frequently regarded with disquiet as threats to be contained' (Cox, p. 4). Whereas in comedy such disquiet could be sublimated through laughter, in tragedy it could not, and such women in the tragedies are portayed as unnatural and their influence on the men disastrous. This was still the attitude to Lady Macbeth in the early nineteenth century when James Boaden expressed admiration for Siddons's portrayal of the character as 'the true and perfect image of the greatest of all natural and moral depravations – *a fiend-like woman*' (Boaden, *Siddons*, vol. II, p. 137). By the middle of the century, however, when anxiety about such issues had become less acute, the interpretation of Lady Macbeth began to change. Helen Faucit portrayed her as a woman devoted to her husband, and Ellen Terry saw her as 'full of womanliness' and 'capable of *affection – she loves her husband*' (Manvell, 'Terry's Lady Macbeth', p. 161). These changes, in turn, affected the interpretation of Macbeth who, as played by Kemble, was an essentially noble man who degenerates under the influence of his wife (played by Siddons), whereas Irving, who partnered Terry, saw him as 'a bloody-minded hypocritical villain' (Furness, p. 470). Most recently, neither character has dominated the other and McKellen and Dench in 1996 were equals who conceived and plotted the murder of Duncan together.

Who took over the role of Macbeth from Burbage after his death in 1619 is not known. In 1642 the theatres were closed by act of parliament and the kind of playhouses for which Shakespeare had written were destroyed. The Globe was demolished in 1644 and the Blackfriars was pulled down later to make way for 'tenements'. When, after the restoration of Charles II in 1660, public theatrical performances started again, they took place in different kinds of theatres and were designed for different kinds of audiences.

RESTORATION 'MACBETH': DAVENANT

Shortly after his return to England, the new king granted two licences, one in his own name and the other in that of his brother, the Duke of York, to form theatrical companies and present plays in public. Such licences were considered necessary as a form of censorship, because plays were said to have been presented which 'do contain much matter of profanation and scurrility, so that such kind of entertainments if well managed might serve as moral instructions in human life' (Thomas and Hare, *Restoration England*, pp. 11–12). One of these patents was granted to Thomas Killigrew, who had been a groom of the King's bedchamber, and who established his company initially at Gibbons' Tennis Court in Vere Street and, in 1663, moved them to the King's House in Drury Lane. The other patent was awarded to Sir William Davenant whose company performed from 1661 at Lisle's Tennis Court, near Lincoln's Inn Fields. Because Killigrew's company included most of the older actors who had worked before the closing of the theatres, they were given exclusive rights to put on pre-Restoration plays, and Davenant was obliged to petition the King in December 1660 for the right to perform at least some old plays. He was thereupon given the rights to eleven plays, nine of which were by Shakespeare (Thomas and Hare, *Restoration England*, p. 13). These included *Macbeth* which the company presented for the first time in 1664, appropriately enough on 5 November (*London Stage*, Part I, p. 85). The text which they used may have been Shakespeare's but was more probably an altered version of the original made by Davenant, who had earlier conflated *Measure for Measure* and *Much Ado about Nothing* under the title *The Law against Lovers* and was later to collaborate with Dryden in a new version of *The Tempest*.

In his alteration of *Macbeth* (published in 1674) the skeleton of Shake-speare's tragedy is clearly visible but Davenant made substantial additions and deletions and revised the dialogue radically throughout (Spencer, *Davenant's 'Macbeth'*, pp. 6–8; Bartholomeusz, *Players*, pp. 15–24). He wrote an additional scene for Lady Macbeth during which she is haunted by the ghost of Duncan in a way designed to parallel the haunting of Macbeth by the ghost of Banquo. But the largest addition was the expansion of the role of Lady Macduff who appears in four new scenes, the first with Lady Macbeth, the second with her husband in which they are visited by the witches, the third in which she tries to dissuade him from opposing Macbeth, and the fourth where, hearing of Banquo's murder, she urges Macduff to flee to England. Her one scene in Shakespeare's original is considerably short-ened and her son's murder does not occur on the stage (see commentary p. 180).

Davenant clearly enlarged Lady Macduff's part in order to provide a foil for Lady Macbeth. Whereas the latter incites her husband to kill Duncan, the former urges Macduff not to oppose Macbeth but to leave vengeance to the hand of God. Unlike Lady Macbeth, who is elated by the witches' prophecy, Lady Macduff urges her husband to disregard them. Davenant obviously attempted to create a contrast between the two women, the one dedicated to evil, the other (who tends to speak in rhymed couplets) to good. At the same time he gave greater opportunities for the actresses who were now appearing on the stage in the roles formerly undertaken by boys. The drunken Porter was excised entirely, as being inappropriate in a tragedy, and the 'England' scene (4.3), considerably shortened, was inexplicably shifted to Birnham Wood.

By now, *Macbeth* had, of course, lost the topical significance it had formerly held for James I, but Davenant gave it a new topicality by creating a parallel between Malcolm and Charles II. It became 'the story of a young prince whose father is murdered, who goes into exile in a foreign court, and who returns to regain the crown that is rightfully his and to reward his followers'. To make sure that the audience noticed the parallel, Davenant 'lengthened the rejoicing at Malcolm's return . . . and brought Fleance, an ancestor of the Stuarts, back to participate in the general rejoicing. He returns not from Ireland but [like Charles II] from France' (Spencer, *Davenant's 'Macbeth'*, pp. 2, 3).

In addition to these alterations, Davenant rewrote much of the dialogue in a style which suited Restoration literary taste. In the Preface to his version of *Troilus and Cressida* Dryden remarks that 'in the present age the tongue in general is so much refined since Shakespeare's time that many of his words, and more of his phrases are scarce intelligible. And of those which we understand, some are ungrammatical, others coarse, and his whole style is so pestered with figurative expressions, that it is as affected as it is obscure' (*Criticism*, p. 159). To judge from his revision of *Macbeth*, Davenant very much agreed with him. When, for instance, the messenger brings news of the advance of Malcolm's army on Dunsinane, Shakespeare's Macbeth cries out

> The devil damn thee black, thou cream-faced loon.
> Where got'st thou that goose-look?   (5.3.11–12)

Davenant's Macbeth merely enquires

> Now, Friend, what means thy change of Countenance? (*Macbeth*, 1674, p. 58)

The dialogue between them which follows is similarly made plainer and more lucid:

(a) IN SHAKESPEARE

SERVANT   There is ten thousand –
MACBETH   Geese villain?
SERVANT   Soldiers, sir.
MACBETH   Go prick thy face and over-red thy fear,
              Thou lily-livered boy. What soldiers, patch?
              Death of thy soul, those linen cheeks of thine
              Are counsellors to fear.

(b) IN DAVENANT

MESS.   There are Ten Thousand, Sir,
MACBETH   What, Ghosts?
MESS.   No, Armed men.
MACBETH   But such as shall be Ghosts ere it be Night.
              Art thou turn'd Coward too, since I made thee Captain:
              Go Blush away thy Paleness, I am sure
              Thy Hands are of another Colour; thou hast Hands
              Of Blood, but looks of Milk.

Davenant replaces Shakespeare's characteristically metaphorical style with a simpler, more literal one. That is no doubt why his version was so popular and held the stage continuously until, seventy years later, Garrick went a long way towards restoring Shakespeare's original.

Before the war, Davenant had managed to win the favour of Charles I by writing masques and entertainments for the court. His *Salmacida Spolia* (1640), in which the King and Queen themselves acted, showed the banishment of Discord by the wisdom of Charles I and, in the concluding spectacle, magnificently designed by Inigo Jones, 'a Heaven opened full of Deities, which celestiall Prospect, with the Chorus below, filled the whole Sceane with apparitions and harmony' (Davenant, *Salmacida Spolia*, D3–D3v; Odell, *Betterton to Irving*, vol. I, p. 93). Presented as it was on the eve of civil war, this was the last real court masque to be performed in England, but Davenant was able to give renewed expression to his taste for spectacle in his productions at Lincoln's Inn Fields after the Restoration. Hence his version of *Macbeth* included extensive additional songs and dances for the witches, who made their entrances and exits 'flying'. Moreover, they were played as buffoons by actors who were well known for their performances in comic roles. At the time when *Macbeth* was originally written, belief in witchcraft was widespread and the trials and burnings of witches were more frequent than at any other time in British history, but by the Restoration, such beliefs had declined and the change is clearly reflected in Davenant's treatment of the weird sisters. They were no longer portrayed seriously as agents of the devil but as 'vaudevillians' (Bartholomeusz, *Players*, pp. 17–18), and Davenant consequently removed from the play the impression that Macbeth and his wife become agents of the supernatural forces of evil.

He also made a number of cuts, including the murder, on the stage, of Macduff's son (4.2.76–82), thereby removing a tragic irony. The scene which immediately follows the killing of the child is the 'England' scene (4.3) during most of which Macduff is unaware of his son's death. It is the revelation of it towards the end of the scene which motivates Macduff to join the rebellion (and ultimately to kill Macbeth). In Davenant's version this motive is absent.

Davenant's version was immensely popular. Pepys saw it in 1666, and was so delighted that he returned ten days later, and found it 'a most excellent play in all respects, but especially in divertisement, though it be a deep tragedy; which is a strange thing in a tragedy, it being most proper here and suitable' (*Diary*, 7 January; vol. VIII, p. 7). Three months later he saw it again and still thought it 'one of the best plays for a stage, and variety of dancing and music, that ever I saw' (*Diary*, 19 April; vol. VIII, p. 171).

Davenant greatly added to the spectacle by introducing movable scenery, again reminiscent of the masques, into the public theatre. This consisted of painted shutters which slid on and off the stage in grooves and, behind them, backcloths which could be raised and lowered (Odell, *Betterton to Irving*, vol. I, p. 91). There were even greater opportunities for music and spectacle when, after Davenant's death, the company moved into a splendid new theatre, the Dorset Garden, built on the banks of the Thames and designed by Wren at the prodigious cost of £9,000 (Nicholl, *English Drama*, vol. I,

p. 330). A production there in February 1673 is described by Davenant's prompter and book-keeper, John Downes:

> The Tragedy of *Macbeth*, alter'd by *Sir William Davenant*; being drest in all it's Finery, as new Cloath's, new Scenes, Machines, as flyings for the Witches; with all the Singing and Dancing in it; THE first Compos'd by *Mr Lock*, the other by *Mr* Channell and *Mr Joseph Priest*; it being all Excellently perform'd, being in the nature of an Opera, it Recompens'd double the Expence; it proves still a lasting Play.   (*Roscius Anglicanus*, p. 33)

The first man to play Davenant's Macbeth was Thomas Betterton, a celebrated actor of wide experience. Rowe, the first Shakespearean editor, claimed that no one was 'better acquainted with *Shakespeare's* manner of Expression and, indeed, he has study'd him so well, and is so much a Master of him, that whatever Part of his he performs, he does it as if it had been written on purpose for him, and that the Author had exactly conceiv'd it as he plays it' (*Works*, vol. 1, p. xxxiv). His style was similar to the easy naturalism attributed earlier to Burbage, and Betterton spoke warmly of Hamlet's advice to the players which he thought 'sufficient to instruct a young Player in all the Beauties of *Utterance*' (Gildon, *Betterton*, p. 83). Since he was better able to express terror than tenderness (Cibber, *Apology*, p. 69), Betterton was probably well suited for Macbeth, but he had an ungainly figure with a large head, a thick neck, fat arms, which he seldom raised higher than his stomach, a corpulent body, and large feet (Aston, *Supplement*, pp. 3–4). Yet Colley Cibber, who had worked with Betterton, declared that he had never heard a line spoken by him in a tragedy 'wherein my Judgement, my Ear and my Imagination, were not fully satisfied' (*Apology*, p. 66).

Cibber also greatly admired the Lady Macbeth of Mrs Betterton whom he thought 'a great Mistress of Nature'. No other actress, he believed (and he seems to be remembering her in the sleep-walking scene) could 'throw out those quick and careless Strokes of Terror, from the Disorder of a guilty Mind . . . with a Facility in her Manner, that render'd them at once tremendous and delightful' (*Apology*, p. 93).

Betterton appeared as Macbeth for the last time in 1709, and he died in the following year. Meanwhile the Macbeth at Drury Lane was George Powell, a man known for his exaggerated, bombastic style who, according to Francis Gentleman, 'lacked the requisite force of expression and proper disposition of features' for the role (*Censor*, vol. 1, p. 110). He was taken out of it after only a few performances, but his successor, John Mills, who played it for the first time in November 1710, went on steadily for twenty-six years. Thomas Davies, who saw his Macbeth, recalled that 'neither his manner of speaking, his action, nor his deportment, made any impression on my mind greatly to his advantage' (*Miscellanies*, vol. II, pp. 131–2). Not surprisingly, few of his contemporaries felt compelled to record their impressions of him.

While Mills was appearing at Drury Lane, a new Macbeth appeared in November 1718 at Lincoln's Inn Fields where a new theatre had been built. This was James Quin, a large, bulky man with a capacious appetite for food and drink (Davies, *Miscellanies*, vol. I, p. 249). Even in private life, his manner was so inflated that he was said to have conversed in blank verse 'which procured him respect from some, but exposed him to ridicule from others, who had discernment to see through his pomp and affectation . . . His airs of importance, and his gait, were absurd; so that he might be said to walk in blank verse as well as talk' (*Biographical Dictionary*, vol. XII, p. 234). His most celebrated role was Falstaff, for which he clearly had the physique, but Davies thought his face and figure also suited him well for Macbeth. His trouble was that he was

> deficient in animated utterance, and wanted flexibility of tone. He could neither assume the strong agitation of mind before the murder of the king, nor the remorse and anguish in consequence of it: much less could he put on that mixture of despair, rage and frenzy, that mark the last scene of Macbeth. During the whole representation he scarce ever deviated from a dull, heavy, monotony.
>
> (*Miscellanies*, vol. II, p. 133)

Smollett also complained of the monotony of Quin's voice which he described as 'a continual sing-song, like the chant of vespers, and his action resembles that of heaving ballast into the hold of a ship' (*Peregrine Pickle*, p. 274). Nevertheless, in spite of his bulk, and heavy, unvaried way of speaking, Quin acted Macbeth more than sixty times and, according to Francis Gentleman, did so 'with considerable applause' (*Censor*, vol. I, p. 109).

GARRICK, MACKLIN, SIDDONS, AND KEMBLE

The first appearance on the London stage in 1741 of David Garrick was the most exciting theatrical event of the century. As Richard III, his first role, said Davies, 'he shone forth like a theatrical Newton' (*Memoirs*, vol. I, p. 44). He was twenty-four at the time, a short, neatly built, well-proportioned man whose way of acting was entirely different from anything the London audiences had seen. Whereas Quin had been ponderous and bombastic, Garrick's delivery was extraordinarily rapid, his gestures subtle, and his whole manner easy and restrained. Garrick and Quin once appeared in the same play, Rowe's *The Fair Penitent*, then very popular. A member of the audience at this production, Richard Cumberland, still remembered years later how 'after long and eager expectation' he first saw Garrick 'then young and light and alive in every muscle and in every feature, come bounding on the stage . . . Heavens, what a transition! – it seemed as if a whole century had been stept over in the transition of a single scene' (Cumberland, *Memoirs*, p. 60).

He was able to interpret a role not only with his voice but with every part of his body. A visitor from Germany, Georg Christoph Lichtenberg, described how when Garrick turned to someone with a bow, it was not simply his head, shoulders, feet, and arms that moved but

> each member helps with great propriety to produce the demeanour most pleasing and appropriate to the occasion . . . It is therefore refreshing to see his manner of walking, shrugging his shoulders, putting his hands in his pockets, putting on his hat, now pulling it down over his eyes and then pushing it sideways off his forehead. (Lichtenberg, *Visits*, pp. 6–7)

All this was performed with the slightest movement of his limbs and with great naturalness. Not everyone admired this attention to detail, however. Charles Macklin, who had no cause to like him personally, was contemptuous of Garrick's incessant movements: '[He] huddled all passions into strut and quickness – bustle was his favourite . . . In *Archer, Ranger, Don John, Hamlet, Macbeth, Brute* – all bustle! bustle! bustle!' (Kirkman, *Macklin*, vol. I, p. 248). This was also the complaint of King George III who saw him act frequently. He told Mrs Siddons on one of her visits to Buckingham House that Garrick 'never could stand still; he was a great fidget' (Siddons, *Reminiscences*, p. 13).

By the time when, having already played Hamlet and Lear, he first undertook *Macbeth* (7 January 1744), Garrick felt so confidently established in the public favour that he took the bold step of abandoning Davenant's version and restoring almost all of Shakespeare's original, which had not been heard since the closing of the theatres over a century earlier. His determination to return to Shakespeare may well have been inspired by Samuel Johnson, whose short-lived school outside Lichfield he had attended as a boy, and who continued to be an intimate friend after they had both moved to London. Johnson was at this time contemplating his edition of Shakespeare's works and was writing his *Miscellaneous Observations on the Tragedy of Macbeth* (1745). Essentially Garrick replaced all Davenant's alterations with the original dialogue but kept some of Davenant's additional 'operatic' scenes with the witches, knowing how popular they were with audiences. He continued to omit the drunken Porter, cut much of the scene with Lady Macduff and her son, including their murders, and substantially abridged the 'England' scene (4.3). Most of his cuts became customary until Phelps restored them in 1844. Like Davenant, Garrick brought Macbeth onto the stage to die and composed for himself a dying speech in which the hero reflects on the vanity of human wishes and is overwhelmed by guilt and despair (see commentary, p. 213).

Shakespeare created Macbeth as a man of supreme courage who is capable of great brutality (especially as he is described by the bleeding Captain in 1.2.15–42) but who also has an innate, imaginative sense of right and wrong and recoils from the idea of killing the King, both when he contemplates the deed and after he has performed it. Actors can be roughly classified into those who emphasise his ruthlessness and those who accentuate his sense of guilt and horror, and Garrick clearly belonged to the latter category. An unidentified reviewer makes this clear:

> It was universally acknowledged that the involved countenance, preserved throughout all the scenes previous to the murder; the astonishing expression of horror after the commission of that execrable deed, the masterly dissimulation of the subsequent scene, through which a consciousness of guilt was suffered to betray itself; with several touches marking the agonies of a tortured mind; particularly the fixed stare, and total inattention in that passage in which Macbeth, after enlarging on the happiness of Duncan, in being removed from all sublunary ills, concludes, 'nothing can touch him further' – were equal to anything that even Mr Garrick has exhibited on the stage.
>
> (Quoted in Stone and Kahrl, *Garrick*, p. 555)

If an actor interprets Macbeth primarily as a man of acute moral sensibility, he must, ideally, play opposite a powerful, dominant Lady Macbeth who can instil into him the determination he needs to carry out the murder. Initially Garrick appeared with several different actresses but finally found his perfect counterpart in Hannah Vaughan Pritchard, a large, imposing woman with 'a natural ease of deportment and grandeur of person' (Davies, *Memoirs*, vol. II, p. 179); in Zoffany's painting of the two of them, as she takes the daggers from Macbeth, she towers over Garrick. Her features, though coarse, were said to be highly expressive (Campbell, *Siddons*, vol. I, p. 138), and her enunciation was so clear that 'not a syllable of articulation was lost' (Davies, *Memoirs*, vol. II, p. 181). Her way of acting, like Garrick's, was 'truly natural' and, like him, she expressed herself in small details. When, for example, in the banquet scene, Macbeth sees the ghost of Banquo (3.4.38–107), she attempted 'by every possible artifice' to hide his consternation from their guests (see commentary, p. 158). 'I will not separate these performers', concluded Davies, 'for the merits of both were transcendent' (p. 148).

Those who saw Garrick's *Macbeth* were so impressed by the two principals that they said little or nothing about his production generally. There is, however, a copy of Bell's 1773 edition of the play, now in the Folger Library, in which a number of manuscript stage directions have been written, perhaps

1 'Give me the daggers' (2.2.56). Henry Fuseli's impression of David Garrick and Hannah Pritchard, Drury Lane Theatre, c. 1766 © 2003 Kunsthaus Zürich.

by William Hopkins, the prompter at Drury Lane, which at least indicate the scene changes. It is clear from these notes that Garrick used movable scenery to indicate changes of location, but, apart from his treatment of the visions, his production seems to have been unremarkable. After his retirement, players accustomed to the splendours of Kemble's productions recalled 'the miserable pairs of flats that used to clap together on even the stage trodden by Mr Garrick; architecture without selection or propriety; a hall, a castle, or a chamber; or a cut wood of which all the verdure seemed to have been washed away' (Downer, *Macready*, p. 21). Garrick apparently made very little attempt to interpret the play visually. The first step in that direction was taken later in the century by Charles Macklin.

Macklin was seventeen years older than Garrick, and when the latter burst onto the theatrical scene, Macklin was already a well-established actor. By far his greatest role was Shylock, which he played in the same year (1741) as Garrick made his debut as Richard III. His success was due partly to his naturally 'saturnine cast of countenance' and 'hollow toned voice' which equipped him well for Shylock. His features are said to have been 'rigid' and his eyes 'colourless', yet 'the earnestness of his manner and sterling sense of his address, produced an effect in Shylock that has remained, with one exception, unrivalled' (Doran, *Servants*, vol. III, p. 76). He also had an easy, familiar way of speaking, an innovation generally attributed to Garrick but which Garrick may well have learned from him. One critic remarked at the time that there was 'more and more nature in playing' and 'nothing of the recitative of old tragedy', an improvement which he attributed to Macklin (Hill, *Actor*, p. 194).

Macklin prepared his production of *Macbeth*, which opened at Covent Garden in 1773, with great care, as may be seen from the notes he made, now preserved in a copy of James Kirkman's *Life of Macklin* in the Harvard Theater Collection. These show that he worked out in detail not simply his own performance but his interpretation of the whole play through the use of sets, music, and costumes. 'His primary aim', says his biographer William Appleton, 'was to recreate the barbaric splendours of early Scottish history' and, hence, he envisaged Dunsinane as a castle 'whose halls were adorned with helmets, dirks, stuffed boars' and wolves' heads' (*Macklin*, p. 171). He visualised the 'cauldron' scene (4.1) as taking place in a 'deep cave' surrounded by high rocks 'and down the back part must be a winding way for Macbeth's [*sic*] to come and meet the witches'. When the cauldron sinks 'there [should] be a great crash of screaming discordant musick – at – an eternal [curse] fall on you – and after Mac says why sinks that cauldron & what noise is this there must be a loud flourish or prelude of musick to introduce the eight visions' (Appleton, *Macklin*, pp. 172–3). He was the first man to attempt to give a production of the tragedy a conceptual unity, far in advance of his time, and to that extent he assumed the role of a modern director.

Macklin broke with the tradition which went back to Davenant's time and represented the witches seriously (*St James's Chronicle*, 28–30 October 1773; Bartholomeusz, *Players*, p. 89). He was also the first producer in London to present *Macbeth* in 'old Caledonian' dress, an idea which Garrick had contemplated but never managed to accomplish.[2] Garrick himself had always worn eighteenth-century court dress with a tie wig, a three-quarter-length embroidered coat, and knee breeches, a costume which, according to a correspondent in the *St James's Chronicle* (28–30 October 1773), made him look, on his entrance into the witches' cave, 'like a Beau, who had unfortunately slipped his Foot and tumbled into a Night Celler [*sic*], where a Parcel of old Women were boiling Tripe for their Supper'. Macklin's dress, on the other hand, was recognisably Scottish. In the first and last acts, he

2   Macklin was not, in fact, the first director to use costumes of this kind for *Macbeth*. There was a production in Edinburgh in December 1757 'with the characters entirely new dress'd after the manner of the ancient Scots' (Dibdin, *Annals*, p. 95).

2 Charles Macklin in 'ancient Scottish dress', Covent Garden, 1773.

wore a Balmoral bonnet with a feather, a knee-length tunic, a tartan plaid tied round his neck and hanging down his back, and calf-length tartan stockings. In Acts 3 and 4 he wore more conventional court dress (Byrne, 'Costuming', p. 55; Appleton, *Macklin*, p. 175).

The idea that theatrical costumes should be those of the time and country in which a play was set had already been put forward as being more true to 'nature'. Thomas Wilkes, in his *General View of the Stage* (1759), protested that audiences had been 'long habituated to . . . glaring impropriety and negligence' in historical plays, and suggested that, if the characters were to be dressed 'according to nature, and what we learn of them from their histories and pictures yet existing, it would let us much more readily into the truth of the story, and greatly beautify the representation' (Odell, *Betterton to Irving*, vol. I, pp. 451–2).

His production of the play in a specifically Scottish setting and in Highland dress was an expression of a growing interest in the Scots and Scottish culture which had begun to appear some thirty years earlier, following the defeat of Charles Edward Stuart ('Bonny Prince Charlie') at Culloden in 1745. 'In 1745 they [the Scots] had been feared as dangerous rebels. But after 1746, when their distinct society crumbled so easily, they combined the romance of a primitive people with the charm of an endangered species' (Trevor-Roper, 'Highland Tradition', p. 25). Recognising that they no longer had any hope of reinstating a Stuart on the throne, the Scots preserved their identity in other ways: by wearing the highland plaid as an expression of their nationality, and the cultivation and imitation of Scottish folk song. The taste for things Scottish spread south, and 'Tory gentlemen in England, who had done little to assist the Rising, wore tartan waistcoats in the House of Commons, and tartan became a fashionable statement of opposition to the government' (Pittock, *Invention*, p. 64). This enthusiasm was encouraged by the immense popularity of James Macpherson's prose poems *Fingal* (1762) and *Temora* (1763), (ten years before Macklin's production) which depicted an idealised, nostalgic, imaginary vision of Scotland's past,

> a strange, remote, exotic, ancient world, peopled by grandly heroic characters who move with a kind of stately dignity across wild and barren landscapes of mountains, crags, rivers, seas, clouds, and mists.
> (Hook, 'Scotland and Romanticism', quoted in Pittock, *Invention*, p. 74)

This was the kind of landscape with which Macklin's *Macbeth* opened.

He was given a very mixed reception. The *Morning Chronicle* was generally approving, especially towards the sets and costumes which were said to 'do Mr Macklin great credit . . . The Quadrangle of Macbeth's castle, and the door which is supposed to lead to Duncan's apartment (both of which are entirely new) are additions of consequence to the exhibition of the play . . . The Banquet was superbly set out, and it must be confessed that the managers seem to have spared neither cost nor assiduity to ornament and add to the effect of the representation' (30 October 1773). Macklin himself was said to have studied the character of Macbeth 'with peculiar and profound attention', and the *London Evening Post* found 'more thinking . . . more *sense* in his emphasis . . . than any other actor I have seen' (Appleton, *Macklin*, p. 179). But he was a difficult, unpopular man and abusive remarks began to appear in the newspapers even before his *Macbeth* opened. On his first entrance he was hissed by what he suspected were supporters of Garrick from Drury Lane. In one review he was ridiculed as 'a clumsy old man who looked more like a Scotch piper than a General and Prince of the blood, stumping down the Stage, at the head of a supposed conquering army' (Cooke, *Macklin*, p. 285), and a correspondent to the *Morning Chronicle* (5 November 1773) described him as 'an old toothless dotard, with the voice of a tired boatswain'. By now he was over seventy and took these comments as personal insults. Before the second performance, he appeared before the audience with a bundle of newspaper cuttings in his hand, and accused his detractors of leading a planned conspiracy against him. Although there were continued tumults among the audience, this particular performance continued, but a week later there was a riot in the theatre, and Macklin was dismissed (*London Stage*, vol. VIII, pp. 1754–7; Appleton, *Macklin*, pp. 178–86). It was a sad end to what had been a brilliantly original conception.

For one London theatrical season, Garrick appeared with the greatest actress of the next generation, Sarah Siddons. Having heard enthusiastic reports of her performances in Cheltenham, he brought her to London in 1775 to play, among other roles, Portia (Siddons, *Reminiscences*, p. 4). Her performance was received only moderately well, and at the end of the season she returned to the provinces. When she came back to Drury Lane eight years later, however, she was given a totally different reception. After her opening performance in *Isabella, or The Fatal Marriage* (a popular tragedy by Thomas Southern, revised by Garrick) 'the house was drenched in tears and the greater part of the spectators were too ill to use their hands in her applause' (*Biographical Dictionary*, vol. XIV, p. 8). In Rowe's tragedy, *Jane Shore*, during that same season, she created an even more sensational effect. 'I well remember', says Boaden, 'the *sobs*, the *shrieks*, among the tenderer parts of her audiences, which manhood, at first, struggled to suppress, but at length grew proud of indulging . . . Fainting fits long and frequently alarmed the decorum of the house, filled almost to suffocation' (*Siddons*, vol. I, p. 327).

She was a tall, imposing woman whose very presence on the stage radiated great power. 'You felt awed when she was before you', exclaimed one admirer (Robson, *Play-goer*, p. 18). For Hazlitt, she was 'the only person who embodied our idea of high tragedy'. To see her for the first time was

an epoch in every one's life, and left impressions which could never be forgotten. She seemed to belong to a superior order of beings, to be surrounded by a personal awe, like some prophetess of old, or Roman matron, the mother of Coriolanus or the Gracchi . . . Her common recitation was faulty. It was in bursts of indignation, or grief, in sudden exclamations, in apostrophes and inarticulate sounds, that she raised the soul of passion to its height or sunk it in despair.

(*Dramatic Essays*, pp. 18–19)

3 Sarah Siddons holding the letter from Macbeth at the opening of 1.5,
Covent Garden, c. 1803.

Her greatest roles were of powerful women subjected to extreme stress: Constance in *King John*, Volumnia in *Coriolanus*, Hermione in *The Winter's Tale*, and Queen Katherine in *Henry VIII*.

She first played Lady Macbeth in February 1785 at Drury Lane but was not, apparently, a complete success and the *Morning Post* (3 February) was lukewarm. This may be attributed to first-night nerves – she was always anxious on opening nights – or the inadequacy of the Macbeth, William 'Gentleman' Smith, an experienced but unremarkable actor. 'I suppose him to have given what he remembered of Garrick', says Boaden, 'He *walked* the character but, though much in earnest, he never *looked* it' (*Siddons*, vol. II, p. 147). It was only when Siddons's brother, John Philip Kemble, took over after Smith's retirement, that she rose to her full greatness and from then onwards was always associated with the role.

She saw Lady Macbeth as a woman 'in whose bosom the passion of ambition has almost obliterated all the characteristics of human nature' and who is able to control her husband by means of 'all the subjugating powers of intellect and all the charms and graces of personal beauty' (Campbell, *Siddons*, vol. II, p. 10), both of which she herself possessed. Nevertheless, she could find nothing in Lady Macbeth's personality with which she could identify herself, and for this reason undertook the role with 'the utmost difficulty, nay terror' (Campbell, *Siddons*, vol. II, p. 37). She was also, she confessed, conscious of being compared with Mrs Pritchard, whose Lady Macbeth was still remembered with admiration.

In spite of these misgivings, it became her greatest role. 'The moment she seized the part, she identified her image with it in the minds of the living generation' (Campbell, *Siddons*, vol. II, p. 56), and many people recorded their impressions of her. The fullest account was written by G. J. Bell, Professor of Scottish Law at Edinburgh University, who wrote a commentary on over sixty passages, describing in detail how she interpreted them.[3] What is striking about his comments is her obvious attention to detail. Her tone and gestures could change half a dozen times in as many lines of verse. Bell's account also shows that her interpretation of the character on the stage was consistent with the view she expressed in her 'Remarks':

> Her turbulent and inhuman strength of spirit does all. She turns Macbeth to
> her purpose, makes him her mere instrument, guides, directs and inspires the
> whole plot. Like Macbeth's evil genius she hurries him on in the mad career of

3   Bell's commentary was published by Fleeming Jenkin, a colleague of his at
    Edinburgh University, in his *Papers Literary, Scientific &c* (2 vols. 1887, vol. I,
    pp. 45–66). Many of Bell's remarks are reproduced in the commentary to this
    present edition.

ambition and cruelty from which his nature would have shrunk. The flagging of her spirit, the melancholy and dismal blank beginning to steal upon her, is one of the finest lessons of true drama. The moral is complete in the despair of Macbeth, the fond regret of both for that state of innocence from which their wild ambition has hurried them to their undoing.   (Bell, 'Siddons', p. 50)

The most extraordinary part of her performance was the sleep-walking scene, which Leigh Hunt called 'sublime': 'the deathlike stare of her coun-tenance, while the body was in motion . . . and the anxious whispering with which she made her exit, as if beckoning her husband to bed, took the audi-ence along with her into the silent and dreaming horror of her retirement' (*Dramatic Criticism*, p. 72). When, during her farewell appearance on the stage in June 1812, this scene concluded, the entire house rose to its feet in an acclamation so prolonged that the performance could not continue. Kemble, the Macbeth, finally quietened the audience and asked if they would hear the rest of the play, but they all shouted 'We can hear no more!' and most of them left the theatre (*Bell's Weekly Messenger*, 5 July 1812).

'In Kemble's hand', wrote Bell, 'Macbeth is only a co-operating part' ('Siddons', p. 50), and Kemble himself acknowledged that, whenever he appeared on the stage with his sister, he was aware of her superiority (Far-ington, *Diary*, vol. VIII, p. 107). The result of their acting together in this play, whether by accident or design, was to alter the balance between the two characters. Whereas Garrick and Pritchard had played as partners and, at least until the end of the banquet scene (3.4), shared the responsibility for their actions, Kemble was dominated and overshadowed by Siddons. Moreover, Kemble regarded Macbeth as initially a good man, the purity of whose heart had hitherto been uncontaminated (Kemble, *Macbeth and Richard*, p. 31). This interpretation suited his inherent gifts and personal-ity. In every role he played, there was 'a blandness, a kindness, a suavity that spoke him to be . . . a good man and a gentleman' (Robson, *Play-goer*, pp. 26–7). Hence Lady Macbeth became largely responsible for her hus-band's corruption, a role which Siddons amply fulfilled. As a result, the audience's sense of justice at Macbeth's downfall was tempered by pity at the ruin of a formerly noble mind. 'Macbeth passes from the scene', remarked the critic of *The Times*, 'leaving a feeling in which pity predomi-nates over justice, and our natural abhorrence of his crimes is sunk in our admiration of the struggles of his virtue' (19 September 1811). Macbeth's decline and death provided the audience with a moral example, and thereby fulfilled Kemble's conception of the function of drama. 'Plays are intended', he declared, 'by employing the united powers of precept and example, to have a good influence on the lives of men' (*Macbeth and Richard*, p. 10).

To judge from the portraits, Kemble and his sister were physically rather similar. Both were tall, commanding figures with features often described as 'classical' or 'Roman' and, as one of her great roles was Volumnia, one of his was Coriolanus. Whereas audiences were unanimous in their enthusiasm for Siddons's Lady Macbeth, however, they were divided in their opinions of Kemble. He had a distinctive, idiosyncratic manner which could arouse either admiration or distaste. He was a detached, intellectual actor whose interpretation of the text was more studied than spontaneous. 'In all he did', recalled Macready, 'the study was apparent' (*Reminiscences*, vol. I, p. 150). Siddons revealed that her brother, even when he expressed violent bursts of emotion, was 'always careful to avoid any discomposure of his dress or deportment'. She herself, on the other hand, 'in the whirlwind of passion, lost all thought for such matters' (Macready, *Reminiscences*, vol. I, p. 149).

Not everyone reacted favourably to Kemble's careful, deliberate style. He had the kind of temperament, says Leigh Hunt, which 'turns everything coolly about in his mind'. But, in spite of this detachment, he could, for many people, be very moving. Hazlitt thought him the best Macbeth he had seen: 'There was a stiff, horror-stricken stateliness in his person and manner, like a man bearing up against supernal influences; and a bewildered distraction, a perplexity and at the same time a rigidity of purpose, like one who had been stunned by a blow from fate' (*Works*, vol. XVIII, pp. 341–2). Hazlitt was particularly impressed by Kemble's delivery of the speech beginning 'My way of life / Is fall'n into the sere, the yellow leaf' (5.3.22–8) which, he said, had a 'fine, thoughtful melancholy . . . The very tone of Mr Kemble's voice has something retrospective about it – it is an echo from the past' (*Works*, vol. V, p. 207).

In 1792 the Drury Lane theatre was closed for enlargements and renovations and it reopened two years later with a production of *Macbeth* in which Kemble and his sister again played the major roles. The text was essentially Shakespeare's to which Kemble had made a number of alterations. Like Davenant and Garrick, he omitted the drunken Porter and, like Garrick, he cut Lady Macbeth's entrance immediately after Duncan's murder. He left out the scene between Lady Macduff and her son, but retained the dying speech for Macbeth which Garrick had added. The witches 'no longer wore mittens, plaited caps, laced aprons, red stomachers, ruffs &c. (which was the dress of those *weird sisters* . . . with Garrick's *Macbeth*) or any human garb, but appeared as preternatural beings, distinguishable only by the fellness of their purposes, and the fatality of their delusions'. The audiences, however, were not always willing to forego the witches' dance. When Kemble toured with his production in the West Country in 1803, the audience in Bristol demanded 'the usual dance' so vociferously that the performance could not continue until their wishes were complied with (Genest, *Account*, vol. VII, p. 596). There were also objections to Kemble's other radical innovation, the omission of Banquo's ghost from the banquet. The apparition, like that of the dagger, became a creation of Macbeth's guilty mind. The disappearance of the ghost, however, was not welcomed by theatre audiences, and Kemble later submitted to popular opinion and brought him back.

When Kemble and his company moved into the enlarged Drury Lane he found that the sets from the old theatre were too small, and was compelled to build new ones (Rosenfeld, *History*, p. 97). Many of them were designed by William Capon, a man who, like Kemble, had a passionate interest in the medieval, and made meticulous sketches of old buildings, such as the Tower of London and Westminster Abbey, on which he based his designs. Kemble deserves the credit, says Rosenfeld, 'for trying to introduce settings more in keeping with the plays and for replacing the old and worn stock scenes that had hitherto been deemed good enough for Shakespeare by fresh settings designed for specific plays' (*History*, p. 100). For his *Macbeth* there were some fifteen new scenes but, 'although the production was spectacular some effort was made to give it an authentic period flavour' (*History*, p. 98). The sets and costumes were the most lavish yet designed for the play. 'The Magnificence of the Dresses', said the *Morning Post* (22 April 1794), 'the grandeur of the Processions, and the picturesque beauty of the Scenery, all correspond with that splendour and elegance, which so peculiarly belongs to this splendid Edifice.'

A fascination with the architecture of the past, and especially of the middle ages, was widespread at the time and influenced all the arts, It originated in the work of the antiquarian Sir William Dugdale who, a century earlier, had published his *Monasticon Anglicanum* (1655–73), a copious account, in three volumes, with engravings, of the medieval buildings and monuments of England. It was received by many with great enthusiasm. Anthony Wood recalls how his 'tender affections and insatiable desire for knowledge were ravish'd and melted downe by the reading of that book' (*Life and Times*, vol. I, p. 209). The *Monasticon* was followed by Dugdale's *Antiquities of Warwickshire* (1656), and numerous accounts by other antiquarians of the ancient buildings of the rest of the country. These, in the next century, inspired the architecture of the gothic revival, the poetry of Keats, Chatterton, and Tennyson, and the painting of the Pre-Raphaelites. As Sybil Rosenfeld points out, 'The desire to recreate past eras, especially in the medieval style, was one of the symptoms of romanticism which Kemble and Capon translated to the stage' (*History*, p. 100).

A good many features of Kemble's production were determined by the size of the new Drury Lane theatre. The stage was the biggest in Europe and the auditorium could hold over three and a half thousand spectators. It was, in fact, the largest theatre in London before the twentieth century (*London Stage*, Part III, p. 1569). Covent Garden was similarly enlarged fifteen years later so that it could hold an audience of 3,000. Such vast amphitheatres invited – indeed, required – casts filled out with extras (there were 'vast crowds of witches and spirits that filled the stage and thundered in the ear a music of dire potency'), and necessitated a style of acting quite unlike Garrick's, as several people pointed out:

> Mr Kemble . . . struggles against a torrent of mummery and machinery and song and spectacle, which the circumstances of the time he lives in, and of the stage he treads, renders it impossible for him to do more than struggle with; it is a turbid torrent that he cannot stem . . . All the intelligence of [Garrick's] eye, the archness of his smile, the movement of his brow, the touching pathos of his undertones, spent in their passage through the misty void, would have failed to reach the outskirts of that greedy theatre; and he would have found himself only understood in the neighbourhood of the orchestra, while the rest of the spectators would have discovered little else in the finest actor that ever lived, but the diminutiveness of his figure.
>
> (Cumberland, 'Retrospectives', p. 100)

It was impossible in such theatres to create the intimacy for which *Macbeth* had originally been designed.

KEAN, MACREADY, AND PHELPS

Shortly before Kemble's retirement, a new star suddenly appeared out of the provinces and, within a year, became the most celebrated actor on the London stage. This was Edmund Kean, a man of obscure origins who was said to have been the son of an itinerant actress who abandoned him in infancy. He was found in a doorway by a good-natured couple who brought him up in their home in Frith Street, Soho. They managed to place him in children's roles at Drury Lane, including one in Kemble's *Macbeth* (in which he misbehaved), but while still a boy, he ran away from home, walked to Portsmouth, and sailed to Madeira as a cabin boy. On his return, he became a tumbler at Bartholomew Fair where he broke both his legs. By the time he was married and had children, he was touring as an actor in the provinces, but his reputation came to the notice of the management of Drury Lane, whose stage manager came to see him in Dorchester. He was offered a contract, insisted that his first role should be Shylock, was given it, and was an instant success. 'No actor has come out in many years at all equal to him' declared Hazlitt (*Morning Chronicle*, 27 January 1814; *Works*, vol. V, p. 179), and in the following season he went on to play Richard III, Hamlet, Othello, and Iago.

He was a small, lean man whose voice did not always have the power to fill the large London theatres, but he was agile and immensely energetic. Hazlitt testifies with enthusiasm to the 'lightness and vigour in his tread, a buoyancy and elasticity of spirit, a fire and animation' (*Morning Chronicle*, 27 January 1814; *Works*, vol. V, p. 179). Indeed, he thought Kean sometimes failed from sheer exuberance of talent and 'dissipated the impression of the character by the variety of his resources' (*Works*, vol. XV, p. 181).

In personality and style he was utterly unlike Kemble, and his originality may, in part, have accounted for his success. Whereas Kemble's way of acting was often called 'gentlemanly', Kean's 'most flagrant defect' was 'want of dignity' (Robinson, *Diary*, vol. I, p. 223). Kemble had been welcomed as a member of fashionable London society, but Kean was a flamboyant ruffian who took up prizefighting, was arrested for brawling in the streets, and sometimes appeared drunk on the stage (Shattuck, *American Stage*, vol. I, p. 38). He died at the age of forty-six as a result of overwork and excessive drinking. A virtue of Kemble's conscientious approach to his roles was that he consistently pondered every word he spoke. Kean, on the other hand, was sketchy and uneven. He was 'the most singular of great actors – so inexpressibly great when successful. He seemed to play by intuition, and if for one moment his inspiration deserted him, he never recovered it' (Macready, quoted in Pollock, *Macready*, p. 32). George Henry Lewes conceded that Kean could be 'tricky and flashy', but also declared him incomparably the greatest actor he had seen.

> Critics who had formed their ideal on the Kemble school were shocked at Kean's want of dignity, and at his fitful elocution, sometimes thrillingly effective, at other times deplorably tame and careless; in their angry protests they went so far as to declare him 'a mere mountebank' . . . [But] it was impossible not to watch Kean as Othello, Shylock, Richard [III], or Sir Giles Overreach without being strangely shaken by the terror, and the pathos, and the passion of a strong spirit uttering itself in tones of irresistible power . . . Small and insignificant in figure, he could at times become impressively commanding by the lion-like power and grace of his bearing.   (*On Actors*, pp. 1–4)

The most celebrated comment on Kean was made by Coleridge who said that to see him act was 'like reading Shakespeare by flashes of lightning' (*Table Talk*, 27 April 1823; vol. I, p. 40). Between the moments of astonishing brilliance, as Coleridge implied, there were long, dull intervals. Kean created the impression of acting spontaneously, but, as Lewes explained, nothing was actually left to chance. He 'vigilantly and patiently rehearsed every detail, trying the tones until his ear was satisfied, practising looks and gestures until his artistic sense was satisfied; and having once regulated these he never changed them'. When he rehearsed on a new stage, 'he accurately counted the number of steps he had to take before reaching a certain spot, or before uttering a certain word' (Donohue, *Theatre*, p. 61).

Kean first played Macbeth during his second season at Drury Lane, on 5 November 1814. As was by now customary, it was a sumptuous production with new scenes, armour, decorations, and dresses. Locke's music, which had been associated with the play since Davenant's time, was now augmented with 'a New Overture and Act Symphonies composed and arranged by Mr Horn'. The banquet was 'not unworthy of a royal festivity' and Kean's three costumes were 'striking for costliness and taste'. The *Times* critic was 'much gratified by the general display' (7 November 1814). It was, however, one of Kean's less successful roles. We can, perhaps, deduce its limitations from a review of his Richard II in which the general fault of his acting was said to be that it is 'always energetic or nothing. He is always at full stretch – never relaxed. He expresses all the violence, the extravagance, the fierceness of the passions, but not their helplessness, and sinkings into despair' (Hazlitt, *Examiner*, 19 March 1815; *Works*, vol. v, p. 224). An actor incapable of expressing helplessness and despair will, at best, achieve a very limited interpretation of Macbeth. Hazlitt complained that 'his movements were too agile and mercurial, and he fought more like a modern fencing-master than a Scottish chieftain of the eleventh century'.

A good deal was written about Kean's unique way of acting, but little about his conception of Macbeth. A review in the *Examiner* (14 November 1814), however, makes it clear that his interpretation was quite unlike Kemble's: 'When he is invested with the title of Thane of Cawdor, nothing could be finer than his start of surprize, and the various workings of his impassioned countenace: we saw already the man hoping and determined to be king.' Again, in response to Lady Macbeth's question 'When [does Duncan] go hence?', Kean 'in an emphatic tone, and with a hesitating look . . . half divulges the secret of his breast' – "Tomorrow as he . . . *purposes*!". In other words, by means of a pause and a stress, he gave the impression that the idea of murdering Duncan had already occurred to him. From then on he appeared not the pawn of his wife's ambition but the master of his own destiny' (Playfair, *Kean*, p. 126). Whereas Kemble portrayed Macbeth as a noble character who degenerates into evil, Kean presented him as a determined, ruthless man who disintegrates through guilt and fear. Though not all the critics agreed with him, F. W. Hawkins thought that Kean did ample justice to the complexity of Macbeth's character, 'a marvellous compound of daring and irresolution, ambition and submissiveness, treachery and affection,

4 Edmund Kean with the bloody daggers (2.2.8), Drury Lane, 1814.

superstition and neglectfulness of his future, a murderer and a penitent'. Hence 'the sternest heart was taken captive', and 'pity predominated over justice' (*Kean*, vol. II, p. 269).

His Lady Macbeth, Mrs Bartley, was not even mentioned by the *Times* reviewer and Miss Campbell, who appeared with him in 1817, was 'altogether too tame and drawling . . . Some attempts at originality failed of effect from the timidity with which they were executed' (Hazlitt, *Times*, 21 October;

Works, vol. XVIII, p. 261). Kean was 'the master of his own destiny' because only he had the power control it.

He created some electrifying incidents, one of which occurred in the scene (2.2) immediately following the murder (see commentary, p. 120), but he rarely showed the steady development of a character through the whole course of a play. His younger contemporary, William Charles Macready, approached the task entirely differently. His performance was the product of rigorous study and analysis of a text, leading to the creation of a whole, consistent character. His biographer, Alan Downer, identifies his distinctive achievement:

> There was not in his finished style the alternation of bursts of volcanic power with level stretches that could barely hold the attention of an audience. At every moment he tried to hold the entire character in view, to maintain that unity of design which he thought the great distinction of Mrs Siddons.
>
> (*Macready*, p. 79)

Macready had never wanted to be an actor. As a boy at Rugby school, his hope was to go to Oxford and prepare himself for a career in the law, but his father, an actor-manager of limited competence, went bankrupt, was sent to gaol, and could, of course, no longer pay for his son's education. Macready was therefore forced to leave school at the age of fifteen but, with characteristic enterprise, he took on the management of his father's company in order to pay off his debts. In this he succeeded and when, on his father's release from gaol two years later, the latter resumed the management of the New Street Theatre in Birmingham, William Charles embarked on what was to become a long acting career by playing Romeo there with considerable success. He quickly became very versatile, and is estimated to have played over seventy parts during the four years he spent with his father's company. He never forgot, however, that he had gone into the theatre against his inclinations and always looked on the profession with distaste. Nevertheless, finding himself, however reluctantly, a member of it, he applied himself diligently to the task. Comparing the achievements of Macready and Kean, George Henry Lewes declared that the latter was 'a type of genius' and Macready 'only a man of talent, but of talent so marked and individual that it approaches very near to genius' (*On Actors*, p. 32). He was, concluded Lewes, 'undeniably a cultivated, honourable, and able man', who 'would have made an excellent clergyman or member of Parliament' (*On Actors*, p. 50). This could certainly not have been said of Kean.

He was tall, strong, and masculine but not handsome. His eyebrows swept upwards, his nose was irregular, his mouth drooped at the corners, and his jaw was large and square. A reviewer in the *News* declared him 'one of the

5 William Macready.

plainest and most awkwardly made men that ever trod the stage', but his eyes were so 'full of fire' that they could divert attention from the 'flatness of the features they irradiated' (Archer, *Macready*, p. 36). He had a rich, powerful voice which could be heard and understood in the huge London theatres of the time. It was 'extensive in compass, capable of delicate modulation in quiet passages (though with a tedency to scream in violent passages), and having tones that thrilled and tones that stirred tears' (Lewes, *On Actors*,

p. 33). His *Diaries* show that he was seldom satisfied with his own performances and, right to the end of his career, he continued to analyse his
shortcomings, and try to correct them. He rehearsed impassioned speeches
with his hands tied down to eliminate unnecessary movement, and in front
of mirrors to make 'intense passion speak from the eyes alone' (Shattuck,
American Stage, vol. I, p. 70), but his primary concern was to convey the sense
of the words: 'His intelligence always made him follow the winding meanings through the involutions of the verse, and never allowed you to feel . . .
that he was speaking words he did not thoroughly understand' (Lewes, *On
Actors*, pp. 33–4). On the other hand, he paid less attention to the flow and
rhythm of the verse, and was said to speak it like prose. 'Mr Macready', said
Leigh Hunt, 'seems afraid of the poetry of some of his greatest parts, as if
it would hurt the effect of his naturalness and his more familiar passages:
but such a fear is not a help towards nature; it is only an impulse towards
avoiding a difficulty' (*Dramatic Essays*, p. 211).

His overriding loyalty was to the play and, as he noted in his *Diaries*,
he attempted 'by giving purpose and passion to the various figures in our
group, to spread over the entire scene some portion of that energy and interest
which, heretofore, the leading actor exclusively and jealously appropriated'
(*Reminiscences*, vol. II, pp. 17–18). The scenery and costumes he used were,
consistently with the taste of the day, historically as accurate as possible, and
he created the kind of elaborate tableaux and processions which audiences
had grown to expect, but he tried not to pursue them as ends in themselves
but to subordinate them to the integrity of the work.

His first attempt at Macbeth was at Covent Garden in June 1820, and,
having performed it regularly throughout his career, he chose it for his
last appearance on the stage over thirty years later. Whereas it is possible
to identify the kind of emphasis given to the role by earlier actors – the
hypersensitivity of Garrick, the ruthless determination of Kean – Macready,
as a result of his concentration on the detail of the text, portrayed Macbeth
as a complex character whose moods fluctuate in response to his experiences.
To begin with, recalled Lady Pollock,

> he was evidently a soldier, although with his rugged aspect and his untheatrical
> walk he did not (on his first entrance) fulfil the classical idea of a tragic hero or
> of a stage warrior . . . He looked like one who had communed with himself
> among the mists of his native mountains with speculative thoughts; and it
> seemed no wonder that the agents of evil fixed upon him as a likely victim.
>
> (*Macready*, pp. 116–17)

To the witches' prophecies, this rough, primitive man was instantly respon-
sive. One could 'instinctively realise that the horrid image that unfixed his
hair and made his seated heart knock at his ribs . . . was the gory image of

the gracious Duncan, his white hair dabbled in blood' (Coleman, 'Facts and Fancies', p. 222). But Macready was also able to convey Macbeth's revulsion from the deed he had himself contemplated: 'nothing could be finer', said Lewes, 'than the indications he gave of a conscience wavering under the influence of "fate and metaphysical aid", superstitious, and weakly cherishing the suggestions of superstition'. 'But', Lewes adds, 'nothing could have been less heroic than his presentation of the great criminal':

> He was fretful and impatient under the taunts and provocations of his wife; he was ignoble under the terrors of remorse; he stole into the sleeping-chamber of Duncan like a man going to purloin a purse, not like a warrior going to snatch a crown.   (*On Actors*, pp. 34–5)

This effect may have been deliberate, an indication of the extent to which the warrior of the opening scenes had debased himself, and others approved what Lewes disliked: 'The crouching form and, stealthy felon-like step of the self-abased murderer . . . made . . . a picture not to be forgotten' (Marston, *Actors*, vol. I, p. 76).

Any actress who took on the role of Lady Macbeth at this time did so under the shadow of Mrs Siddons. She had retired only eight years before Macready mounted his first production of the play, and he appears to have looked for someone whose interpretation would most closely resemble hers. He engaged a number of different actresses, but was most satisfied with Mary Amelia Huddart (later Mrs Warner) who appeared with him at the beginning of his career, and, again, at the end of it. Both he and Phelps believed that she was 'the only possible [Lady Macbeth] since Siddons' (Coleman, 'Facts and Fancies', p. 204).

Like Siddons she excelled in 'severe, majestic characters' such as Volumnia in *Coriolanus*, Queen Gertrude in *Hamlet*, and Queen Katherine in *Henry VIII*, but although her interpretation of Lady Macbeth was similar to that of Siddons, it lacked her depth and authority. Westland Marston regarded it as a 'somewhat surface exhibition'. In the first two acts she was 'stern, set, decisive and, when the need was, impetuous and scornful', but she seemed detached from the role and was not 'seized by the will and inspired by its energy'. Nevertheless she created 'so to speak, such a consistent *physique* of Lady Macbeth . . . that she was held for years to be its most satisfactory representative' (*Actors*, vol. I, pp. 276–7).

It was while she and Macready were acting in Dublin in 1842 that Warner fell ill and he turned for help to Helen Faucit, who agreed to undertake Lady Macbeth for the first time after only one rehearsal. Faucit broke completely with tradition and, for the first time in the history of the play, portrayed Lady Macbeth as a gentle, affectionate character who, far from being driven by personal ambition, is motivated essentially by devotion to her husband. The Irish dramatist William Carlton wrote shortly after seeing her performance,

> I said to myself: this woman, it seems to me, is simply urging her husband forward through her love for him, which prompts her to wish for the gratification of his ambition, to commit a murder. This, it would appear, is her sole object . . . She perceives that he has scruples; and it is necessary that she should work upon him so far as that he should commit the crime, but at the same time prevent him from feeling revolted at the contemplation of it, and this she effects by a sanguinary sophistry that altogether hardens his heart.
>
> (Martin, *Faucit*, p. 177)

In Faucit's version, once Duncan had been murdered, Lady Macbeth had fulfilled her purpose and, from the end of the banquet scene, she became a broken, exhausted, melancholy woman. A friend wrote to her that she had made 'quite a new thing' of Lady Macbeth: 'The banquet scene, strange to say, was terribly pathetic' (Martin, *Faucit*, p. 109). This appears to have been the most moving part of her performance, and not the sleep-walking scene where she made no attempt to become the monumental tragic figure of Siddons, but 'a great lady sick to death' (Martin, *Faucit*, p. 312).

A more imposing actress was the American Charlotte Cushman of whom Macready heard when he was touring the United States in 1843. She was a tough, determined woman, physically tall, big boned, and with a raw, husky voice. With these inherent qualities she undertook several male roles, including Romeo, Hamlet, and Smike in an adaptation of Dickens's *Nicholas Nickleby*. With her forceful temperament and impressive physique, her interpretation of Lady Macbeth at the Princess's in 1846 was similar to that of Siddons, but she lacked Siddons's subtlety and variety. According to Marston,

> Her performance, it must be admitted, was powerful and greatly applauded. But inasmuch as in the guilty Queen we need the gradual and varied development of character and passion, Miss Cushman's unrelieved, level earnestness of manner . . . gave her Lady Macbeth a sameness of gloom which fatigued admiration.   (*Actors*, vol. ii, pp. 69–70)

Two years later, Macready took on another Lady Macbeth, Fanny Kemble, daughter of Charles and niece of John Philip Kemble and Sarah Siddons, whose idea of the character was slightly different. Like Cushman, she saw Lady Macbeth as possessing qualities conventionally thought of as masculine – 'energy, decision, daring, unscrupulousness; a deficiency of imagination, a great preponderance of the positive and practical mental elements; a powerful and rapid appreciation of what each exigency of circumstance demanded, and the coolness and resolution necessary for its immediate execution' (Fanny Kemble, *Notes*, p. 57). Her Lady Macbeth had none of the love and devotion which, to Faucit, had been the key to her character. On the contrary, Kemble saw her habitual tone as 'a sort of contemptuous compassion towards the husband whose moral superiority of nature she perceives and despises' (*Notes*, p. 69). She dies, not of remorse but of wickedness: 'I think her life was destroyed by sin as by a disease of which she was unconscious' (*Notes*, p. 51).

Fanny Kemble was, as she frankly admitted, far from satisfied with her own performance, perhaps because, like many of Macready's associates, she found him personally very difficult. In the letters she wrote to her friends, she conceded that he could create wonderful effects: 'All the pieces that were put on the stage under his supervision were admirable for the appropriate harmony of the scenery, decorations, dresses, and whole effect; they were carefully accurate, and extremely beautiful' (*Later Life*, vol. III, p. 377). On the other hand, his 'artistic vanity and selfishness were unworthy of a gentleman, and rendered him an object of dislike and dread to those who were compelled to encounter them' (p. 378):

> Macready . . . comes in when one is in the middle of a soliloquy, and goes off when one is in the middle of a speech to him. He growls and prowls, and roams and foams, about the stage, in every direction, like a tiger in his cage, so that I never know on what side of me he means to be; and keeps up a perpetual snarling and grumbling like the aforesaid tiger, so that I never feel quite sure that he *has done*, and that it is my turn to speak.   (*Later Life*, p. 386)

Each of them found the other painful to work with and three years later Macready turned again to Warner.

A notable member of Macready's company was Samuel Phelps, who was to become the most distinguished actor-manager of the next generation. He began his career by touring for a decade in the provinces, went on to play mostly secondary and minor roles with Macready for six years, and then took on the management of Sadler's Wells. This was made possible by the repeal in 1843 of the patent theatres monopoly, originally introduced by Charles II, whereby the performance of legitimate drama was restricted to Covent Garden, Drury Lane, and, later, the Haymarket. With the end of the monopoly, the actors became free to perform wherever they chose.

The Sadler's Wells theatre originated shortly after the Restoration when Thomas Sadler discovered a medicinal spring in his garden in Islington and created around it first a pleasure garden and then a music room for concerts. The original wooden building was replaced in 1765 by an attractive stone theatre capable of holding 2,500 people (Allen, *Phelps*, p. 82), and in 1804, a large tank was installed on the stage which was used for aquatic drama, such as shipwrecks, storms, and sea battles, which were popular at the time. The district surrounding the theatre was densely populated and shabby, full of 'small shops, taverns, cheap lodging-houses and slums' and the local population consisted of 'small tradesmen, mechanics, the commoner kind of clerks, peddlers and innumerable wage-earners of different kinds' (Allen, *Phelps*, pp. 247–8). 'There is good evidence that the lower middle class had not been seen at serious dramatic performances within living memory' and the critics never ceased to be surprised that they 'learned to appreciate Shakespeare with a discriminating taste not found in any other theatres' (Allen, *Phelps*, pp. 249–50). Phelps was applauded by John Morley for teaching 'an audience mainly composed of hard-working men, who crowd a sixpenny gallery and shilling pit, heartily to enjoy the sweetest and the noblest verse man ever wrote' (Morley, *Journal*, p. 162).

The enterprise was an immediate success. The company opened on 27 May 1844 with *Macbeth*, 'got up . . . in a style which elicited audible exclamations of astonishment from the usual visitors in the boxes. Such, too, was the curiosity excited, that it was necessary to pile up elevated forms in the lobbies for the literally overflowing audience; where, we conjecture, they could see little and hear less' (*Athenaeum*, 1 June 1844, p. 507). Although he regularly put on the work of other dramatists, it was, as he said in his farewell speech, 'the object of my life and the end of my management to represent the whole of Shakespeare's plays. I have succeeded in placing on the stage thirty-four of them, and they have been acted between three and four thousand nights' (Phelps and Forbes-Robertson, *Phelps*, p. 213).

According to Coleman, who knew him, Phelps had a mass of light brown hair which he wore in bunches over his ears. His mouth and chin were 'firm and well cut, brow square and well balanced, face oval, figure a little over middle height, slender rather than sturdy, voice deep and resonant'. He was praised for his 'ruggedness', his masculinity, his 'honest reliance on his own powers'.

> Into his acting he generally threw immense energy. He could be intense, fiery, vigorous, rough, refined, ineffably mean or magnificently grand, as occasion required. All kingly and soldierly qualities he could manifest in his matchless bearing, as his Henry V, Melantius, and Macbeth bear ample testimony and, above all, he threw into such characters a pathos which was unapproachably manly and grand.   (Phelps and Forbes-Robertson, *Phelps*, pp. 29–30)

His productions reflected Macready's influence, especially in their ensemble playing and their avoidance of spectacle for its own sake. These were the qualities singled out by Henry Morley:

> A main cause of the success of Mr Phelps in his Shakespearean revivals is, that
> he shows in his author above all things the poet. Shakespeare's plays are always
> poems, as performed at Sadler's Wells. The scenery is always beautiful, but it is
> not allowed to draw attention from the poet, with whose whole conception it is
> made to blend in the most perfect harmony. The actors are content also to be
> subordinated to the play, learn doubtless at rehearsals how to subdue excesses
> of expression that by giving undue force to one part would destroy the balance
> of the whole, and blend their work in such a way as to produce everywhere the
> right emphasis . . . Shakespeare is not fairly heard when he is made to speak
> from behind masses of theatrical upholstery, or when it is assumed that there is
> but one character in any of his plays and that the others may be acted as
> incompetent performers please.   (*Journal*, pp. 152–4)

It was also one of Phelps's achievements to return more closely than
any of his predecessors to the original texts, as he did in his production of
Macbeth. The witches' dialogue was confined to the words printed in the
Folio, and Locke's music and the songs initially added by Davenant were
abandoned. As a result the witches were no longer a crowd of singing and
dancing hags but 'three dim apparitions who breathed evil with their quiet
words' and became 'a pervading influence over the whole play' (Allen, *Phelps*,
p. 232). The first part of the Porter's monologue was restored but the second was omitted because of its obscenity, and the dialogue between Lady
Macduff and her son, and the son's murder on the stage, were brought
back. Finally, Macbeth was killed off stage and his head brought in on a
pole in accordance with the original stage directions (*Athenaeum*, no. 1040,
2 October 1847, p. 1036). Some people found these restored passages offensive, especially the murder of Macduff's son, and they were omitted in later
performances, but the audience were given the opportunity to see the whole
of *Macbeth*, with no additions, for the first time in more than two hundred
years. Phelps also abandoned as anachonistic the tartan costumes originally brought in by Macklin and replaced them with more primitive-looking
clothing made from a heavy, dark material which fell from the shoulders
in folds.

His first Lady Macbeth was Mrs Warner, who, of course, knew the role
well, having played it opposite Macready, but when Phelps revived the play
on 20 March 1850, he chose Isabella Glyn, a more powerful actress who had
been an impressive Cleopatra a year earlier. 'With her wealth of raven black
hair, her dark flashing eyes, her magnificent figure and demeanour', recalled
John Coleman, 'she was in person the very beau ideal of Lady Macbeth or
Cleopatra' ('Facts and Fancies', pp. 231–2). She delivered the opening soliloquy with 'an electric power', and 'in the murder and banquet scenes she was
self-possessed, appalling, sustained, triumphant – the very heroine of crime'

(*Illustrated London News*, 23 March 1850, p. 194). Her interpretation was clearly similar to that of Siddons, to whom she was inevitably compared.

CHARLES KEAN, IRVING, AND HISTORICAL AUTHENTICITY

Macready did some historical research and supervised all the details of his productions scrupulously, but he was not slavishly bound to historical authenticity, preferring to create the tone and atmosphere of a play and to produce a unity of effect (Rosenfeld, *History*, p. 117). The first actor-manager to apply himself wholeheartedly to historical detail was Charles Kean (the son of Edmund) in his productions at the Princess's Theatre in the 1850s.

Kean had been more or less forced into the theatrical profession. While he was still a schoolboy at Eton, his temperamental father suddenly insisted that he should accept a post with the East India Company and, when Charles refused, his father removed him from school, stopped his allowance, and left him with no means of support. On the strength of his father's reputation, however, he was offered an engagement as an actor at Drury Lane, which he accepted out of necessity, but for which, it quickly became apparent, he had no ability, as George Henry Lewes explains:

> Laughed at, ridiculed and for many years, terribly handled by critics, both in public and privately, he has worked steadily, resolutely, improvingly, till his brave perseverance has finally conquered an eminent position. He began by being a very bad actor; he has ended by forcing even such of his critics as have least sympathy with him to admit that in certain parts he is without a rival on our stage.   (*On Actors*, p. 13)

These 'certain parts', according to Lewes, did not include the great tragic roles: 'I must confess', he said, 'that it has never been an intellectual treat to me to see Charles Kean play tragic heroes, but I doubt whether even his great father could have surpassed him in certain melodramatic parts' (*On Actors*, p. 14). (The melodramatic roles were presumably in such popular plays as Boucicault's *Louis XI* and *The Corsican Brothers*, which were in his repertoire.) 'He has none of those terrible looks', said Lewes, 'which made his father terrible to fellow-actors no less than to spectators. There has never been the smallest danger of his frightening an actress into fits, as Edmund Kean is said to have frightened Mrs Glover' (*On Actors*, pp. 16–17).

Kean's audiences, however, were not nearly as critical as Lewes was. His first performance of Macbeth at Covent Garden in 1820 was received with tremendous enthusiasm. 'His success', according to the *Morning Post*, was

6 'Give me the daggers' (2.2.56). Photograph of Ellen and Charles Kean,
Princess's Theatre, 1853.

'one of the most brilliant which has ever been recorded in the annals of the
drama.' Several years later he presented it before Queen Victoria at Windsor,
and when, having assumed the management of the Princess's Theatre, he
revived it there (14 February 1853), it was given three times a week for twenty
weeks. The houses were 'crowded to the roof' and hundreds of people had
to be turned away (Cole, *Charles Kean*, vol. II, p. 52). Ellen Kean's Lady

Macbeth was even favourably compared to Siddons's (and she does appear to have been a much better actor than her husband): 'In simple pathos, in natural bursts of indignation when urged beyond patience, in the gentle, unartificial, and purely woman-like features of the character . . . [Siddons] is exceeded by Mrs C. Kean' (Cole, *Charles Kean*, vol. II, p. 150).

Her expression of Lady Macbeth's womanly qualities, which recalls Faucit, also impressed Lewes who did not agree with her view of the role but admitted, 'at any rate she *has* a view, and realises it with vulture-like ferocity. In no scene was she weak; in the sleep-walking scene she was terrific' (*Dramatic Essays*, p. 238), but Kean could not be said to take any view of Macbeth at all.

> He tries to embody the various feelings of each situation; taking, however, the literal and unintelligent interpretation, so that almost every phase of the character is falsified . . . In Charles Kean's Macbeth all the tragedy has vanished; sympathy is impossible, because the mind of the criminal is hidden from us. He makes Macbeth ignoble – one whose crime is that of a common murderer, with perhaps a tendency towards Methodism. It is not, however, so much the acting as the 'getting up' of Macbeth which will attract the public.
>
> (*Dramatic Essays*, p. 238)

Kean's 'getting up' of the play was apparent in the eighteen specially painted scenes listed in the playbill which included a 'Distant View of Iona by Moonlight', and he always worked to produce the most sensational effect (see commentary, p. 80). For the hall in which the banquet scene took place, there was a sloping timber roof supported by Saxon pillars and, above that, a minstrels' gallery in which seven bards played on harps. Kean was criticised for the coarse simplicity of the actual banquet which seemed to compare unfavourably with the 'splendid fruits and gorgeous dish-covers' used by Macready, but he defended his choice on the grounds that such food was appropriate for the household of a highland chieftain of the eleventh century.

This care for historical correctness was a striking feature of the production – and, indeed, of all Kean's productions at the Princess's. He appended a fly-leaf to the playbill in which he specified the various authorities he had consulted. Admitting that there was little or no information about the dress worn by the Scots in Macbeth's own time, he explained that he had borrowed materials 'from those nations to whom Scotland was continually opposed in war'. The sets were also based on pre-Norman architecture, for advice on which he consulted a member of the Society of Antiquaries, to which he was later elected. He was motivated not only by his own personal passion for archaeology but also by 'a Victorian passion for education' (Rosenfeld, *History*, p. 120), and he was commended for making the theatre into 'a brilliant, living museum for the student'.

7 Banquo's ghost appears at the banquet in a transparent column (3.4.88), Princess's Theatre, 1853.

At the time when Kean was mounting his productions of Shakespeare at the Princess's, the Italian actress Adelaide Ristori appeared in an Italian translation of *Macbeth* at the Lyceum (11 July 1857). She was, by then, a celebrated international star who had acted throughout Italy and in Paris, and went on to make several tours of the United States. She was a great beauty with a commanding personality, and was celebrated for her performance of regal roles such as Marie Antoinette, and Mary Queen of Scots in Schiller's *Maria Stuart*. 'When she came on the stage', recalled John Coleman, 'she seemed to fill it with her majestic presence' ('Facts and Fancies', p. 232). She did not simply rely on the expansiveness of her personality, however, but, as a dedicated artist, prepared her roles with a meticulous attention to detail. Although she played the role in translation, her performance was finely judged and, at the end, very moving. One can understand why, in her own lifetime, she was called 'the Siddons of modern Italy'.

She portrayed Lady Macbeth as a woman who exercised complete contol over her feelings. She was 'watchful, self-contained and fights against compunctious visitings of nature without letting a stir be seen or any note of aches within to escape her lips until her heart too sorely charged gives way under the weight it is forced secretly and silently to bear' (Morley, *Journal*, p. 158). The change in Lady Macbeth's personality began to appear towards the end of the banquet scene (3.4.122–44) when, left alone with her husband, her strength and determination started to fail and she appeared totally exhausted. This change was a preparation for the sleep-walking in which 'her look is haggard . . . her whole aspect is spectral, her action slow and painfully nervous in its manner, her voice low, full of such weariness as follows acute and exhausting pain' (Morley, *Journal*, p. 161).

The Macbeth, Vitaliani, on the other hand, was portrayed as a weak man, totally dominated by his wife, 'who cannot keep his troubles to himself who gives all his emotions tongue who when he shrinks with his mind, shrinks with his body also, who when he is startled mentally starts bodily, and so, instead of being self-contained, is always pouring himself out, even at the very finger-tips' (*ibid.*). The contrast between the two of them could not have been more extreme, and Vitaliani's nervous animation was so exaggerated as to become ridiculous. By overshadowing Macbeth and making the play entirely hers, Ristori 'deprived it of a tragic hero' (Bartholomeusz, *Players*, p. 192).

Kean's productions were so expensive to mount and the scenery so cumbersome to erect that he found it necessary to give them long, continuous runs and not, as had hitherto been the custom, to have several plays alternating in repertory. For the same reasons, Henry Irving's productions of Shakespeare at the Lyceum, of which he assumed the management in 1871, ran continuously for as many performances as there were audiences to attend them. His first production of *Macbeth*, which opened in September 1875, ran for eighty nights, and his revival, in December 1888, for six months.

Irving often employed more than a hundred supernumeraries, and the theatre had a chorus, a corps de ballet, and a thirty-piece orchestra. It has been estimated that six hundred people regularly worked for him (Hughes, *Shakespearean*, p. 16). Under the influence of his scholarly designers, his productions also became increasingly exact historically. The costumes and props for *Macbeth* were designed by Charles Cattermole, a well-known water-colourist, who 'searched the museums for authority for every article of costume, weapon, furniture and domestic utensil down to every nail, button and blade' (Hughes, *Shakespearean*, p. 17). The sets, designed by Hawes Craven, were also archaeologically correct, but their most prominent feature was their solid, three-dimensional massiveness. Macbeth's castle at Inverness, for example, was 'rough-textured to represent stone' and, as Duncan and his retinue approached the cavernous gate, 'they climbed a great, sloping bridge, which suggested that the castle was indeed situated on a rocky summit. Retainers lined the ramp, lighting the scene with torches, women bowed as Lady Macbeth swept down to meet the King' (Hughes, *Shakespearean*, p. 100), and the entire scene was accompanied by 'serene and beautiful music' written by Arthur Sullivan whom Irving had commissioned as the composer for the production.

It was estimated that over four hundred costumes were made for the production in the workshops attached to the theatre, 'including 165 for soldiers (115 Scotch and 50 English), 80 for the "Flight of Witches", 40 for lords and ladies, 16 for waiting women, 8 for kings, 5 for cooks and so forth. Besides these are the dresses for the principals, with their "changes", all wrought in the house' (M. H. Spielman, *Magazine of Art*, January 1889, p. 99). The costumes were made of brown leather, fur and woollens of a dull, bronze colour, dark red, green, blue, and purple. These, together with the subdued lighting, 'blended together to compose a dark, massive, dangerous world' (Shattuck, *American Stage*, vol. II, pp. 181–2).

Unlike Charles Kean, Irving did not cultivate spectacle as an end in itself. As Sybil Rosenfeld points out, 'he strove towards a unity in which all elements would coalesce to express the mood of the drama and whilst using spectacle, processions and antiquarianism more sparingly than Kean, he sought from his painters primarily beauty and artistry' (*History*, p. 133). Irving himself described his desire for unity in an article in the *Boston Evening Transcript* (24 October 1884) where he explained that Shakespeare's characters are studied so close to life, the influence of time, place and social atmosphere is so strong upon them, that emphasising their suroundings in a scenic way has really an illustrative force. A carefully-studied and truthful *mise-en-scene* becomes an actual functional part of the drama itself, and gives additional vitality and intelligibleness to the action.

(Quoted in Shattuck, *American Stage*, vol. II, pp. 164–5)

The heavy, solid sets of *Macbeth* and the profound gloom in which the action took place were a visual expression of the play.

Irving was a wonderfully dedicated, imaginative director, but his acting was eccentric. Unlike his predecessors, from Burbage and Garrick onwards, he did not attempt to 'become' the character he was playing. He saw the actor's function as that of a creative artist: 'The actor's interpretation of a part, what he made of it by filtering it through himself, was more important than the part as it appears "in the book"' (Shattuck, *American Stage*, vol. II, p. 160). Hence each of the characters he played was 'a fresh development of his own individuality, not, as is the case with mimetic actors, a study from the life' (Archer, *Actor and Manager*, p. 77). This attitude towards his art perhaps accounts for his extraordinary personal mannerisms which were clearly recognisable no matter what role he might be playing. His walk was odd and ungainly. According to William Archer, who often saw him,

It seems as though locomotion with Mr Irving were not a result of volition, but of an involuntary spasm. Under certain circumstances, it is complicated by the most extraordinary sidelong and backward skirmishings . . . [He] rapidly plods across the stage with a gait peculiar to him, a walk somewhat resembling that of a fretful man trying to get very quickly over a ploughed field.

(Archer, *Actor and Manager*, pp. 63–72)

There were even stronger protests against his vocal mannerisms which, for an American critic, 'made a great part of his performance wholly unintelligible . . . He so mouthed and mumbled his lines that their sense was lost', and 'more than once, at great crises in the action, ripples of half-suppressed laughter ran round the house' (Jeanette Gilder in the *Critic*; Shattuck, *American Stage*, vol. II, pp. 177–9). The *Athenaeum* said of his first production of *Macbeth* that 'his slow pronunciation and his indescribable elongation of syllables bring the whole near burlesque' and predicted that if these mannerisms were not checked, they would eventually ruin his career (no. 2501, 2 October 1875, p. 448). Henry James regarded him as 'a very superior amateur' who had received no proper training (*Scenic Art*, pp. 36–7).

With such deficiencies, it is hard to understand why he was so popular, and earned so much respect that he became the first actor to be awarded a knighthood. Part of his success is attributable to the quality of his productions. He had, says William Archer, 'the art of inspiring to the verge of genius his scenic artists and machinists, which may possibly be the reason why he has so little inspiration left over for himself' (*Actor and Manager*, p. 96). But as an actor he had a charismatic quality which surpassed his eccentricities. 'It is his face and his brain that have made him what he is', said Archer – 'his glittering eye and his restless, inventive intellect.' Indeed, Archer believed that Irving's mannerisms 'increased rather than diminished his success. They heighten his individuality, if not its magnetism. They are, indeed, the over-development of his individuality' (*Actor and Manager*, pp. 88; 71).

His interpetation of Macbeth provoked much criticism. Irving saw him not as an inherently good man who succumbs to the influence of his wife (the John Philip Kemble view) but, in his own words, as 'a bloody-minded, hypocritical villain' (Furness, p. 470). The witches, he believed, did not suggest the murder to Macbeth but were emanations of an idea which already existed in his own mind. He had, moreover, already proposed the idea to his wife, as she implies in her words, 'What beast was't then / That made you break this enterprise to me?' (1.7.47–8). Far from being influenced by her, Irving said, 'it is quite possible that Macbeth led his wife to believe that she was leading him on. It was part of his nature to work her moral downfall in such a way' (Shattuck, *American Stage*, vol. II, p. 177). His disintegration during and after the murder was brought about not by guilt and remorse but by terror of its consequences.

Henry James believed that this was a perfectly possible interpetation and one which suited Irving's personality:

> Mr Irving has great skill in the representation of terror, and it is quite open to him to have thrown into relief this side of his part. His best moment is his rendering of the scene with the bloody daggers . . . [He] is here altogether admirable and his representation of a nature trembling and quaking to its innermost recesses really excites the imagination.   (*Scenic Art*, pp. 36–7)

The critic of the *Athenaeum*, on the other hand, complained that his Macbeth was not a tragic figure:

> [He] shows us an abject and unheroical being, in whom we find no trace of the soldier. His moaning and complaining are less than manly, and his mental struggles are those of a commonplace nature. There is no warrant in the text for the excessive cowardice Mr Irving displays . . . There is not a point at which the character is adequately masculine.   (No. 2501, 2 October 1875, p. 448)

The final effect of his performance was not to create an impression of an inherently noble man who had been corrupted but a coward whose 'abject

8 Ellen Terry carrying a candle in the sleepwalking scene (5.1.15), Lyceum Theatre, 1888.

terror and remorse make death at the hands of the man he has most injured a welcome consummation' (Laurence Irving, *Actor and his World*, p. 260).

Kate Bateman, the Lady Macbeth of Irving's 1875 production, made little attempt to fulfil her role as Irving had conceived it, but was the conventionally powerful, ruthless woman in the manner of Siddons and Cushman, and not the tool of her husband that Irving believed she should be. The Lady

Macbeth of his revival in 1888, however, was Ellen Terry, not only a very much greater actress but one who was better equipped temperamentally to express his conception of her role. She was essentially 'feminine', domestic, deeply devoted to her husband and therefore ambitious for him. At the Ellen Terry Museum at Small Hythe in Kent, there are two bound copies of the play which Irving gave her, and with the text interleaved with blank pages on which she wrote a great many comments on how she thought she should play the role.[4] In the flyleaves at the end of the play, she writes of Macbeth, 'With all his rant and bombast he had "lucidity" – and never belittled his crime – he never said "a little water clears us of this deed." He was far-seeing – therefore he had less excuse – for his crime was more deliberate – The witches turned his head (as witches will do!). His aim was kingdom.' But Lady Macbeth, she says, 'is full of womanliness' and is 'capable of *affection – she loves her husband –* Ergo – *she is a woman* and she knows it, and is half the time *afraid* whilst urging Macbeth not to be afraid as she loves a *man*. Women love *men*' (Manvell, 'Terry's Lady Macbeth', p. 161). In her first scene, she read Macbeth's letter in her sitting room by firelight and, when she had finished, 'threw herself back in the long oaken chair to dream of the arrival and the fortunes of her king and lover'. She addressed the soliloquy to his miniature and concluded by kissing it. When he entered, she 'rushed forward to greet him with a long embrace' (Hughes, *Shakespearean*, p. 100). 'Conjugal sympathy and self-sacrifice are the keynotes of her character', said the *Spectator* (5 January 1889). Her deep affection for and dependence on her husband also became the cause of her tragedy. As Macbeth embarked on successive crimes, she became increasingly isolated from him and, as the *Illustrated London News* remarked, was 'punished by utter loneliness, by the forfeiture of her husband's love, and she dies, maddened by remorse, of a broken heart' (5 January 1889). Some people thought her interpretation was at odds with the role as Shakespeare had written it, and one reaction to her performance during the murder was, 'What on earth is this graceful, amiable, and picturesque woman doing in these shambles? . . . How did she get there? And being there, why doesn't she faint or go off into hysterics? . . . It is rather Lady Macbeth adapted and modified to suit the peculiar individuality of the actress, than Miss Terry sinking that individuality in Shakespeare's creation' (*Spectator*, 5 January 1889).

In 1876, a year after Irving's first production of *Macbeth*, Tommaso Salvini, the great Italian actor, appeared in the title-role in Edinburgh, and

4   Extracts from the notes Terry wrote in her copy are quoted in Manvell, 'Terry as Lady Macbeth', *Listener*, 2 February 1967, and in Alan Hughes, *Henry Irving, Shakespearean*, Cambridge, 1981.

returned with it to Covent Garden eight years later. He had begun his career by acting in Italian plays but, as he grew older, created a name for himself as an interpreter of Shakespeare's tragic roles, including Hamlet, Othello, and Lear with which he toured the major cities of Latin America and the United States. He was broad-shouldered and heavy set, but surprisingly lightfooted, quick, and graceful and claimed that his muscular strength, fostered by constant exercise, was such that he could lift a man seated in a chair and place him on a billiard table. 'He needed only to step onto any stage to command it' (Shattuck, *American Stage*, vol. II, pp. 148–9). He was also a dedicated actor who studied his roles carefully and, with his expressive, flexible voice, exercised great control over the verse. 'His massive, barbaric costumes as Macbeth were designed by Gustave Doré, who visited Scotland to arrive at "historical accuracy"' (Shattuck, *American Stage*, vol. II, p. 155).

To Salvini, Macbeth's greatness consisted largely of his courage and physical strength – what R. L. Stevenson called 'the royalty of muscle', a quality seldom seen on the British stage. On his first entrance, wrote Stevenson, 'he arrives with Banquo on the heath, fair and red-bearded, sparing of gesture, full of pride and the sense of animal well-being, and satisfied after the battle like a beast who has eaten his fill'. But in spite of his physical power, his Macbeth had a 'moral smallness'. He was easily controlled by his wife for whom he was 'little more than an agent, a frame of bone and sinew for her fiery spirit to command'. He always gave way to her allurements, and yet 'his caresses . . . are singularly hard and unloving. Sometimes he lays his hand on her as he might take hold of anyone who happened to be near him at a moment of excitement. Love has fallen out of the marriage by the way and left a curious friendship' (*Academy*, 15 April 1876). His whole performance was 'full of gusto and a headlong unity', but his most subtle effect was to convey the change which had come over Macbeth by the fifth act. He was still, apparently, 'the big, burly, fleshly, handsome looking Thane . . . But now the atmosphere of blood, which pervades the whole tragedy, has entered into the man and subdued him to its own nature; and an indescribable degradation, a slackness and puffiness, has overtaken his features. He has breathed the air of carnage and supped full of horrors' (*ibid.*). Unfortunately, his Lady Macbeth was simply not up to the part. 'Not to succeed in the sleep-walking scene', said Stevenson, 'is to make a memorable failure. As it was given, it succeeded in being wrong in art without being true to nature' (p. 367).

The most celebrated actor of the next generation, Johnston Forbes-Robertson, was also highly gifted, but his endowments were of an entirely different, much more English, kind. Early in his career he was fortunate enough to work with Phelps, who coached him in verse-speaking for which he became much admired. His biographer, Hesketh Pearson, remarks that he and Ellen Terry were the only two players in his experience 'who delivered the language of Shakespeare as if it were their natural idiom and whose beauty of diction matched the beauty of the words' (*Actor-Managers*, pp. 1–2).

For several years he was a member of Irving's company, playing Claudio to Irving's Benedick, and when Irving played Wolsey, he was Buckingham. During Irving's frequent tours in America in the autumn, Forbes-Robertson took over the management of the Lyceum where, in his first season, in 1895, he produced *Romeo and Juliet* with Mrs Patrick Campbell as Juliet. It was there that he played Hamlet, which was his greatest success, and for which he was naturally very well suited. He was a tall, slim man with aristocratic, sensitive good looks and an elegant dignity. He conveyed effortlessly Hamlet's analytical intelligence, and his performance seemed perfectly natural, 'nobly well-bred, ideally graceful, flawlessly spoken, and so charming that one could see it again and again, and twice in a day, yet never tire of it' (Pearson, *Actor-Managers*, p. 1).

The qualities which suited him well for Hamlet did not help him when he played Macbeth (17 September 1898). As the critic in *The Times* pointed out, 'The very scholarliness, the preachiness that accord with the character of the philosophic Dane are drawbacks to the shaggy warrior.' He managed to look the part very well, and created a fine impression of 'rugged strength, a type which might have been placed on canvas by a great painter who remembered that the uncouth Scottish thane of the 11th century was as likely as not to be half-Norwegian in blood, and ruddy with the ruddiness of the Scandinavian stock'. His appearance, however, was at odds with his natural gifts as an actor, 'so that he becomes loutish where he should be stalwart and massive, and almost cowardly in manner where he should be perplexed and overawed. The part, in short, does not fit in with Mr Robertson's special gifts of intellectual refinement and subtlety' (*Times*, 19 September 1898).

As Lady Macbeth, Mrs Patrick Campbell, certainly looked splendidly barbaric in a bodice like a coat of mail, covered in blue, green, and gold sequins which suggested serpent's scales (Batholomeusz, *Players*, p. 212) and she seemed about to interpret the part in the ruthlessly determined style of Siddons and Cushman, but she tried to play it as a 'cajoling, feline adventuress'. The critic of the *Academy* (24 September 1898) found her 'one of the most hopelessly uninspiring Lady Macbeths that I remember to have seen. Her murderous counsels are delivered without conviction, while her remorse is without a shred of plausibility or pathos. Nothing in her rendering of the part conveys the smallest thrill or shudder to the house.' She also had obvious difficulty in enunciating Shakespeare's words (*Times*, 19 September

1898). Both she and Forbes-Robertson were remarkable actors, but in this particular play they were both, predictably, miscast.

Several years earlier, in 1884, London had received a visit from the celebrated French actress Sarah Bernhardt. Her repertoire consisted mainly of French plays, but she also appeared three times in *Macbeth* in a French prose translation which, according to *The Times*, transformed it from a tragedy into 'a dull and somewhat vulgar melodrama' (5 July 1884). She portrayed Lady Macbeth as 'a siren-like creature by whose fascinations men are enslaved' (*Pall Mall Gazette*, 5 July 1884). Hence the Macbeth, Marais, became seduced by passion rather than ambition (Aston, *Bernhardt*, p. 77). When attempting to persuade her husband to murder Duncan, 'she wraps him in a clinging embrace, as if she would play upon his senses rather than his reason', and, as a result, 'she wheedles but she never masters him' (*Times*, 5 July 1884). Her performance was violently histrionic, as when she rushed up the steps to smear the faces of the grooms with blood, uttering great cries and gesticulations, and in the sleep-walking scene, which she played with bare feet and in a clinging night-dress, she was equally violent. 'After apostrophising the "damned spot", she fell back shrieking hysterically, and finally rushed off to the wings, calling out lustily, "To bed, to bed!" (*Au lit, au lit!*)' (Bartholomeusz, *Players*, p. 209; *Times*, 5 July 1884). The *Times* critic said that he had never seen 'a more inadequate and unsatisfactory performance of a Shakespearean play'.

Herbert Beerbohm Tree was born in the same year (1853) as Forbes-Robertson but was much more passionately committed to the theatre, and whereas Forbes-Robertson retired some twenty years before his death, Tree went on acting and directing almost to the end. He was a sociable, witty, entertaining man, tall, slim, sandy-haired, and flamboyant in manner, and (the half-brother of Max Beerbohm) an inventive comic actor. Mrs Patrick Campbell thought him the best character comedian of his day. He was a brilliantly funny Malvolio, but lacked the depth and substance necessary for the most challenging tragic roles and never attempted Lear. He became manager of the Haymarket theatre where he made his reputation in popular comedies and melodramas, including George Du Maurier's *Trilby* in which he played the sinister Svengali. This and other productions were so profitable that he was able to build his own theatre, Her Majesty's, just down the street from the Haymarket. His limitations as a Shakespearean actor did not discourage him from mounting many of the plays, including *Hamlet*, *The Merry Wives of Windsor*, *Henry IV Part 1*, *King John*, *Antony and Cleopatra*, and *The Merchant of Venice*, in all of which he played the leading roles. In 1905 he started an annual Shakespeare festival, during which he showed six of his productions in six days, an enterprise which was so successful that it was eventually extended to three months, and other actor-managers were invited to bring their productions to his theatre.

The critic of the *Athenaeum* (9 September 1911) approved of his Macbeth, but thought that Tree over-emphasised 'the dreamy and irresolute side of Macbeth at the expense of that of the soldier and man of action . . . Horror of self – of the newly-discovered possibilities of self – is what this Macbeth is constantly expressing, and Sir Herbert contrives often enough to give that idea by mere looks.' This last remark looks like a tactful way of saying that, vocally, he was not expressive. Bernard Shaw put it more bluntly: 'Blank verse, as such, had no charm for him; nor, I suspect, did he credit it with charm for anyone else' (Shattuck, *American Stage*, vol. II, p. 187). Assessments of his performance varied. The *Athenaeum* declared that, within the two previous decades, no Macbeth had been more thoughtful and imaginative, but the *Academy* found him 'unconvincing and disappointing' (9 September 1911): 'Sir Herbert gives you what he can – sweetness, perfect taste, romantic melancholy, a sense of beauty. He interests and charms you but never dominates or thrills.' According to the *Daily News*, Tree's 'sallow face and long, drooping moustache denote a mind ill at ease from the moment of his first entry with Banquo. His gasps and contortions pointed to some deep-seated nervous disorder . . . Sir Herbert did not suggest, nor did he at any point give one the impression of the physically brave and skilful soldier' (6 September 1911). As for Violet Vanbrugh, her Lady Macbeth was beautiful and pathetic, but 'when she has violent words to say, her whole demeanour gives the lie to them' (*Times*, 6 September 1911).

There was, however, some powerfully theatrical staging. At Macbeth's first entrance, for example, he did not simply walk on but stood on a crag, holding a flaming torch above his head while the witches crouched below him in the heather. For the sleep-walking scene, the stage was empty apart from a bare flight of stone steps with no balustrade, leading from the highest visible point of the stage to the ground, and set close against a stone wall. It was down these steps that Lady Macbeth walked (see commentary p. 191).

As a director, Tree, following the style of his time, believed that the plays should be presented with all the resources which the theatre could offer: 'We must grant [to Shakespeare] the crowds and armies, the pride, pomp and circumstance which he calls for everywhere in his work' (Shattuck, *American Stage*, vol. II, p. 194). There were fifteen different scene changes in his *Macbeth*, the banquet was preceded by a torch dance, an episode was added in which Duncan was escorted to bed by a train which included a harper, and there was singing which turned into a hymn as the King blessed the kneeling company (Crosse, *Playgoing*, p. 39). These additions and the complicated changes of scene all took up time. The intervals between

No. 3778. VOL. CXXXIX SATURDAY, SEPTEMBER 16, 1911. SIXPENCE.

THANE OF GLAMIS! THANE OF CAWDOR! KING!—SIR HERBERT TREE AS MACBETH AT HIS MAJESTY'S.

A STUDY BY FRANK HAVILAND.

9 Herbert Beerbohm Tree about to enter Duncan's bedchamber (2.1.62),
His Majesty's Theatre, 1911.

scenes and acts added up to an hour, and one of Shakespeare's shortest plays took four hours to perform. The production therefore fell into a series of disconnected episodes and, to compensate for its length, about a third of the text was cut, far more than had been omitted from previous productions. Sir Herbert 'has sought to achieve a pictorial, not a dramatic effect' said *Blackwood's Edinburgh Magazine*. The complaint was made, as it had often been since Kemble's production over a century earlier, that so much time and effort were spent in creating spectacle that the performance was 'too often slow and monotonous' (*Illustrated London News*, 9 September 1911).

THE RETURN TO SHAKESPEARE'S STAGE

By now audiences began to tire of the prevailing style of Shakespearean production, to complain that the actors were given second place to the scenery, and that, for all their splendour, performances were becoming tedious and exhausting. Moreover, the style of production in Germany was remarkably similar, and there were similar calls for a return to Shakespeare and simplicity. It was in Germany that the reaction originated. Ludwig Tieck, the translator of the standard German version of Shakespeare, put on four of the plays as early as 1821–51 on a kind of Elizabethan stage with a permanent setting, and, in 1889, a 'Shakespeare Stage' was built at the Munich Residenz theatre with an extensive forestage projecting out beyond the proscenium arch, on which the plays were performed without cuts and with a minimum of scenery (Kennedy, *Looking*, p. 36). Towards the end of the century, boldly original, non-representational sets were designed in Germany by Adolphe Appia who 'at one swoop cleared the clutter of proscenium arch, painted scenery and stage machinery' (Rosenfeld, *History*, p. 146).

In England the movement started later and was slower to take effect. It was led by William Poel, the founder of the Elizabethan Stage Society who, in reaction against the work of Irving and Tree, began to produce the plays as far as possible as they had been in Shakespeare's time. 'All kinds of elaborate attempts at stage illusion', he declared, 'tend . . . to divert a careful observance of the acting, while they are of no real service to the imagination of the spectator' (Poel, *Theatre*, p. 7). In the Elizabethan playhouse, people's thoughts 'were not being constantly diverted and distracted by those outward decorations and subordinate details which in our day so greatly obliterate the main object of a dramatic work' (Poel, *Theatre*, p. 8). To allow the audience to concentrate entirely on a play, the stage should be stripped bare of scenery, and brought as far as possible into the auditorium so that the slightest modulations of the actors' voices could be heard and the lines spoken without exaggeration. Acting 'should follow the laws of speaking, not those of singing' (Poel, *Theatre*, p. 57).

Poel put on *Macbeth* for six performances at the Grand Theatre, Fulham, in June 1909, with Lillah McCarthy, and Hubert Carter, 'a young actor of taurine physique with a strong, flexible voice' (Speaight, *Poel*, p. 189). He thought this the most Elizabethan of Shakespeare's tragedies: 'the blood-guiltiness of Holyrood and Fotheringay darkens the corridors of Dunsinane . . . There is barbarism in *Macbeth* but it is the barbarism of Bothwell, not of Boadicea' (quoted in Speaight, *Poel*, p. 184). The cast wore Elizabethan dress rather than the kind of primitive garments used by Irving and Tree, and they played the complete Folio text, uncut, for the first time since Phelps's production more than sixty years earlier.

Poel's revival of Elizabethan staging was revolutionary, but its influence was not immediate. 'Forbes-Robertson gave his farewell performances in the old style. And Tree continued in his stately way, sublimely indifferent to the growing belief that it was out of date' (Crosse, *Playgoing*, p. 49). There was one director, however, who, as an actor, had worked with Poel, and was immediately influenced by his methods. Harley Granville-Barker, in a letter to Max Reinhardt, said that Poel had 'taught him more about the staging of Shakespeare than anyone else in Europe' (Kennedy, *Looking*, p. 38). He produced three of Shakespeare's plays at the Savoy Theatre, *The Winter's Tale* and *Twelfth Night* in 1912, and *A Midsummer Night's Dream* two years later. For these he used an apron stage, full texts, rapid speaking, and only one interval. He used very simple permanent sets with no attempt at historical authenticity, which alternated with painted curtains decorated with formal patterns (Byrne, 'Fifty Years', p. 8). Some people were outraged by what Barker had done. The critic of the *Athenaeum* (28 September 1912) declared that, 'in a distressful striving after the artistic,' he had achieved 'that mingling of discordant, ill-related elements, that impossible jangling of different keys, which can never be far removed from vulgarity', but the majority were delighted. The critic of *The Times* found Barker's *Twelfth Night* the most enjoyable he had seen.

At the age of forty, however, Barker retired from the theatre and devoted himself to writing. His *Prefaces to Shakespeare* (1927–47) are commentaries on nine of the plays as scripts designed for performance in the kind of theatre for which they were written. It was these, probably more than his productions, which radically changed the style in which they were put on, and his influence can still be recognised at the present day in the architectural permanent sets now regularly used in Shakespearean productions. Poel's 'dry, antiquarian, amateurish experiments began to transform the look of Shakespeare' (Kennedy, *Looking*, p. 38), and his influence can still be seen in the open stages at Stratford, Ontario, at Chichester, and in the Elizabethan theatres at Stratford-on-Avon (the Swan) and in London (Shakespeare's Globe). His conviction that acting 'should follow the laws of speaking, not those of singing' radically changed the way in which the verse was treated in the twentieth century.

Barker was briefly the manager of the Court theatre and, during his time there, produced three plays of Shakespeare in which small roles were played by Lewis Casson, and when Casson directed a full text of *Julius Caesar* in Manchester, very much under Barker's influence, he used a modified apron stage and a permanent set. The production was received unfavourably, however, and in his *Macbeth* at the Prince's Theatre in 1926, he returned to the old style. It was beautiful to look at but, as James Agate complained, 'the curtain descends some two and twenty times, which gravely disperses the interest instead of concentrating it' (*Chronicles*, p. 218). Sybil Thorndike's Lady Macbeth was authoritative and moving. Gordon Crosse thought it 'the top of her achievement':

> In her reading of the letter, her voice rather deepened from its natural pitch, amazement and excitement were blended, the latter prevailing as the emotion heightens . . . In the sleep-walking scene she spoke in a dull, flat voice, sometimes breaking into a wail of utter misery. I have never known wretchedness presented on the stage as she presented it.   (*Playgoing*, p. 53)

The Times, however, was less impressed, and attributed the weakness of her performance to the frequent breaks in the action: 'In strength or fear she has a fierceness of attack or a subtlety of approach that compels unceasing admiration . . . If she fails nevertheless to stir the blood or to freeze it . . . the reason must be that her own part, like the play itself, is broken up and robbed of its cumulative force' (28 December 1926).

The two predominant styles of Shakespearean production in the early twentieth century, the Victorian, pictorial style with its historically based sets and costumes, and the austere style of the Elizabethan revival, both located the plays firmly in the past, and, as a result, gave to both of them an antiquarian quality which was thought to distance them from contemporary experience. An attempt was now made to break even further from tradition, and give them a modern relevance by locating them in the present. The first attempt of this kind in England was made by Barry Jackson, the founder of the Birmingham Repertory Theatre, who in 1925 put on a modern-dress *Hamlet* there ('*Hamlet* in plus-fours'), directed by H. J. Ayliff. It was generally thought to throw new light on the play, but his *Macbeth* three years later was ridiculed.

Ayliff's *Macbeth* was set in the period of the first world war, and the battle scenes with which it opened and closed were brought up to date with exploding shells and rattling machine guns. Macbeth was dressed in khaki uniform with riding-breeches, high, polished boots, and a chest covered in medal ribbons, Lady Macbeth appeared in a short, sleeveless cocktail dress, and Lady Macduff and her son were murdered over a cup of afternoon tea by killers who entered through a casement window. Macduff received the news of their deaths wearing a lounge suit and a felt hat (Styan, *Revolution*, p. 150). 'According to the promptbook . . . Duncan's arrival at Inverness, that classic moment of irony and foreshadowing, was announced by "three hoots" of a motorhorn' (Kennedy, *Looking*, p. 112). The actors, however, assumed not only the dress of the twentieth century but also its rapid, clipped, low-keyed way of speaking. As a result the poetry of the play was destroyed and the anachronisms called attention to themselves. 'The spiritual home of Miss Mary Merrall's Lady Macbeth', said James Agate,

> is obviously the more exclusive portions of Finsbury Park . . . I confess that I never sought to see the speech beginning, 'What beast was't then / That made you break this enterprise to me?' with the speaker reclining in abandonment and luxury in the arms of her Sheik on an art-coloured divan with a distant gramophone playing the opening of the first act of *Carmen*.
>
> (*Chronicles*, pp. 224–5)

In spite of its failure, however, Jackson's modern-dress productions were influential internationally, and it is now customary for directors to set a Shakespearean play, especially the comedies, in whatever place or period they believe will illuminate it.

The setting for the production of *Macbeth* at the Old Vic in 1930, in which John Gielgud played the central role for the first time, was simple, basic, and austere. The austerity – some people called it 'dowdiness' – was determined largely by financial restrictions. Under the management of Lilian Baylis, the Old Vic was run on a shoestring, and the budget for sets and costumes was only £20 (the equivalent of about £600 today), and the leading actors were paid £10 a week. At the same time the simplicity suited the taste of Gielgud and the director, Harcourt Williams, both of whom admired Granville-Barker. Artistic policy and financial stringency justified each other. In spite of these constraints, the production was a great success. James Agate thought it the best production he could remember, and found Gielgud 'vocally superb . . . For the first time in my experience Macbeth retained his hold on the play till the end' (*Chronicles*, pp. 225–7). 'The settings were simple enough to keep the play moving at the pace the Old Vic tradition has set, but the simplicity had more than mere expediency to recommend it' (*Times*, 18 March 1930). *The Times* said nothing of the Lady Macbeth, Martita Hunt, but Agate, though he admired her 'intelligence, subtlety and artistry', found her 'always too likeable'.

Gielgud had much in common with Forbes-Robertson. They were both tall, slim, elegant figures, admired for their sensitivity to the verse, and both had their greatest successes as Hamlet. In their reviews of Gielgud's 1942 production of *Macbeth* at the Piccadilly, the critics remarked, as they had of Forbes-Robertson, that 'in verbal modulation, in splendour of declamation [he] is incomparable' (*Observer*, 12 July 1942), but he was 'conspicuously lacking in soldierly quality' (*Times*, 9 July 1942). He managed to convey a martial impression in his first scene, 'though low in tone, gaunt and sombre like an El Greco', but came fully into his own when contemplating the murder, where his feeling for the poetry wonderfully expressed Macbeth's nervous anxiety, his struggle between determination and doubt, and 'his collapse after the murder was a masterpiece of nerves well matched by the truly magnificent virtuosity of the Banquet Scene, where the actor went all out' (Agate, *Chronicles*, p. 245). *The Times* agreed that he became 'truly exciting between one murder and another' where 'he falls a prey to his wildly superstitious nature and paints imaginary horror in words that seem to have been dipped in the witches' cauldron' (9 July 1942). The Lady Macbeth, Gwen Ffrangcon-Davies, was thought to have been miscast. She was a gifted comic actress but for this role was physically too slight, and lacked sufficient power and range. 'Scorn is the deepest note of this actress's register; scorn accompanied by an expression of faint disgust. She can neither speak daggers nor look them' (Agate, *Chronicles*, p. 245).

Gielgud directed *Macbeth* again in June 1952 at Stratford-on-Avon with Ralph Richardson and Margaret Leighton in the leading roles, and this time created a setting which was not historical but symbolic, an expression of the darkness and evil created by the language. It was 'an unlocalised setting of blackest night. Torches flare against it. Here is the battleground of the powers of evil and good' (*Illustrated London News*, 5 July 1952). 'The clever arrangement of dark clanking passages leading from the castle hall is as full of doom as could be wished' said *Punch* (25 June 1952). The conception was a good one, but the execution was not, and Sir Ralph Richardson, whose Falstaff had been called 'definitive', was a failure.

> The Macbeth Sir Ralph presented to us could never have won a battle at all, unless one were to suppose that in the fighting before the play he had received the last of a series of severe concussions. That would explain why he should meander, punch drunk, through the events which followed . . . The immense varieties and subtleties of the verse were overborne by a kind of dazed monotony of delivery that wore us down.   (*New Statesman*, 21 June 1952)

This Macbeth, said the *Spectator*, 'to the literal-minded playgoer must give the impression of having been hit very hard on the head just before the curtain went up' (20 June 1952). Margaret Leighton gave 'a performance of conspicuous intelligence and great virtuosity', but she was thought to be too slight and feminine: 'Frown as she will, her Lady Macbeth never chills our blood. Her charms are too innocent for out-and-out ruthlessness; we cannot believe her capable of cold-blooded villainy' (*Punch*, 25 June 1952).

The designs for all these post-war productions, with the exception of Jackson's modern-dress version, followed the familiar English conventions then thought appropriate for the national poet. In Europe, however, all kinds of experiments were being tried, especially in Germany, following the radical innovations in design introduced by Appia and Gordon Craig, who had abandoned realism in favour of abstract shapes and the expessive use of light and darkness. The average British playgoer was unaware of these developments, and was therefore astonished when, in April 1933, a European *Macbeth* suddenly appeared at the Shakespeare Memorial Theatre. It was directed by Theodore Komisarjevsky, a Russian who had left his home country after the revolution, and was acquainted with what had been happening across the channel. The most striking innovations were the sets:

> [Komisarjevsky] carried some of the feeling of Soviet constructivism into a metaphoric structure of burnished aluminium with curved screens, scroll work, and turning staircases. Though it had the initial appearance of a unit set, its sections could be moved so that the action occurred in an adjustable abstract architecture, suggesting by turns a castle exterior, an interior or the open plain.
>
> (Kennedy, *Looking*, p. 129)

Other accounts amplify these impressions of 'twisted forms and bright metal rearing up amidst subdued lights and dark shadows against a backdrop of clouds, now pale, now suffused with crimson, with stairs leading offstage to unseen entrances and exits' (Mullin, 'Komisarjevsky's *Macbeth*', p. 23).

The design was expressionistic in the sense that it conveyed the feelings of guilt and hallucination in Macbeth's consciousness. Consistently with this, the supernatural elements were eradicated. The witches had no special powers but became old hags plundering the corpses on the battlefield and, when they prophesied Macbeth's future, they read his hand like palmists. Banquo's ghost did not put in an appearance but became Macbeth's own shadow enlarged and projected on the aluminium wall, and the cauldron scene was not shown at all. 'After the banquet Macbeth went to bed on the stage and had a nightmare in which he heard some of the speeches in that scene [4.1] spoken "off"' (Crosse, *Playgoing*, p. 97).

The whole action took place against a background of war. 'The great lords and generals are habited in steel helmets, field grey and long cloaks very like those of German staff officers' and 'dark muzzles of field guns protrude from the stockades, [and] firearms are carried by the troops' (*Punch*, 10 May 1933). The costume worn by Fabia Drake, the Lady Macbeth,

> incorporated a considerable amount of iron-mongery and was much ridiculed. Her crown in the banquet scene was made of saucepan scourers . . . [and] her breasts were covered by what appeared to be saucepan lids . . . The actors were encouraged to speak their lines swiftly and sharply, which the critics disliked: 'A series of spasmodic rushes', commented the *Morning Post*, 'which destroys the music and rhythm of the verse'   (Beauman, *Royal Shakespeare*, pp. 131–2)

The production was generally not well received: 'A good set of players were apparently so bewildered by the oddities of the production that they gave a very poor performance', said Gordon Crosse (*Playgoing*, p. 97), but not all the reactions were hostile. Some of the critics felt that it was 'a thing of genius, boldly brilliant and true' (*Birmingham Gazette*, 19 April 1933), which had 'the force of an entirely new conception' (*Scotsman*, 21 April 1933). 'When once we have grasped the producer's conventions and intentions', said Joseph Thorp in *Punch*, 'all, or nearly all fell into place naturally and inevitably. The old play was given a new cutting edge' (10 May 1933).

'MACBETH' ON FILM

By now a great many films had been made of Shakespeare's plays, beginning in 1899 with four scenes from *King John* (of which only one has survived) with Beerbohm Tree as the King. Sixteen films were made of *Macbeth* between 1909 and 1994 (Rothwell, *Screen*), many of them silent and most of them now forgotten. Orson Welles's version (1948) is interesting because of the strongly personal interpretation he gave to the play. He saw it as a struggle between Christian law and order and the forces of chaos and hell, and emphasised this idea by creating a new character, the Holy Father, who speaks the lines of various minor characters, including the Old Man, Ross, Angus, and Lennox, and is the presiding presence in the England scene. This is played in front of a stone Celtic cross which is used throughout as a symbol of Christianity. The English soldiers carry a great sea of crosses as they advance on Dunsinane and these are contrasted with the satanic, forked crosses carried by the witches.

The production is designed to be Scottish. The set, which is not at all naturalistic, consists of rough, massive rocks under a dark sky and the actors, who speak with unconvincing Scottish accents, are dressed in skins and rough, woollen garments, the men with medieval helmets. Welles himself wears a huge, square-shaped crown. More than half the text is cut and is rearranged so that Welles, a heavy, gloomy presence with large, rolling eyes, often shown in close-up, dominates the play. He appears haunted, neurotic, and agonised from the start and therefore has little room to develop. The Lady Macbeth, Jeanette Nolan, had previously acted only in radio plays. Her personality is slight and makes little impression, even in the sleep-walking scene, at the end of which she is woken by a kiss from Macbeth, runs off screaming, and jumps to her death from a cliff. Technically the production is uneven and much of the dialogue is scarcely audible, but its greatest weakness is the slow, unvaried pace at which it is taken.

The most radically original film of *Macbeth* is Akira Kurosawa's *Throne of Blood* (1957), a free adaptation of Shakespeare's play translated into Japanese. It departs from the original in a number of ways: there is no 'letter' scene (1.5), though the dialogue between Macbeth and his wife makes it clear that they have already discussed the murder; there is no equivalent of the 'England' scene (4.3) and Macbeth is killed not in single combat but by a shower of arrows shot at him by his own men, one of which goes through his throat. There is only one witch, a kind of oracle who is discovered spinning amid a heap of human bones as she sings of the futility of human ambition and, though she is referred to as 'she', she has a deep masculine voice.

Washizo (Macbeth) is a very large, virile man, unmistakably a military leader and an impressive horseman. His moral struggles are conveyed not in soliloquies but by the tortured, haunted expressions of his face. His wife's face, by contrast, is impassive and expressionless as she glides along in a formal, floor-length dress. It is she who quietly instigates the murder, drugs Duncan's guards, and hands the murder weapon, a long spear, to Macbeth. She says the words of the sleep-walking scene while kneeling in front of a basin of water and her agony of conscience is made more striking by comparison with the calm she has shown earlier.

The most powerful feature of the film is the setting. Duncan's fort is remote and isolated and must be reached through a tangled and confusing forest, Cobweb Forest, in which the characters are hopelessly lost. Their confusion is worsened by a fog which hangs permanently over the landscape and the film opens with a wild thunderstorm. Cobweb Forest, the equivalent of Birnam Wood, surrounds the castle, and when it appears to move it can be seen from the castle walls. The transposition of the play from Scotland to Japan and the unfamiliar Asian costumes give the play a new emphasis. It appears not to be a dramatisation of a series of historical events (an impression increased by the frequent use of Scottish costumes), but a timeless myth or morality play in which the evil hero is punished for his misdeeds. It is, of course, not Shakespeare's *Macbeth* but it is a magnificent film which in some ways illuminates the moral significance of the original.

In Roman Polanski's film version (1971) both Macbeth (Jon Finch) and his wife (Francesca Annis) are young – well under thirty – and very good-looking, to the extent that in the opening scenes Macbeth has a look of innocent naivety and finds the witches' prophecies genuinely baffling. She is slim and willowy with long, golden hair. Both are physically attracted to each other but she is the instigator of the murder, persuading him not by being a domineering woman, but a charming, alluring wife who is highly ambitious but also shallow in that, unlike Macbeth, she fails to foresee the consequences of their crime. Both are increasingly possessed by anxiety and regret, especially Macbeth whose face darkens during the course of the action.

The sets are thoroughly naturalistic. Dunsinane castle (filmed at Lindisfarne in Northumberland) looks delightful, perched on the top of a little hill, and, for once, gives credibility to Duncan's remark that it 'hath a pleasant seat' as he approaches it in the distance. This realism extends to the violence of the play, especially the scenes which are reported by Shakespeare but are actually shown by Polanski, such as the torture and execution of Cawdor (who is tied in chains and forced to leap from the battlements), the murder of Duncan and his grooms, the killing of Lady Macduff and her little son, who is naked and taking a bath when the murderers enter, and the decapitation of Macbeth whose head, shown in close-up, rolls down a flight of steps outside the castle. Polanski's *Macbeth* is bloodier than Shakespeare's and, at the end, less reassuring. After Malcolm is made King, his brother Donaldbain, who walks with a limp, secretly goes off to consult the witches and, as the film concludes, is shown entering their cave. There is no sense of redemption; the cycle of ambition and murder is about to begin again.

A 'SLIGHTLY DISAPPOINTING' PLAY?

During its theatrical history, a number of critics have remarked that, in performance, *Macbeth* has seldom been successful. In 1869, F. W. Hawkins asked the question, 'Why does the character of Macbeth usually produce so poor an impression when placed on the stage?' (*Kean*, vol. 1, p. 269), and James Agate, reviewing Gielgud's production of 1930, said he found the play 'always slightly disappointing' (*Chronicles*, p. 225). The difficulty, it was said, lay in the apparent contradictions in the leading role which is 'a host of incompatibles. He is at once poet and murderer, dreamer and doer, tyrant and sniveler, warrior and philosopher, Shelley and Himmler' (*Saturday Review of Literature*, 17 April 1948). During the first half of the century, 'the most eminent actors . . . either failed, or did not try, to capture the mighty opposites in Macbeth's character' (Bartholomeusz, *Players*, p. 251). Another difficulty lies in the complexity of Lady Macbeth, who is both unfeelingly ambitious, especially in the first part of the play, and yet genuinely affectionate towards her husband, and few actresses have managed to express both sides of her personality. Whereas Siddons and Cushman were ruthless and domineering, Faucit and Terry were tenderly devoted. Yet another difficulty arises from the way that *Macbeth* is constructed. It moves rapidly forward towards the murder and on to the end of the banqueting scene so that, as Agate put it, 'the play goes up like a rocket', but then 'comes down like the stick' (*Chronicles*, p. 225). This drop in tension is attributed to the 'England' scene, the longest in the play and the most static, which many directors, including Garrick and Irving, tried to overcome by substantially cutting it.

The inability of the actors and directors to surmount these difficulties probably accounts for the disappointment felt by the reviewers. Hence Gielgud, though he spoke Shakespeare's poetry expressively, never gave the impression of being a strong fighting commander, and Martita Hunt, though undoubtedly intelligent and subtle, was always 'too likeable' (Agate, *Chronicles*, p. 228). Malcolm Keen, who played Macbeth at the Old Vic in 1932, successfully presented him as a tyrant but failed to do justice to his contemplative intelligence, and his Lady Macbeth, Margaret Webster, was said to have simplified the character and made her into a melodramatically evil woman (Bartholomeusz, *Players*, p. 237). Two years later, Charles Laughton was said to lack Macbeth's tragic stature, and had no feeling for the expressiveness of the verse. 'Listening to Mr Laughton', said Ivor Brown, 'you may wonder whether *Macbeth* was written in poetry at all' (*Observer*, 8 April 1934). Flora Robson, 'terribly handicapped by a reddish wig and robe the colour of tinned salmon at its tinniest', was so much more successful that she was said to have dwarfed Laughton. Like Fanny Kemble, she saw Lady Macbeth as 'deficient in imagination', unable to grasp the seriousness of the crime on which she had embarked, and she was a warmly affectionate wife who became desolated by the widening gap between herself and her husband. She had 'all the baleful horror of a Medusa', said the *Daily Telegraph*, 'and yet managed to suggest also a pitiful humanity' (3 April 1934). Michael Redgrave, in 1947, had a masculine, commanding presence, but, according to *The Times*, 'the plainest reason for [his] failure to move us is the monotonous hoarseness of his speech' (19 December 1947). A critic in an unidentified newspaper cutting in the London Theatre Museum agreed that Redgrave 'leaves Macbeth the poet almost unnoticed. Speeches and phrases are hurled out in a kind of martial rage.' There was general approval, however, for the production in which Redgrave appeared. The American director Norris Houghton managed to shape his cast into a coherent company, and, as a result, the predominant impression was of the play and not the characters: 'They play as a group, subordinated to the overriding pressure of an idea which they all appear to share, an idea of the play as a whole . . . A consistency of underlying pattern props up even the weakest and gives to the whole a unity unlike anything we have seen in London for some years' (*New Statesman*, 27 December 1947).

THE PLAY IN PRODUCTION SINCE 1950

One of the few actors capable of embracing the whole range of Macbeth's character was Paul Rogers. 'Here', said Ivor Brown, 'is the whole Macbeth, reflective word-spinner as well as noble scoundrel, with a voice to render it and the physique to endure this most exhausting of the great roles.' He was 'a superb Macbeth. Never have I seen the part grow so vividly through nervous ambition to uneasy triumph and then to ageing disillusion and the bravest end' (*Observer*, 29 August 1954). The production, by Michael Benthall, opened at the Edinburgh Festival and, after a spell in London at the Old Vic, moved on to New York where Rogers was again warmly acclaimed. 'Mr Rogers,' said Brooks Atkinson in the *New York Times*, 'an intelligent actor with a resonant voice . . . catches the whole range of the character from the mannerly though guarded beginning to the reckless brutality of the end' (30 October 1956). What united this Macbeth with his wife was certainly not love, but 'a fierce connubial bond', a mutually shared attraction towards evil. On her first entrance, Coral Browne, who played Lady Macbeth in New York, was 'a sensual, baleful woman of grace and authority who sends a shudder through the whole play', and by the end she had become 'a worn, dishevelled, glassy-eyed creature who has tumbled over the brink into madness' (*New York Times*, 30 October 1956).

The production was distinctively Scottish. It began with the sound of bagpipes and was dressed in leather cloaks and grey kilts ('specially made by the firm that supplies the Duke of Edinburgh'), and the witches appeared in a wild landscape against a background of towering rocks. 'The set (by Audrey Cruddas) was no more than a rough-hewn square arch, on either side of which appeared, as necessary for the interior scenes, doorways, recesses, the lower treads of a sharply ramped and angled staircase. Through the opening of the arch was seen, dimly, the bleak heath or the dark inward of the castle and, suddenly, for the English scene, a dazzling rain-washed sky – the most moving visual effect in the play' (David, 'Tragic Curve', p. 123). Benthall's production, like Houghton's, was said to be very straightforward, 'a bloody tale of brutish people', 'a rushing macabre melodrama'. It was very noisy; 'Every entry was clamorously accompanied by pipe and drum, or by the pipes at full blow' (David, 'Tragic Curve', p. 123), but the pace and excitement were achieved at the expense of the play's tragic pathos. It 'leant very much towards the melodramatic', said Richard David, and 'the audience was never called upon to agonize for a tragic hero, but only to witness with excitement and approval the cornering of a dangerous criminal by the forces of the law' ('Tragic Curve', pp. 123–4).

Among members of the theatrical profession, *Macbeth* is thought to be an unlucky play. Since it is the most sustained study of evil in the whole of Shakespeare – perhaps in the whole of literature – it is not difficult to see how such a notion came about, but exactly when it arose is uncertain. There appears to be no reference to it in the eighteenth or nineteenth centuries, but by 1937 it was common knowledge. In November of that year, the opening of a production by Michel St Denis (in which Olivier made his first attempt at the title-role) coincided with the death of Lilian Baylis, the manager of the Old Vic where it was shown. As Bartholomeusz remarks, the coincidence 'seemed to confirm the superstition among theatre people that productions of the play were doomed to attract disaster, a suspicion entertained by Lilian Baylis herself' (*Players*, p. 245). Thirty years later it was rumoured that Peter Hall, then the Artistic Director of the Royal Shakespeare Company, had invited Peter Brook to direct the play, but that Brook had refused 'on the grounds of superstition', and Hall undertook the direction himself. The superstition seemed to be be proved right when, during rehearsals, Hall became so ill that the opening night had to be delayed by more than a month.

Laurence Olivier returned to the role at Stratford in 1955. In this production, according to *The Times*, he focused with such penetration on the hero's mind that the 'usual difficulty of reconciling the tough warrior with the superstition-ridden neurotic seems scarcely to exist' (8 June 1955). The outstanding feature of his performance was the care and concentration with which he spoke the words. He deliberately did not say them 'beautifully', as Gielgud appears to have done, but

> his control is perfection, his range stupendous, and his instinctive feeling for the language sure and exact. He makes every syllable, every consonant and vowel do its maximum of work, he has appreciated every nuance of the weight and feel of the words, never underplays them – or indeed overplays them; they are, all of them, relished in the speaking for their value in carrying us to where we are going; in that sense they are all of them enjoyed. . . . One thing I particularly admired about Sir Laurence's superbly relished delivery was his ability to use the pause, the perfectly timed pause, without breaking the rhythm.
>
> (*New Statesman*, 18 June 1955)

He was said to be the greatest Macbeth since Macready, and he certainly displayed Macready's concentration on the detail of the text, but, in so doing, and unlike Macready, he did not turn the poetry into prose.

His Macbeth was not initially an obviously noble man, as Kemble's had been, but nor did he give the impression, as Irving had, that he was inherently evil and had considered killing the King before his meeting with the witches. He achieved something more subtle. In his first scene, he conveyed the impression that Macbeth's mind was already filled with unspecific 'dangerous thoughts and desires which it dare not formulate till the Weird Sisters give them voice', and, in the early scenes with Lady Macbeth, he suggested vividly the hope that 'the latent nobility of character may yet assert itself against the fatal lure of ambition' (*Times*, 8 June 1955). As the play developed, 'the black and dominating figure of Sir Laurence . . . led us slowly but surely to the very heart of the dark and the dreadful, and has discovered there, too, something that others have missed, that streak of self-hatred that adds yet another shade to the sombre palette of remorse' (*New Statesman*, 18 June 1955). Some of the critics complained that Olivier seemed not to care whether he killed Duncan or not, an impression which Richard David believed to be deliberate. 'The hideous deeds presented to his will seemed, like the air-drawn dagger, unreal; his intellect rejects them, and yet he remains under a terrible and inescapable compulsion to do them.' It was Olivier's achievement, says David, 'to make the audience share this possession, to bring them under the same spell, so that they experienced Macbeth's progress from the inside and themselves travelled the tragic curve' ('Tragic Curve', p. 125). He was also physically very agile ('sinuous' and 'tigerish' said the *Financial Times*). At the second appearance of Banquo's ghost in the banquet scene, he leapt onto a table, and he undertook the fight against Macduff with 'breathtaking courage'. Olivier, it seems, had all the necessary gifts to make his one of the greatest Macbeths in theatrical history.

Opinions of Vivien Leigh's Lady Macbeth were less positive. She was thought by some to be too slight for the part, and certainly did not attempt Siddons's grand manner, but she was 'tough, pertinacious', 'sharp and hard as nails' and, in a 'serpent-green' gown, had 'the personal magnetism that will mesmerically sway her hesitant hero to the supreme treachery and the risk of doom' (Brown, *Memorial Theatre*, p. 9).

The text was played almost complete with only the (probably spurious) Hecate scene (3.5) and the scene between Lennox and a Lord (3.6) left out. The settings created a realistically 'medieval' impression:

> the heath was authentically heathery, the castle had indeed a pleasant seat
> overlooking a loch-filled glen, and for the last scenes of the play we were on the
> very battlements with a distant view of snow-covered Grampians. Particularly
> effective was the narrow, cloister-like corridor at the far end of which suddenly
> appeared the spark of the sleep-walker's taper.   (David, 'Tragic Curve', p. 126)

10 Lady Macbeth demands to be given the daggers (2.2.56). Laurence Olivier and Vivien
Leigh, Shakespeare Memorial Theatre, Stratford-upon-Avon, 1955.

Glen Byam Shaw's direction was dismissed as inadequate ('oddly unin-
spired') by some critics, but defended by others for its 'vigour and clarity'.
In a close analysis of the performance of the scene between Macbeth and his
wife before the murder (1.7), Richard David has shown how each move and
gesture by the actors exactly expressed the changing relationship between
the two characters ('Tragic Curve', p. 128; see commentary, p. 110).

Donald McWhinnie's 1962 production, also at Stratford, was simple and straightforward, played on a wide, sloping platform in front of a broad stone arch, but Irene Worth's Lady Macbeth was both unorthodox and entirely plausible. Initially she emphasised her practical, homely qualities, and the first impression she made was one of domesticity (*Plays and Players*, August 1962, p. 19). 'Her smile at persuading her husband has only to be widened an inch or so in order to greet Duncan' and her sleep-walking scene 'has the pathos of a stupid person unhinged and she talks of daggers as if they were table knives' (*Times*, 6 June 1962). Eric Porter's Macbeth was a thoroughly intelligent performance which strongly established his soldier-like personality. 'His Macbeth is clearly eaten up by ambition, but had he married differently he would probably have got by honourably, and died in his bed' (*Punch*, 29 June 1962). The production received general approval, and was considered competent and efficient but lacking in passion.

William Gaskill's 1966 production at the Royal Court was said to be his 'most uncompromisingly Brechtian. Hard white light beats down even in the night scenes and Banquo's murderers fumble about in imagined dark-ness in full view of the audience. The style is resolutely anti-illusionist' (*Times*, 21 October 1966). Sir Alec Guinness and Simone Signoret were ill-suited to each other. She looked magnificent, 'a lazily imperious giantess with a mouth like a wound', but the short, lightweight Guinness played 'like a dynamic mannikin': 'much of his performance suggests a mating rite between a spirited male bird and a large, broody female'. The production was further impeded by Signoret's French–American accent and her voice was not powerful enough to carry even in that relatively small theatre.

Peter Hall's 1967 production at Stratford was considered 'disappointing', largely on account of the performance of Paul Scofield from whom some-thing remarkable had been expected. Scofield is one of our greatest actors with a magnetic presence and a distinctive, lucid voice, but on this occa-sion he seemed not to be giving a finished performance but experimenting with different ways of speaking his lines, as though searching for one that would satisfy him. 'I find his performance very interesting and absolutely convincing,' said B. A. Young in the *Financial Times*,

> but he plays such tricks with the words, inserting long 'Macready pauses' in the most unlikely places, throwing the accents on to the most unexpected words, inflecting what have always seemed to me quite straightforward sentences with the most inappropriate inflections (and quite often with none) that all the meaning is lost. 'Duncan is IN his grave,' he says: and 'Oh full of scorpions. Is my mind'; 'My way of life is fallen into the sere. The yellow leaf.' What's it all about?   (17 August 1967)

This was, of course, a review of a very early performance and it may be that Scofield settled into a steadier reading as he became more comfortable with the part. Vivien Merchant, the Lady Macbeth, was criticised for delivering her longer speeches in a 'neatly clipped and drilled' way, 'as if conscious of the beady eye of an elocution mistress at her back'. 'With this pair of dummies running the castle', said Hilary Spurling in the *Spectator*, 'the production has small sense of direction, time or place' (25 August 1967).

Like Welles, Hall interpreted *Macbeth* as a Christian play – or, rather, a play about the nature of evil, seen from a Christian point of view. In the opening scene, the weird sisters were shown as huge silhouettes inverting a crucifix on which they poured blood; a cross was carried behind Duncan and, later behind Malcolm; Duncan wore the white robes of consecrated kingship, and when later Macbeth appeared in the same robes, 'the blasphemy was shocking' (Robert Speaight, *Shakespeare Quarterly*, Autumn 1967, p. 394). The 'England' scene, with its accounts of Edward the Confessor's miraculous powers of healing and Malcolm's enumeration of the 'king-becoming graces', often omitted in earlier productions, was given in full and with considerable weight in a much-praised performance by Ian Richardson. There is no doubt that *Macbeth* is full of Christian, religious images and that Hall gave expression to what is present in Shakespeare's text, but, as Irving Wardle pointed out in *The Times* (17 August 1967), such an interpretation 'casts no light on the two main characters. It does nothing to explain what hold Lady Macbeth had over her husband; nor their separate ways of development after the murder. Such things still can be approached only in direct human terms.'

Hall's use of visual symbolism showed the influence of the kind of interpretation of Shakespeare which had first appeared about thirty years earlier in the critical writings of Wilson Knight, with which Hall had probably become acquainted when he studied English Literature at Cambridge. Knight had little interest in the customary interpretation of the plays in terms of character, and replaced it with analyses of metaphors, symbols, and themes. To judge from Irving Wardle's comments, this emphasis was reflected in Hall's production.

His successor as Artistic Director of the RSC, Trevor Nunn, was also a Cambridge graduate in English, and his interpretation of *Macbeth* had some similarities to Hall's. He directed it twice, first with Nicol Williamson and Helen Mirren in 1974, and then with Ian McKellen and Judi Dench two years later. The two productions were quite dissimilar. The first was shown in the company's main theatre and appeared to be a development of Hall's 'religious' reading, an interpretation made very clear from the set. It consisted of a dark, oak interior which looked like a cathedral in which were mimed the coronations of Duncan, Macbeth, and Malcolm, 'setting a pattern of ritual virtue to a blazing organ accompaniment while the rest of the play turn[ed] to a grinding discord' (*Times*, 30 October 1974). Duncan, dressed in white, was presented as a High Priest as well as a king, and Macbeth's usurpation took on the character not only of regicide but of sacrilege. As in Hall's production, the England scene took on a central significance. 'Malcolm and Macduff conversed in choir-stalls in front of a standing crucifix, so that one felt the inspiration of Edward the Confessor behind the forces mustering for the tyrant's overthrow' (Speaight, *Shakespeare Quarterly*, Winter 1976, p. 16).

Nicol Williamson charted Macbeth's slow disintegration carefully, creating the impression of a man going ever more deeply into crime. 'At the end of the play one hardly recognised the exemplary soldier one had seen at the beginning' (Speaight, *Shakespeare Quarterly*, Winter 1976, p. 17). An unidentified review of his performance in New York complained that the Macbeth described by his wife as being too full of the milk of human kindness is not 'a Macbeth that we catch any fugitive glimpses of in Williamson; on the contrary, he is a man already in dire want of psychiatric attention. (So, eventually, is Lady Macbeth.)' Helen Mirren, a young Lady Macbeth, played her as a morally trivial woman, as Poel had believed she should be, who 'made the most atrocious actions sound like an enchanting game' (*Times*, 30 October 1974), and who exercised over her husband a sexual control and a will of iron. It was she who lured Macbeth into murder. The closeness of their relationship having been strongly established, the split between them half-way through the play became very clear and Mirren 'showed with great subtlety, how the crime which brought Macbeth and Lady Macbeth together ineluctably drew them apart'. 'Each performance', said Robert Speaight, 'became a study in loneliness' (*Shakespeare Quarterly*, Winter, 1976, p. 17).

When the production moved to London a year later, Nunn had greatly simplified it, substituting for the cathedral-like setting a kind of magic circle round which the actors sat on crates watching the performance until they were needed to play their parts in it and this he repeated in 1976 in a new production with fresh actors. This time it was shown not in the company's main house but at the Other Place, a disused garage that had been converted into a simple studio theatre. There was no raised stage and the actors performed on a bare floor. The audience – less than two hundred of them – sat on three sides of the acting area, two rows deep and elevated above the floor by scaffolding. As in the revival of Nunn's first production, the acting area was defined by a black painted circle round which the actors sat on packing-crates when not engaged in the performance. The audience could thereby see the witches outside the circle as they watched Macbeth fulfilling their prophecies, and see Macduff sitting ignorantly as his family is slaughtered (*New York Times*, 5 February 1978). The cast was reduced to fourteen (about the number used when *Macbeth* was first performed) and there was some doubling. The audience was, in fact, considerably smaller than it must have been at the Globe and they were so close to the actors that an extraordinary intimacy was created between them, and the words could be spoken quietly and subtly. There was no intermission, and the playing time was just over two hours (half the time taken by Tree's production). With virtually no set, Nunn largely abandoned the religious symbolism of his earlier version, and the play was not so much about damnation as about the minds of the characters, the way in which Macbeth and his wife will themselves to evil and, in the process, destroy themselves. In such plain, austere surroundings, the success of the production rested entirely on the actors.

As Lady Macbeth, Judi Dench wore a simple grey shift and a head-scarf, and Ian McKellen, in dark riding-breeches, boots and black tunic, and with sleeked hair, was a coldly murderous Macbeth who looked like 'an intense 1930s fascist' (Kennedy, *Looking*, p. 254). 'What we see', said Michael Billington of the *Guardian* (17 September 1976), 'is the gradual tearing away of Macbeth's public mask until we reach the driven psychopath beneath.' He achieved 'a blend of the practical – in, for instance his briefing of Banquo's murderers – and the introspective; and establishes with his wife a rich relationship full of affection, desire, awe, inspiration and protectiveness' (*Sunday Times*, 12 September, 1976). The closeness of their relationship was apparent from the rapturous embrace with which she welcomed her husband on his return home from battle, and in the intimacy of their dialogue, and their obviously close understanding of each other there was a strong sexual element, but McKellen's Macbeth was not simply seduced into crime. The plotting of Duncan's death was something which they shared, a decision which they reached as a result of their two minds working together. Dench played the sleep-walking scene with 'feverishly writhing hands, only still when they are held for a long moment to the candle and scrutinised' and she glided out with a 'sudden, startling agility' which 'brought the scene to a high pitch of excitement' (David, *Theatre*, p. 88). In the England scene, Roger Rees, an innocent, earnest Malcolm, dressed in white in contrast to the prevailing black, described the 'king-becoming graces' with a profound seriousness which made them central to the interpretation of the play.

The spareness of the production had disadvantages. In the final scenes the opposing armies did not appear on the stage but remained in the wings, 'from which their voices, as they planned their campaign, echoed round Macbeth who, having fortified himself within the inner ring with a noisy and desperate piling of beer-crates, remained on view throughout, demonstrably "tied to

11   Ian McKellen and Judi Dench (2.2.8), The Other Place, Stratford-upon-Avon, 1976.

the stake" ' (David, *Theatre*, pp. 86–7). There was no triumphant celebration of victory at the end. The troops, utterly exhausted after their struggle, sat with heads hanging and swords slumped at their sides while Malcolm, shaken and trembling, announced his impending coronation.

In Adrian Noble's 1986 production in the main theatre at Stratford the Macbeth was Jonathan Price who did not follow the tradition of presenting him as a great warrior. On the contrary his Macbeth was essentially a little man who depended for his strength on his relationship with his wife. It was impossible to imagine him as 'Bellona's bridegroom' and he was constantly, nervously explaining and attempting to justify himself. His interpretation, as Stanley Wells pointed out was 'anti-Bradleian in its denial of Macbeth's poetic imagination' (*Shakespeare Survey*, vol. XLI, 1988, p. 170). The strongest emotion he expressed was the fear that he displayed on his first encounter with the witches, when he collapsed in a dead faint on hearing their prophecy that he would be 'King hereafter'. He reacted to the news of his wife's death not resignedly as some Macbeths had done but by breaking down in naked grief and terror, and when told by the Messenger that Birnham Wood was advancing on Dunsinane he became hysterical and overturned a table and chairs. Lady Macbeth (Sinead Cusack) was young and beautiful but also vulnerable, and she expressed her gradual disintegration very movingly. The set was designed basically as a backgound for the actors, a simple black box, the walls of which closed in on Macbeth during the final scenes, emphasising the way in which he had become trapped and isolated.

The headline in the *Daily Telegraph* to the review of Richard Eyre's production in 1993 was 'Macbeth is Murdered at the National Theatre' and the critics generally had few favourable things to say about it. 'It was', wrote Peter Holland, 'awe-inspiring only in its awfulness.' Their most severe criticism was directed against the Macbeth, Alan Howard, whose lines were 'screamed and chanted, twisted and fragmented, stretched and gabbled into a nonsense that harked back to the satiric descriptions of the worst nineteenth-century barnstorming styles' (*Shakespeare Survey*, vol. XLVII, 1994). 'He uses [his voice] like a showy soloist giving a display of vacuous virtuosity . . . It's as if Howard himself cannot understand the character he's playing and is forced to hide behind hollow histrionics' (*Daily Telegraph*, 5 April 1993). This weakness was partially redeemed by his delivery of the 'tomorrow and tomorrow' soliloquy which was thrilling. The Lady Macbeth, Anastasia Hille, 'simply lacked the technique for such a demanding role'. She played her as 'a neurotic bimbo on the make, clad in a translucent nightie' (*Daily Telegraph*, 5 April, 1993). The production, moreover, was full of 'directorial flourishes' which interfered with the reception of the play.

Derek Jacobi's Macbeth in Adrian Noble's production at the Barbican Theatre a year later was generally applauded. He was 'one of those highly trained, sensitive military men who love the army for its discipline and order' (*Times Literary Supplement*, 14 January 1994). Because he was 'above all, ordinary' it was not strange that he was susceptible to his wife's persuasions, but, having given way to them, he appeared out of his depth, dismayed by the nightmare in which he was living' (*Shakespeare Quarterly*, Fall 1995, vol. 46, no. 3). He spoke his words with intelligence and discrimination, but there was 'nothing of the *daemon*'. The violence and savagery required in the final scenes seemed out of his range 'except when he carefully hacked off Young Siward's arms and legs before breaking his neck in an act of casual indulgence in violence'. Cheryl Campbell, a wayward, seductive Lady Macbeth, was 'a woman discovering not only her own power but also the sapping of her nature by that very power'. The setting, like that in Adrian Noble's previous production, was simple and functional, a pair of great doors leading in from the wings on either side between which a platform on a bridge slid up and down. This gantry 'descended with the witches on it and left them peering down at the action; it was on this platform that Banquo was murdered, his corpse left there until it needed to reappear at the feast. But the mechanics were a distraction from the performance and did nothing to suggest the supernatural. They inhibited rather than helping the witches' (Peter Holland, *Shakespeare Survey*, vol. XLVIII, 1995).

Both the costumes and the setting for Tim Albery's 1996 production, also at the main house in Stratford, were severely functional. 'The chairs and table for the banquet were of the most basic design; there was no throne for Macbeth to sit on, no crown for him to wear, no cauldron for the witches' (Robert Smallwood, *Shakespeare Survey*, vol. L, 1997, p. 207) and the set was of the simplest: brown papered walls and, at the rear, four plain brown doors. Some of the critics found it inexpressive, as, indeed, it was, but others realised that the audience's concentration was confined to the characters and their relationships. Even these were distanced from them, however, by a series of small, box-like platforms along the front of the stage, suggesting the battlements of a castle. The effect of this plain setting was to discourage us from being moved or excited and to force our concentration solely on the behaviour and words of the suffering human beings in front of us. 'It was', says Smallwood, 'an attempt to provide the intensity of studio Shakepeare in a fifteen-hundred seat theatre' (p. 207).

The costumes, also functional, did not call attention to themselves. For much of the play Macbeth (Roger Allam) wore plain, dark trousers and a white shirt (vividly splashed with blood after the murder). The two women wore simple, straight, dark dresses over which were black smocks. These were neutral and suggested no particular historical period. It is hard to imagine a production visually less like those of the nineteenth century.

Allam's Macbeth was initially confident, sociable, and cheerful, especially in his comradely relationship with Banquo, but this self-confidence was irrevocably destroyed when he was greeted by Ross as Thane of Cawdor (1.3.103) and he never regained it. Brid Brennan, 'a tiny Celtic waif', became confident and determined as a result of reading the letter and it was she who gave her husband the strength to commit the murder. She became distant from him during the banquet, however: they grew further apart and, at the end of the scene, they went off separately. The conclusion was far from triumphant and Malcolm, the new King, delivered the final lines in 'an emotionless monotone'. It was, like the rest of the production, comfortless and bleak. The director had clearly thought out the play afresh and given it a new emphasis which some people found unacceptable. Both the characters and the action were entirely consistent, however, and others welcomed the opportunity to see the play in a fresh light.

In November 1999, the Royal Shakespeare Company again presented *Macbeth*, this time directed by Gregory Doran and played in a small auditorium, the Swan Theatre, a Jacobean-style playhouse holding about four hundred people seated on three levels round an apron stage. The actors were mostly dressed in black battledress (like 'Balkan guerillas'); Lady Macbeth wore a series of simple but elegant long dresses and the sainted Duncan appeared in dazzling gold and white brocade. The sets were minimal, and much of the action took place in a half light or darkness so that when Birnam Wood came to Dunsinane, 'it does so in such a crepuscular swirl that for a moment it really does appear as an eerie event, rather than as a few actors wagging twigs of privet' (*Observer*, 21 November 1999). The horror and violence of the play were emphasised by the sound of frequent, deep, loud, drumming. The dialogue, only slightly cut, was spoken rapidly, and with one scene running seamlessly into another and no intermission, the performance took just over two hours. The pace was so fast that, according to the *Observer*, 'You are made to feel with Macbeth that there is no going back.'

The Macbeth was Antony Sher, a lean, agile, sinewy man who had recently played Richard III and Tamburlaine, and who immediately conveyed the impression of a self-confident, genial, unhesitatingly violent soldier. Playing close to the audience, he was able to convey 'the full nuance of an emotionally complex speech without seeming laboured or actorly in doing so' (*Financial Times*, 18 November 1999). The most distinctive quality of his interpretation was its ironic detachment. His reaction to the witches' prophecies was 'a big, disbelieving laugh ... He grins a lot, and shakes the hand of his rival Malcolm on the latter's promotion to Prince of Cumberland; he turns his speech after the discovery of Duncan's murder into a well-prepared public oration', and ends 'the awesome passage about wading ever deeper in blood [3.4.136–7] with an ironic chuckle' (*Times*, 18 November 1999). The irony became increasingly sardonic, so that, when he had dismissed life as a tale told by an idiot (5.5.25–7) 'he walks off the stage into the audience with a flourish of disdain' (*Observer*, 21 November 1999). The detachment which was central

12 Antony Sher and Harriet Walter, Swan Theatre, Stratford-upon-Avon, 1999.

to his interpretation, however, inhibited his expression of Macbeth's inner turbulence and misery:

> 'I have supped full of horrors,' says the doomed Macbeth, but Sher has done little more than nod knowingly at them as he passed their tables. They have not chilled his spine or prickled his scalp . . . You don't feel his mind is full of scorpions, as he claims, or even dizzy with insomnia, as his wife suggests.
>
> (*Times*, 18 November 1999)

'You can fault neither Sher's energy nor the care with which he appoaches every line', said *The Times*, 'but where's the darkness within?'

Harriet Walter's Lady Macbeth was tall, slim, poised, not at all the domineering tragedy queen, but an intelligent woman, rather aristocratic, dedicated to the promotion of her husband's career and content to play a secondary role as the commanding officer's wife. As such she was entirely credible. She summoned the spirits of darkness (1.5.38–52) 'not with the ease of someone beckoning her consorts, but as one who needs an injection of cruelty' (*Observer*, 21 November 1999) and, from the start, gave an impression of frailty and hesitation so that, as she and Macbeth went more deeply into evil, she seemed to be on increasingly unfamiliar ground. Hence when, after the murder and the banquet, her controlled facade began to crack, her disintegration was not unexpected. 'She grimaces with nervousness when she greets the King; she gasps as she takes the daggers from her husband' (*Observer*, 21 November 1999), and, by the time of the sleep-walking scene, had gone over the edge into madness. Her performance was more genuinely tragic than Sher's in that she was an immediately recognisable, sympathetic woman, whose loyalty to her husband led her gradually into depths of evil which her frail nature could not endure.

The Royal Shakespeare Company's productions at the Other Place and the Swan, with almost complete texts and little or no scenery, marked a return to something like the conditions in which *Macbeth* was played in Shakespeare's time. They certainly fulfilled William Poel's injunction that the stage should be stripped bare of scenery and brought as far as possible into the auditorium so that the lines could be spoken without exaggeration. Such productions, however, lacked one central element to which audiences were accustomed. There were no visual effects other than those created by the positioning of the actors. There could be none of the dark, primitive scenery of the kind created by Irving and Tree, which was a visual expression of the play and the minds of the characters. The success of such productions depends exclusively on the ability of the actors to express Shakespeare's words. Moreover, they are possible only in small theatres where the audience, also small, are seated close to the actors. The production style could not be transferred successfully to a large, more conventional theatre, where the audience must be seated further away from the actors, and where a bare stage calls attention to itself and can be a distraction. In such conventional theatres settings, however simple and functional, are unavoidable and will no doubt continue to be used in the future.

LIST OF CHARACTERS

Speaking characters in order of first appearance:

Three WITCHES

DUNCAN, *King of Scotland*

MALCOLM, *Duncan's elder son, later Prince of Cumberland, later King of Scotland*

CAPTAIN *in the Scottish forces*

LENNOX, *a thane*

ROSS, *a thane*

MACBETH, *Thane of Glamis, later Thane of Cawdor, later King of Scotland*

BANQUO, *a thane*

ANGUS, *a thane*

LADY MACBETH, *Countess of Glamis, later Countess of Cawdor, later Queen of Scotland*

ATTENDANT *in the household of Macbeth*

FLEANCE, *Banquo's son*

PORTER *in Macbeth's household*

MACDUFF, *Thane of Fife*

DONALDBAIN, *Duncan's younger son*

OLD MAN

Two MURDERERS *employed by Macbeth*

SERVANT *in the household of Macbeth*

THIRD MURDERER *employed by Macbeth*

HECATE, *goddess of the moon and of sorcery*

A LORD, *a Scot, opposed to Macbeth*

FIRST APPARITION, *an armed Head*

SECOND APPARITION, *a bloody child*

THIRD APPARITION, *a Child crowned*

LADY MACDUFF, *Countess of Fife*

SON *to Macduff and Lady Macduff*

MESSENGER, *a Scot*

Two MURDERERS, *who attack Lady Macduff and her Son*

DOCTOR *at the English court*

DOCTOR OF PHYSIC *at the Scottish court*

WAITING-GENTLEWOMAN *who attends Lady Macbeth*

MENTEITH, *a thane opposed to Macbeth*
CAITHNESS, *a thane opposed to Macbeth*
SERVANT *to Macbeth*
SEYTON, *gentleman loyal to Macbeth*
SIWARD, *general in the Anglo-Scottish forces*
MESSENGER *in Macbeth's service*
YOUNG SIWARD, *Siward's son, in the Anglo-Scottish forces*

Silent characters:
Attendants in Duncan's entourage
Musicians (players of hautboys)
Torch-bearers
Sewer } *in Macbeth's household*
Servants and Attendants
Ghost of Banquo
Three Witches, accompanying Hecate
Eight kings, appearing to Macbeth
Drummers and bearers of colours (flags) in the Anglo-Scottish forces
Soldiers in the Anglo-Scottish forces
Drummers and bearers of colours (flags) in Macbeth's forces
Soldiers in Macbeth's forces

MACBETH

ACT I, SCENE I

Thunder and lightning. Enter three WITCHES

0 SD   *Thunder and lightning. Enter . . .* 'Thunder and lightning was the conventional stage
language . . . for the production of effects . . . from the tiring house that would establish a
specifically supernatural context in the minds of the audience' (Thomson, '*Thunder and
Lightning*', p. 11). In Davenant's version, the witches were portrayed as buffoons and were
played by men whose reputations had been made in comedy (see p. 8; Bartholomeusz,
Players, pp. 17–18). They were dressed in 'mittens, plaited caps, laced aprons, red
stomachers [and] ruffs' and carried broomsticks (Oulton, *History*, vol. II, p. 139). Garrick
wanted them to be evil, sinister creatures but dared not break with tradition for fear of
offending the gallery (Burnim, *Director*, p. 109). Macklin was the first director in England to
present them seriously (1773), and in Kemble's production, they were depicted as
'preternatural beings distinguishable only by the fellness of their purposes, and the fatality
of their delusions' (Oulton, *History*, vol. II, p. 139). In the German translation by Schiller and
Goethe, produced in Weimer in 1800, the witches are 'statuesque like the norns of Nordic
mythology or the Roman sybils, impressive, impassive foretellers of the future . . . They
were played by veiled men wearing classical drapes . . . They sow the evil seed in
whomever is "valiant, upright and good" which they consider Macbeth to be' (Williams,
German Stage, p. 95). Macready's witches had beards and wore short kirtles. The curtain
rose on a darkened stage, in the centre of which they could be dimly seen, conferring
inaudibly as the thunder clapped. They rushed apart, one to the right, another to the left,
the third to the back. Then the witch at the back cried out the opening lines, 'full voiced,
male and malevolent' (Downer, *Macready*, p. 319). In Phelps's production 'the stage was
darkened to a much greater degree than usual, so much so that but the imperfect outlines
of the weird sisters were visible. In front only a dim, lurid light played, and as the hags
stepped backwards, the darkness, aided by a combination of gauze screens, procured one
of the most perfect effects of vanishing we ever saw' (*Lloyd's Weekly London News*, quoted
in Phelps and Forbes-Robertson, *Phelps*, p. 100). The curtain rose in Irving's 1888
production on darkness, thunder, and rain. A flash of lightning revealed the witches
silhouetted against the sky, standing on a 'rocky eminence', and, at the end of the scene,

FIRST WITCH When shall we three meet again?
　　　　In thunder, lightning, or in rain?
SECOND WITCH When the hurly-burly's done,
　　　　When the battle's lost, and won.
THIRD WITCH That will be ere the set of sun.　　　　　5
FIRST WITCH Where the place?
SECOND WITCH Upon the heath.
THIRD WITCH There to meet with Macbeth.
FIRST WITCH I come, Graymalkin.
SECOND WITCH Paddock calls.　　　　　　　　　　　10
THIRD WITCH Anon.
ALL Fair is foul, and foul is fair,
　　　　Hover through the fog and filthy air.

Exeunt

more lightning showed them flying 'through the fog and filthy air' (Hughes, *Shakespearean*, p. 94). Komisarjevsky's witches in 1933 were 'old hags who were discovered plundering the slain after the battle'. Michel St Denis's witches wore grotesque masks and scaly costumes suggestive of sea-monsters' (Crosse, *Playgoing*, pp. 97, 102). Norris Houghton introduced, in addition to the witches, three tall, masked figures who gave the impression of being the supernatural powers of whom the witches were the agents (Gilder, 'New York', p. 131). Benthall's 'noisy' *Macbeth* 'opened with a wild and raucous cry, as a battle-casualty, leaving the field . . . staggered onto the stage and fell, to be ghoulishly seized upon by the witches in the guise of ragged camp-scavengers' (David, 'Tragic Curve', p. 123). Glen Byam Shaw's witches 'seemed to be magically suspended in a swirling mist between heaven and earth' (*New Statesman*, 18 June 1955). 'A weird high sound like the howling of the wind – but more unearthly – continues throughout the scene . . . A cat screeches, a toad croaks, and the witches vanish into darkness' (Mullin, *Macbeth Onstage*, p. 23). Hall's 1967 production began with a huge white canopy which hung over the stage and fluttered away at the first flash of lightning. It revealed a blood-red, heather-like carpet from under which the witches emerged carrying an inverted crucifix (*Shakespeare Survey*, vol. XXI, 1968, pp. 119–20). Nunn distinguished between the witches, two of whom were old and the third young. 'It was the young one, strangely possessed, who had the gift upon which they depended. Her look of open-mouthed vacancy changed to agony as the perceptions came upon her. She may have lacked virtue's protection as the dark forces clutched at her, but she was an innocent who gazed aloft like an ecstatic saint . . . It was she who made the critical announcement that Macbeth would be king; and later it was she, and not the Second Witch, who felt the approach of Macbeth like the pangs of childbirth' (Williams, *Text and Performance*, p. 62).

13　The word 'hover' may imply that the witches made their exit 'flying'. See note to 1.3.76–9 below.

ACT I, SCENE 2

Alarum within. Enter King [DUNCAN], MALCOLM, DONALDBAIN, LENNOX, *with Attendants, meeting a bleeding* CAPTAIN

0 SD   *Enter* . . . Macready's Promptbook shows that in his production this scene opened with a flourish of drums and trumpets, followed by a procession: 'Two chamberlains come first, walking backwards and bowing to King Duncan, who moves to the middle of the stage for his opening lines. He is followed by Malcolm and Donaldbain together, a physician, Ross, Lennox, three officers, and six lords. The procession is halted by the appearance, from downstage left, of the Bleeding Officer, supported by two soldiers' (Downer, *Macready*, p. 319). A watercolour in Charles Kean's Promptbook shows the setting as a 'Camp near Forres, site of Sweno's pillar' (a kind of obelisk). In his production, 'Duncan's camp at Forres . . . was discovered in night and silence, a couple of semi-savage armed kerns were on guard prowling to and fro with stealthy steps. A distant trumpet-call was heard, another in reply, another and yet another; a roll of the drum – an alarum. In an instant the whole camp was alive with kerns and gallowglasses, who circled round the old king and the princes of the blood. The Bleeding Sergeant was carried in on a litter, and the scene was illuminated with the ruddy glare of burning pine-knots' (Coleman, 'Facts and Fancies', p. 225). Irving cut the scene from his 1875 production but restored it in 1888 when a gauze was withdrawn to reveal 'a green and whin-clad hillside, with the tents of Duncan's army in the middle distance, seen through a group of Scotch firs overreaching the foreground'. When the gauzes closed again at the end of the scene 'distant thunder muttered and the sky grew lighter' (Hughes, *Shakespearean*, pp. 89, 94). Glen Byam Shaw began the scene with an assembly. 'Duncan and his sons entered P[rompt] S[ide] with a "Royal Standard Bearer" and two soldiers carrying banners; then come Lennox, Menteith, Caithness, and three more soldiers with banners, then an officer and two more soldiers. The King and his assembled entourage form a picture of an ordered society, a dramatic image P[rompt] S[ide] balanced by the excited entry of the wounded Sergeant O[pposite] P[rompt Side]' (Mullin, '*Macbeth* at Stratford', p. 278). 'Throughout this scene we hear the sounds of battle in the distance . . . We can now see the heath, its gray expanse broken only by rough-edged boulders' (Mullin, *Macbeth Onstage*, p. 23).

DUNCAN What bloody man is that? He can report,
As seemeth by his plight, of the revolt
The newest state.
MALCOLM   This is the sergeant
Who like a good and hardy soldier fought
'Gainst my captivity. Hail, brave friend;   5
Say to the king the knowledge of the broil
As thou didst leave it.
CAPTAIN   Doubtful it stood,
As two spent swimmers that do cling together
And choke their art. The merciless Macdonald –
Worthy to be a rebel, for to that   10
The multiplying villainies of nature
Do swarm upon him – from the Western Isles
Of kerns and galloglasses is supplied,
And Fortune on his damnèd quarrel smiling,
Showed like a rebel's whore. But all's too weak,   15
For brave Macbeth – well he deserves that name –
Disdaining Fortune, with his brandished steel,
Which smoked with bloody execution,
Like Valour's minion carved out his passage
Till he faced the slave,   20
Which ne'er shook hands, nor bade farewell to him,
Till he unseamed him from the nave to th'chaps
And fixed his head upon our battlements.
DUNCAN O valiant cousin, worthy gentleman.
CAPTAIN As whence the sun 'gins his reflection,   25
Shipwrecking storms and direful thunders,
So from that spring whence comfort seemed to come,
Discomfort swells. Mark, King of Scotland, mark,
No sooner justice had, with valour armed,
Compelled these skipping kerns to trust their heels,   30
But the Norwegian lord, surveying vantage,
With furbished arms and new supplies of men
Began a fresh assault.

1b–3a   Cut by Nunn.
   4   ('Who like . . . soldier') 'That', Nunn.
8–9a   Cut by Nunn.
10–12a Cut by Nunn.
10–12   Cut by Forbes-Robertson.
18–19a ('. . . minion') Cut by Forbes-Robertson.
25–8a   ('. . . swells') Cut by Forbes-Robertson and Nunn.

DUNCAN Dismayed not this our captains, Macbeth and Banquo?
CAPTAIN Yes, as sparrows, eagles, or the hare, the lion.   35
If I say sooth, I must report they were
As cannons over-charged with double cracks;
So they doubly redoubled strokes upon the foe.
Except they meant to bathe in reeking wounds
Or memorise another Golgotha,   40
I cannot tell.
But I am faint, my gashes cry for help.
DUNCAN So well thy words become thee as thy wounds;
They smack of honour both. Go get him surgeons.

> [*Exit Captain, attended*]

Enter ROSS *and* ANGUS

Who comes here?
MALCOLM   The worthy Thane of Ross.   45
LENNOX What a haste looks through his eyes! So should he look
That seems to speak things strange.
ROSS   God save the King.
DUNCAN Whence cam'st thou, worthy thane?
ROSS   From Fife, great king,
Where the Norwegian banners flout the sky
And fan our people cold.   50
Norway himself, with terrible numbers,
Assisted by that most disloyal traitor,
The Thane of Cawdor, began a dismal conflict,
Till that Bellona's bridegroom, lapped in proof,
Confronted him with self-comparisons,   55
Point against point, rebellious arm 'gainst arm,
Curbing his lavish spirit. And to conclude,
The victory fell on us –
DUNCAN   Great happiness! –
ROSS   That now Sweno,
The Norways' king, craves composition.
Nor would we deign him burial of his men   60
Till he disbursèd at Saint Colm's Inch
Ten thousand dollars to our general use.

36–41   Cut by Charles Kean and Forbes-Robertson.
45b–7   Cut by Charles Kean.
46–7a   Cut by Forbes-Robertson.
46b–7a ('So . . . strange') Cut by Nunn.
54b   ('lapped in proof') 'brave Macbeth', Nunn.

DUNCAN No more that Thane of Cawdor shall deceive
Our bosom interest. Go pronounce his present death
And with his former title greet Macbeth.   65
ROSS I'll see it done.
DUNCAN What he hath lost, noble Macbeth hath won.

Exeunt

ACT I, SCENE 3

Thunder. Enter the three WITCHES

FIRST WITCH Where hast thou been, sister?
SECOND WITCH Killing swine.
THIRD WITCH   Sister, where thou?
FIRST WITCH A sailor's wife had chestnuts in her lap
       And munched, and munched, and munched. 'Give me',
          quoth I.
       'Aroint thee, witch', the rump-fed runnion cries.   5

0 SD   *Enter . . .* In Macready's production, 'The backscene of the heath is masked by a huge
opaque cloud, in turn made misty by curtains of gauze clouding which hang in front of it.'
As the three witches assemble and begin to dance, 'the opaque cloud rises slowly and the
light begins to increase'. Then, during the witches' dialogue, 'a marching tune can be heard
in the far distance . . . The witches dance, the lights continue to rise, the march grows louder
and the mists and clouds have dispersed to reveal the barren rocky heath stretching toward
a distant sunset. Two spindling trees, one at right and one just left of center, accent the
barrenness. In the distance, on the right, part of Macbeth's army can be seen' (Downer,
Macready, p. 320). Phelps had 'a bleak, mournful landscape' here, 'just as the Scottish
highlands really are. On a low rise, between two ancient pines that represent the only
vegetation on the heath, stand the three witches. The discord of their hoarse voices is
orchestrated into a kind of melody, like the cries of old and young ravens' (Fontane, *London
Theatre*, p. 82). Phelps placed the witches on a rock back stage behind a green gauze
thickened below which obscured them totally when it rose, and then they were seen
floating in the air, whilst lightning revealed the advancing army (Rosenfeld, *History*, p. 118).
Charles Kean's staging, in 'a desolate place with a few bare trees', also used a combination
of lowered lights and gauzes for the entance of the witches (Promptbooks). In Irving's
revival of 1888, the witches' speeches were declaimed against a background of music which,
together with their voices, produced 'the wildest and uncanniest effect'. Then the rhythm
developed into a march, heralding the approach of Macbeth (Hughes, *Shakespearean*,
p. 95).

1–25   Cut by Komisarjevsky in order to eliminate the supernatural powers of the witches (Mullin,
'Komisarjevsky's *Macbeth*', p. 27).

    Her husband's to Aleppo gone, master o'th'Tiger:
    But in a sieve I'll thither sail,
    And like a rat without a tail,
    I'll do, I'll do, and I'll do.
SECOND WITCH I'll give thee a wind.   10
FIRST WITCH Thou'rt kind.
THIRD WITCH And I another.
FIRST WITCH I myself have all the other,
    And the very ports they blow,
    All the quarters that they know   15
    I'th'shipman's card.
    I'll drain him dry as hay:
    Sleep shall neither night nor day
    Hang upon his penthouse lid;
    He shall live a man forbid.   20
    Weary sennights nine times nine,
    Shall he dwindle, peak, and pine.
    Though his bark cannot be lost,
    Yet it shall be tempest-tossed.
    Look what I have.
SECOND WITCH   Show me, show me.   25
FIRST WITCH Here I have a pilot's thumb,
    Wrecked as homeward he did come.
          Drum within
THIRD WITCH A drum, a drum;
    Macbeth doth come.
ALL The weïrd sisters, hand in hand,   30

10–17   Cut by Nunn.
20   Cut by Nunn.
26   A manuscript note in Macready's Promptbook says, '*March* – Very distant – L[eft] – commencing with the kettledrums – This was played in the Green Room, and the Door opened and shut occasionally, to give the idea of the winds wafting the sound to and fro. The mist has, by this time, dispersed, discovering the extent of Heath, and part of the Army in the distance. Sunset.'
30–5   The stage direction at this point in Richard Cumberland's *British Theatre* (c. 1829) reads '*The Witches join hands and turn whilst they repeat these lines; they continue turning, until the second gets into the C., facing the audience; she then bends her head thrice over the hands of the other two, and speaks; after which the third and first do the same, and part hands as they retire to R.*' (Sprague, *Actors*, p. 227). In Charles Kean's production, just before Macbeth's entrance, 'the three witches joined their crutches and went round in a circle, then stood still, pointing to Macbeth' (Bede, '*Macbeth* on the Stage', p. 21).

Posters of the sea and land,
Thus do go, about, about,
Thrice to thine, and thrice to mine,
And thrice again, to make up nine.
Peace, the charm's wound up.   35

Enter MACBETH *and* BANQUO

35 SD   *Enter . . .* According to Simon Forman's 'Bocke of Plaies', in a peformance at the Globe
Playhouse, Macbeth and Banquo entered on horseback. (See Introduction, p. 2, n. 1).
Davenant gave Macbeth an additional opening line, 'Command they make a halt upon the
Heath', to give the impression that he and Banquo had left their soldiers off stage. Garrick,
whose entrance was preceded by a 'Scotch March', kept this line and followed it with the
words 'Halt, halt, halt', spoken by a soldier 'within' (Burnim, *Director*, p. 110). Macklin
developed the idea further and brought on a group of 'officers drums Fifes standards, &
other warlike characters & Insignia of the van of an army on the march' (manuscript notes).
They remained on the stage throughout the rest of the scene (*St James's Chronicle*, 28–30
October 1773). Kemble introduced a procession of twenty-four officers, soldiers and
standard-bearers with Macbeth and Banquo: 'They pass over the bridge . . . and form in two
Divisions across the back of the stage and down L[eft]. [Last soldiers] remain on bridge'
(Promptbook). Macready retained Davenant's opening line but spoke it off stage; Phelps cut
the line but Irving restored it. 'Irving was praised for the artistic disposal of his troops – "an
endless procession", straggling by in small groups' (Sprague, *Actors*, p. 230). Garrick,
following established tradition, wore a tie wig and contemporary regimental uniform.
Macklin introduced Scottish costume for the first time in the play's history, at least in
England. His Macbeth was 'booted, in russet, broadsword, Pistols, at his side, dirk, a cap
imitating a Bonnet, a ruff. – hair tied behind but short. – Soldiers half stockinged'
(manuscript notes). Kemble followed his example (Scott, 'Kemble', p. 219) and wore 'a
scarlet habit, plaid cloak and scarlet breeches', which were said by the *Morning Chronicle*
(17 October 1788) to have been 'characteristic', 'the bold military habit of the ancient Scots'
(Donohue, 'Kemble and Mrs Siddons', p. 71). Macready wore a short, black wig, and his
clipped beard and moustache outlined his mouth and jaws. He wore a knee-length garment
like a kilt, a bonnet with a feather and a plaid scarf thrown over his shoulder (Downer,
Macready, p. 320). Charles Kean's costume consisted of 'a chocolate coloured shirt, tight
sleeves; hauberk or coat of mail . . . grey leggings, bound round the ankles with straps of buff
leather; buff leather shoes; steel helmet with two eagle feathers in socket in front . . . party
coloured [*sic*] mantle' (Promptbook). Irving wore a 'wrap-over tunic . . . bordered with dark,
shaggy fur, and his leg straps were of leather with metal studs and buckles' (Jones, 'Stage
Costume', in Foulkes, *Victorian Stage*, p. 66). His face was lined and haggard and his
'restless movements, his wild and wandering eye' and his wiry, red moustache gave him

MACBETH So foul and fair a day I have not seen.
BANQUO How far is't called to Forres? What are these,
So withered and so wild in their attire,
That look not like th'inhabitants o'th'earth,

'a thoroughly unreliable look . . . He was even now contemplating murder as a means to the throne which his victories had brought almost within his reach' (Hughes, *Shakespearean*, p. 95). Salvini's Macbeth 'arrives with Banquo on the heath, fair and red-bearded, sparing of gesture, full of pride and the sense of animal well-being, and satisfied after the battle like a beast who has eaten his fill' (Stevenson, 'Salvini', p. 367). He was dressed in skins and woollens, and wore a spiked helmet with towering wings. Most of the Scots in Tree's production had 'reddish, auburn or flaxen hair'; both Macbeth and Macduff had 'huge, fiercely-flowing moustachios, length, indeed, being characteristic of the chevelure employed generally' (*Boston Evening Transcript*, 15 September 1911). Tree introduced a crash of thunder as Macbeth and Banquo entered, and, 'against the background of lightning-riven sky, rocks toppled and a stout oak-tree, rent to the roots, fell to earth. The shriek of the blast mingled with the sound of distant trumpets, and after the elements had run riot for a while, a final flash of lightning showed the figure of Macbeth poised on a boulder' (Pearson, *Tree*, p. 213). In Glen Byam Shaw's production, 'there was a boulder mid-stage on which the witches huddled side by side to exchange their sinister confidences. At the sound of Macbeth's drum they shrank into the prompt corner . . . Macbeth [Olivier], entering stage right, advanced to the centre and stepped up onto the boulder, where he stood in a strong light as of the setting sun . . . Thus all attention was concentrated on the face of Macbeth as he stiffened at the sight of the witches and as, guarded still, he listened to their prophecies. All the tension was gained by this device of focusing' (David, 'Tragic Curve', p. 127). At the RSC's Swan Theatre in 1999, 'Macbeth and Banquo, dressed like Balkan guerrillas, are carried onto the bare stage on the shoulders of their triumphant troops' (*Times*, 18 November 1999).

36 'The very first words Macbeth utters . . . show the natural vivacity of his character, and its tendency to be divided in its feelings; and the way in which these were spoken did not augur well for [Macready's] performance. "So fair and foul a day I have not seen", says the good-humoured conquering general, looking cheerily up at the sky, and playing, as it were, with the harmless struggle of the elements. Mr Macready delivered the words like a mere commonplace' (Leigh Hunt, *Dramatic Essays*, p. 211).

37b–45a 'It seemed as if [Macready] could scarcely repress his impatience during the six or eight lines of interrogatory [*sic*] which came from his co-mate in command, and it was in a quick imperious tone that he dashed over to the centre of the stage and exclaimed, "Speak, if you can! What are you?" The sinister prophecies of the weird sisters seemed to thrill through the man's body and soul as he started away, and, for a moment, "stood rapt in the wonder of it"' (Coleman, 'Facts and Fancies', p. 222).

And yet are on't? – Live you, or are you aught   40
That man may question? You seem to understand me,
By each at once her choppy finger laying
Upon her skinny lips; you should be women,
And yet your beards forbid me to interpret
That you are so.

MACBETH   Speak if you can: what are you?   45
FIRST WITCH All hail Macbeth, hail to thee, Thane of Glamis.
SECOND WITCH All hail Macbeth, hail to thee, Thane of Cawdor.
THIRD WITCH All hail Macbeth, that shalt be king hereafter.
BANQUO Good sir, why do you start and seem to fear
Things that do sound so fair? – I'th'name of truth   50
Are ye fantastical, or that indeed
Which outwardly ye show? My noble partner
You greet with present grace and great prediction
Of noble having and of royal hope
That he seems rapt withal. To me you speak not.   55
If you can look into the seeds of time
And say which grain will grow and which will not,
Speak then to me, who neither beg nor fear
Your favours nor your hate.

FIRST WITCH Hail.   60
SECOND WITCH Hail.
THIRD WITCH Hail.
FIRST WITCH Lesser than Macbeth, and greater.
SECOND WITCH Not so happy, yet much happier.
THIRD WITCH Thou shalt get kings, though thou be none.   65
So all hail Macbeth and Banquo.
FIRST WITCH Banquo and Macbeth, all hail.
MACBETH Stay, you imperfect speakers. Tell me more.
By Finel's death, I know I am Thane of Glamis,
But how of Cawdor? The Thane of Cawdor lives   70
A prosperous gentleman, and to be king
Stands not within the prospect of belief,

40b–1a   In Cumberland's *British Theatre* (c. 1829), at this point there is the stage direction, '*Each
Witch lays the fore-finger of her right hand on her lips, and, with her left hand, points to
Macbeth.*' Then, at the last hail, '*Each Witch drops on her knee. They continue to point at
Macbeth, till Banquo adjures them "I' the name of truth", at which they all start up.*'
Sprague (*Actors*, p. 230) points out that the kneeling of the witches is at least as old as
Kemble's time.

69   ('Finel's') 'my father's', Nunn.

No more than to be Cawdor. Say from whence
You owe this strange intelligence, or why
Upon this blasted heath you stop our way   75
With such prophetic greeting? Speak, I charge you.

Witches vanish

BANQUO The earth hath bubbles, as the water has,
And these are of them. Whither are they vanished?

76 SD *Witches vanish* Banquo's words, 'The earth hath bubbles', imply that the witches vanished
through trapdoors, but Macbeth's 'Into the air', the witches' 'hover' (1.1.13), and Lady
Macbeth's 'they made themselves air' (1.5.4), could suggest that, in the original
performances, they made their exit 'flying'. This is unlikely, however, because, as Hodges
points out, there are only three instances in Shakespeare's plays of the use of a flying
machine: at the end of *Macbeth*, Act 3, Scene 5, where Hecate flies aloft in a 'foggy cloud',
and in two Blackfriars plays, *Cymbeline*, where Jupiter descends, mounted on an eagle
(Act 5, Scene 4), and *The Tempest* (Act 4, Scene 1) where Juno descends and joins Iris
(*Globe Restored*, p. 76). In all these cases only one single character is involved, and,
moreover, the Hecate scene, which is probably spurious, may have been added to the text
when *Macbeth* moved to the Blackfriars. If we discount the Hecate scene as a late addition,
then entrances and exits 'flying' were never called for at the Globe, perhaps because there
was no machinery for the purpose at that particular playhouse (Beckerman, *Globe*,
pp. 93–4). Davenant's witches certainly flew on and off, as the stage directions in his
printed text of 1674, '*Ex. flying*' (1.1.13) and '*Enter . . . flying*' (1.3.0), make clear, and the
production of his version at Dorset Garden in 1673 is described as having 'new Scenes,
Machines, as flyings for the witches' (Downes, *Roscius Anglicanus*, p. 33). Garrick's witches
'*sink*' at the end of the first scene and '*rise from under the stage*' through traps at the
opening of the third, but in Phelps's revival at Sadler's Wells in 1847, 'the Weird sisters
seemed to grow out of a supernaturally induced mist and to merge once more into it'. The
effect was apparently created by 'gauzes, the thickening folds of which produced the effect
of the Sisters' vanishing' (Sprague, *Actors*, pp. 226–7). Phelps also arranged that 'after the
disappearance of the witches it grows light, the mists disperse, and we have a clear view
across the Scottish landscape. In the sunshine troops march on while the remarkable music
[of drums and violins] . . . is heard' (Fontane, *London Theatre*, p. 82). Charles Kean used
gauze curtains in all the witches' scenes and they vanished upwards (Bede, '*Macbeth* on the
Stage', p. 21). In Glen Byam Shaw's production, 'as Macbeth fixed on the second witch the
first slid like a lizard from the scene; when attention shifted to the third the second was
gone; and as Macbeth and Banquo turned on each other in eager surmise the third too
vanished' (David, 'Tragic Curve', p. 128).

MACBETH Into the air, and what seemed corporal,
        Melted, as breath into the wind. Would they had stayed.   80
BANQUO Were such things here as we do speak about?
        Or have we eaten on the insane root,
        That takes the reason prisoner?
MACBETH Your children shall be kings.
BANQUO   You shall be king.
MACBETH And Thane of Cawdor too: went it not so?   85
BANQUO To th'selfsame tune and words – who's here?

Enter ROSS *and* ANGUS

ROSS The king hath happily received, Macbeth,
        The news of thy success, and when he reads
        Thy personal venture in the rebels' sight,
        His wonders and his praises do contend   90
        Which should be thine or his. Silenced with that,
        In viewing o'er the rest o'th'selfsame day,
        He finds thee in the stout Norwegian ranks,
        Nothing afeard of what thyself didst make,
        Strange images of death. As thick as tale   95
        Came post with post, and every one did bear
        Thy praises in his kingdom's great defence,
        And poured them down before him.
ANGUS   We are sent
        To give thee from our royal master thanks;
        Only to herald thee into his sight,   100
        Not pay thee.

79   'When [Macready] spoke "Into the air", we could almost see the hags pass away, and like a
      wreath of vapour dissolve into the invisible element. Afterwards he was rapt; thick-coming
      fancies seemed to crawl through his brain . . . Scarcely conscious of the presence of Banquo
      and his friends when once hailed Thane of Cawdor, his words to them dropped hurriedly
      and impatiently: it was the sublime of preoccupation' (Pollock, *Macready*, p. 118).

80   '[Irving] dissembled his excitement, betraying himself for a moment by the intensity of
      "Would they had stayed"' (Hughes, *Shakespearean*, p. 95).

88b–98a   Cut by Nunn.

91b–5a   ('Silenced . . . death') Cut by Forbes-Robertson.

100–1a   Cut by Nunn.

ROSS And for an earnest of a greater honour,
        He bade me, from him, call thee Thane of Cawdor:
        In which addition, hail most worthy thane,
        For it is thine.
BANQUO   What, can the devil speak true?   105
MACBETH The Thane of Cawdor lives. Why do you dress me
        In borrowed robes?
ANGUS   Who was the thane, lives yet,
        But under heavy judgement bears that life
        Which he deserves to lose.
        Whether he was combined with those of Norway,   110
        Or did line the rebel with hidden help
        And vantage, or that with both he laboured
        In his country's wrack, I know not,
        But treasons capital, confessed and proved,
        Have overthrown him.
MACBETH [*Aside*]   Glamis, and Thane of Cawdor: 115
        The greatest is behind. – Thanks for your pains. –
        [*To Banquo*] Do you not hope your children shall be kings,
        When those that gave the Thane of Cawdor to me
        Promised no less to them?
BANQUO   That trusted home,
        Might yet enkindle you unto the crown,   120
        Besides the Thane of Cawdor. But 'tis strange,
        And oftentimes, to win us to our harm,
        The instruments of darkness tell us truths;
        Win us with honest trifles, to betray's
        In deepest consequence. –   125
        Cousins, a word, I pray you.
MACBETH [*Aside*]   Two truths are told,
        As happy prologues to the swelling act
        Of the imperial theme. – I thank you, gentlemen. –

103   Charles Kean started when Ross addressed him as Cawdor, 'his right hand clenched against
        his breast, the fingers of his left hand opening convulsively' (Bede, '*Macbeth* on the Stage',
        p. 21). Ross's announcement 'aroused such a series of emotions [in Irving] that Macbeth's
        companions noticed his abstraction. Awe gave way to exultation as he contemplated "the
        swelling act / Of the imperial theme" and to terror at the thought of murder' (Hughes,
        Shakespearean, p. 95).

112b–13a   ('or that . . . wrack') Cut by Forbes-Robertson.

                          This supernatural soliciting
                          Cannot be ill, cannot be good. If ill,   130
                          Why hath it given me earnest of success,
                          Commencing in a truth? I am Thane of Cawdor.
                          If good, why do I yield to that suggestion,
                          Whose horrid image doth unfix my hair
                          And make my seated heart knock at my ribs   135
                          Against the use of nature? Present fears
                          Are less than horrible imaginings.
                          My thought, whose murder yet is but fantastical,
                          Shakes so my single state of man that function
                          Is smothered in surmise, and nothing is,   140
                          But what is not.
BANQUO   Look how our partner's rapt.
MACBETH If chance will have me king, why chance may crown me
                          Without my stir.
BANQUO   New honours come upon him
                          Like our strange garments, cleave not to their mould,
                          But with the aid of use.

129–30a   'From this moment on, Macbeth [Macready] is an altered man, shaken by dark emotions,
          the slave of fate … Unconscious of his companions, with glassy eye and dreamlike
          expression, he walks across the stage with an uncertain gait, until they break in upon him'
          (Downer, *Macready*, p. 322).

138–41a   In a letter to a correspondent who objected to Garrick's pausing after the word 'single',
          Garrick replied, 'My idea of the passage is this – Macbeth is absorbed in thought, & struck
          with ye horror of ye murder, tho but in Idea (fantastical) and it naturally gives him a slow –
          tremulous – under tone of voice, & tho it might appear that I stop'd at Every word in ye line,
          more than Usual, yet my intention, was far from dividing the Substantive from its adjective,
          but to paint ye horror of Macbeth's Mind, & keep ye voice suspended a little – wch it will
          naturally be in such a Situation' (*Letters*, vol. 1, p. 350).

142–3a   Irving spoke these words 'with a sigh of such relief as is felt only by the irresolute when they
          see a hope that events may spare them the dreaded necessity of making up their minds'
          (Hughes, *Shakespearean*, p. 95–6).

MACBETH   Come what come may,   145
   Time and the hour runs through the roughest day.
BANQUO Worthy Macbeth, we stay upon your leisure.
MACBETH Give me your favour. My dull brain was wrought
   With things forgotten. Kind gentlemen, your pains
   Are registered where every day I turn   150
   The leaf to read them. Let us toward the king.
   [*To Banquo*] Think upon what hath chanced and at more
    time,
   The interim having weighed it, let us speak
   Our free hearts each to other.
BANQUO   Very gladly.
MACBETH Till then, enough. – Come, friends.   155
             Exeunt

146 As an example of the care with which Macklin had studied his role, the *Morning Chronicle* (30 October 1773) points out that 'Garrick says
   Time and the *hour* runs through the roughest day . . .
This is flat tautology. Macklin reads,
   Time, – and the hour (i.e. opportunity)
   Runs through the roughest day.
In the former, the line is of no import; in the latter, it is characteristic, and marks a mind intensely bent upon the idea of murder which had engrossed his imagination.'
Bartholomeusz adds that Macklin's interpretation of the line follows the punctuation of the First Folio, which has a comma after 'Time', indicating a pause, and a comma after 'hour':
   Time, and the Houre, runs through the roughest Day.
         (*Players*, p. 85).

151 In Macready's and Charles Kean's productions, Banquo here gestured to the army waiting off stage. The martial music resumed loudly and the curtain fell on the general exeunt (Downer, *Macready*, p. 322; Charles Kean, Promptbook).

155 SD *Exeunt* 'On his exit, Irving's barbaric soldiers followed him to the sound of a wild march, they swarm along almost at a "double," in the most open order, or rather disorder, their spears, carried at all possible angles, forming a sort of fantastic fretwork against the fiery sky. Their weariness could be felt and shared; each man individualized, they seemed to number thousands' (Hughes, *Shakespearean*, pp. 96–7).

ACT I, SCENE 4

Flourish. Enter King [DUNCAN], LENNOX, MALCOLM,
DONALDBAIN, *and Attendants*

DUNCAN Is execution done on Cawdor, or not
     Those in commission yet returned?

MALCOLM   My liege,
     They are not yet come back. But I have spoke
     With one that saw him die, who did report
     That very frankly he confessed his treasons,   5
     Implored your highness' pardon, and set forth
     A deep repentance. Nothing in his life
     Became him like the leaving it. He died
     As one that had been studied in his death,
     To throw away the dearest thing he owed   10
     As 'twere a careless trifle.

DUNCAN   There's no art
     To find the mind's construction in the face.
     He was a gentleman on whom I built
     An absolute trust.

Enter MACBETH, BANQUO, ROSS, *and* ANGUS

             O worthiest cousin,
     The sin of my ingratitude even now   15
     Was heavy on me. Thou art so far before,
     That swiftest wing of recompense is slow

---

0 SD   *Flourish. Enter . . .* As the curtain rose on this scene, Macready repeated the royal march
       with which the second scene had opened, then a procession entered from the right which
       included Duncan, Malcolm, and Donaldbain and, at line 14, a second procession came on
       from the left, consisting of Macduff, Lennox, Macbeth, Banquo, and six lords, one of whom
       carried two banners rolled together which he placed at the King's feet as a sign of victory
       (Downer, *Macready*, p. 322). Charles Kean set the scene in an interior with a low ceiling
       and heavy pillars on either side (Promptbook).

1b–3a   ('or not . . . But') Cut by Nunn.

To overtake thee. Would thou hadst less deserved,
That the proportion both of thanks and payment
Might have been mine. Only I have left to say,   20
More is thy due than more than all can pay.
MACBETH The service and the loyalty I owe,
In doing it, pays itself. Your highness' part
Is to receive our duties, and our duties
Are to your throne and state, children and servants,   25
Which do but what they should by doing everything
Safe toward your love and honour.
DUNCAN   Welcome hither.
I have begun to plant thee and will labour
To make thee full of growing. Noble Banquo,
That hast no less deserved, nor must be known   30
No less to have done so, let me enfold thee
And hold thee to my heart.
BANQUO   There if I grow,
The harvest is your own.
DUNCAN   My plenteous joys,
Wanton in fullness, seek to hide themselves
In drops of sorrow. Sons, kinsmen, thanes,   35
And you whose places are the nearest, know:
We will establish our estate upon
Our eldest, Malcolm, whom we name hereafter
The Prince of Cumberland, which honour must
Not unaccompanied invest him only,   40
But signs of nobleness like stars shall shine
On all deservers. [*To Macbeth*] From hence to Inverness

18b–20a   ('Would thou . . . mine') Cut by Nunn.
23b–7a   ('Your highness' . . . honour') Cut by Forbes-Robertson.
29b–32a   Of Salvini's reaction to these lines, R. L. Stevenson writes, 'The moral smallness of [his
          Macbeth] is insisted on from the first, in the shudder of uncontrollable jealousy with which
          he sees Duncan embracing Banquo' ('Salvini', p. 367).
33b–5a   ('My plenteous . . . sorrow') Cut by Forbes-Robertson.
35b–42a   When Duncan proclaimed Malcolm as his successor, Macready's manner combined
          'bewilderment and agitation'. Duncan moved up stage, speaking to Banquo, and the rest of
          the court followed, leaving Macbeth alone to express his inner thoughts (Downer,
          Macready, p. 322). The Duncan in Glen Byam Shaw's production took a coronet from a
          cushion and placed it on Malcolm's head (Mullin, *Macbeth Onstage*, p. 25).

       And bind us further to you.
MACBETH The rest is labour which is not used for you;
       I'll be myself the harbinger and make joyful   45
       The hearing of my wife with your approach.
       So humbly take my leave.
DUNCAN   My worthy Cawdor.
MACBETH [*Aside*] The Prince of Cumberland: that is a step
       On which I must fall down, or else o'erleap,
       For in my way it lies. Stars, hide your fires,   50
       Let not light see my black and deep desires,
       The eye wink at the hand. Yet let that be,
       Which the eye fears when it is done to see.   *Exit*
DUNCAN True, worthy Banquo, he is full so valiant,
       And in his commendations I am fed;   55
       It is a banquet to me. Let's after him,
       Whose care is gone before to bid us welcome:
       It is a peerless kinsman.
                     Flourish

                         Exeunt

43 ('And . . . you') 'And lodge this night with our beloved Macbeth', Nunn.

ACT I, SCENE 5

Enter [LADY MACBETH] *alone, with a letter*

Setting Macklin, under the heading 'Inside of the Castle', notes 'Every room must be full of Pictures of warriors, swords, helmet [*sic*], Targets dirk – escutchions, & the hall, bores stufft, wolves – & full of Pikes and broadswords' (manuscript notes). Ellen Terry, in Irving's production, was discovered reclining in a chair, and reading the letter by firelight. 'When you first saw Lady Macbeth [Violet Vanbrugh], she was reading the letter at a low window which revealed a sunlit landscape – brilliant against the sombre frame of the castle wall. That picture dwells in the memory as one of the chief things of the play' (*Times*, 6 September 1911).

0 SD *Enter* . . . Although Macklin wore Scottish costume, his Lady Macbeth wore fashionable contemporary dress. In her first scene, Siddons wore 'a long, dark undergown of floor length; over this a white knee-length gown of light material with an unobtrusive lace border . . . gathered with a cincture high in the waist; a long, dark-coloured mantle falls down the back and trails on the floor behind; and a head-band, holding back profuse amounts of hair, completes the costume' (Donoghue, 'Kemble's *Macbeth*', p. 72). Charles Kean's Lady Macbeth (his wife, Ellen), had 'a light blue dress, the skirt diversified in colours from the knee; party coloured [*sic*] mantles fastened by fibula on right shoulder; coronet of gold over kerchief, or head covering' (Promptbook). Ellen Terry's costume on her first appearance was the one in which she is depicted in Sargent's celebrated portrait. She wore 'a gown of thirteenth-century pattern, crocheted in a yarn of green silk and blue tinsel, which gave the effect of scales. This was sewn all over with real green beetle wings and a narrow border in Celtic designs worked out in rubies and diamonds. To this was added a cloak of shot velvet in heather tones, upon which great griffins were embroidered in flame-coloured tinsel' (Laurence Irving, *Irving*, pp. 501–2). Long plaits of deep red hair fell from under a purple veil. 'The hair was complemented by a pallid complexion highlighted by ruddy cheeks, intended to "mark her as a daughter of the North, a Saga-heroine"' (Hughes, *Shakespearean*, p. 98). Oscar Wilde was said to remark of Ellen Terry's costume that 'Lady Macbeth seems an economical housekeeper and evidently patronizes local industries for her husband's clothes and the servants' liveries, but she takes care to do all her own shopping in Byzantium' (Hughes, *Shakespearean*, p. 98). Her notes, written in a copy of the play, comment at this point 'Steady. Breathe hard. Excited. Not too quick' (Manvell, 'Terry's Lady Macbeth', p. 160). Mrs Patrick Campbell, playing opposite

LADY MACBETH [*Reads*] 'They met me in the day of success, and
   I have learned by the perfectest report they have more in
   them than mortal knowledge. When I burned in desire to
   question them further, they made themselves air, into which
   they vanished. Whiles I stood rapt in the wonder of it, came   5
   missives from the king who all-hailed me Thane of Cawdor, by
   which title before these weïrd sisters saluted me and referred
   me to the coming on of time, with "Hail, king that shalt be."
   This have I thought good to deliver thee, my dearest partner of
   greatness, that thou mightst not lose the dues of rejoicing by   10
   being ignorant of what greatness is promised thee. Lay it to thy
   heart and farewell.'

Forbes-Robertson, wore 'a bodice like a coat of mail, covered with blue, green, and gold sequins almost suggesting a serpent's scales' (Dent, *Campbell*, p. 162). In William Poel's production the Lady Macbeth, Lillah McCarthy, had bright red hair and a flushed complexion. 'Her eyelids were painted a light green and there were flecks of gold under her eyes. Her mouth was very clear and carmined. Her neck and hands were white tinted with blue. She carried her head high, with straightened back and squared shoulders, and she moved with a slight swing.' Poel visualised her as aged about thirty-five (Speaight, *Poel*, p. 188). Violet Vanbrugh, playing opposite Tree, wore 'a long robe of a dull wine colour, decorated down the front with green embroidery', and had 'a brilliant scarlet veil which fell to her feet and a scarlet gauze scarf' (*Westminster Gazette*, 8 September 1911). Judi Dench wore a simple grey shift and a headscarf, and Harriet Walter a long, elegant, black evening dress (*TLS*, 26 November 1999). Dench gave the impression that she already knew the contents of the letter so well that she scarcely needed to look at it.

4   '[Siddons's] first novelty was a little suspension of the voice, "they made themselves – air": that is, less astonished at it as a miracle of nature, than attentive to it as a manifestation of the reliance to be built upon their assurances' (Boaden, *Siddons*, vol. II, p. 133). Knowles comments, 'In the look and tone with which she delivered that word ['air'], you recognised ten times the wonder with which Macbeth and Banquo actually beheld the vanishing of the witches' (*Lectures*, p. 166). Ristori, by the intonation of these words, expressed 'the deep awe which supernatural occurrences awaken in her. She is not less sensitive than Macbeth to the terror they produce' (Morley, *Journal*, p. 187).

5   Ellen Kean 'in reading the letter paused at "vanished", and then continued to read, with an air of great wonder, to "King that shalt be". Here she made a long pause, looking puzzled, and sweeping her hand over her eyes. Then she resumed the reading with rapid energy' (Bede, '*Macbeth* on the Stage', p. 21).

12   When she had finished reading the letter, Terry 'threw herself back in the long oaken chair to dream of the arrival and the fortunes of her king and lover'. She addressed the soliloquy to his miniature and concluded by kissing it (Hughes, *Shakespearean*, p. 98).

Glamis thou art, and Cawdor, and shalt be
What thou art promised; yet do I fear thy nature,
It is too full o'th'milk of human kindness   15
To catch the nearest way. Thou wouldst be great,
Art not without ambition, but without
The illness should attend it. What thou wouldst highly,
That wouldst thou holily; wouldst not play false,
And yet wouldst wrongly win. Thou'dst have, great
      Glamis,   20
That which cries, 'Thus thou must do' if thou have it;
And that which rather thou dost fear to do,
Than wishest should be undone. Hie thee hither,
That I may pour my spirits in thine ear
And chastise with the valour of my tongue   25
All that impedes thee from the golden round,
Which fate and metaphysical aid doth seem
To have thee crowned withal.

Enter [ATTENDANT]

13–14a   '[Siddons] read the whole letter with the greatest skill, and, after an instant of reflection, exclaimed,

    Glamis thou art, and Cawdor, AND SHALT BE
    What thou art *promised*.

The amazing burst of energy upon the words *shalt be* perfectly electrified the house. The determination seemed as uncontrollable as *fate* itself' (Boaden, *Siddons*, vol. II, p. 133). Bell recalls that she said this line and a half in an 'exalted, prophetic tone, as if the whole future were present to her soul' and also with 'a slight tincture of contempt' ('Siddons', p. 51). Terry spoke them in a whisper (Manvell, 'Terry's Lady Macbeth', p. 160).

14b–23a 'The searching analysis of Macbeth, which she makes, was full of meaning – the eye and hand [of Siddons] confirmed the logic. Ambition is the soul of her very phrase: –

    Thou'dst have, great Glamis

Great Glamis! this of her *husband*! – metaphysical speculation, calculated estimate – as if it had regarded Caesar or Pompey. He is among the means before me – how is such a nature to be worked up to such *unholy* objects?' (Boaden, *Siddons*, vol. II, pp. 133–4).

23b–24   '[Siddons] starts into higher animation' (Bell, 'Siddons', p. 52).

26–28a   'Mrs Siddons used to elevate her stature, to smile with a lofty and uncontrollable expectation, and, with an arm raised beautifully in the air, *to draw the very circle she was speaking of*, in the *air about her head*, as if she ran her finger round the gold' (Hunt, *Dramatic Essays*, p. 212).

28 SD   *Enter* . . . Charles Kean's and Nunn's Attendant was Seyton (Promptbooks).

                                                   What is your tidings?
ATTENDANT The king comes here tonight.
LADY MACBETH   Thou'rt mad to say it.
     Is not thy master with him? Who, were't so,   30
     Would have informed for preparation.
ATTENDANT So please you, it is true: our thane is coming.
     One of my fellows had the speed of him;
     Who almost dead for breath, had scarcely more
     Than would make up his message.
LADY MACBETH   Give him tending,   35
     He brings great news.

                                   Exit [Attendant]
                    The raven himself is hoarse
     That croaks the fatal entrance of Duncan
     Under my battlements. Come, you spirits
     That tend on mortal thoughts, unsex me here

29b–30   'After the violence of the exclamation, [Siddons] recovered herself with slight alarm, and, in
         a *lowered* tone, proposed a question suited to the new feeling:
              Is not thy master *with* him?'
         (Boaden, *Siddons*, vol. II, pp. 134–5).
         Bell also notes that here Siddons was 'soft, as if correcting herself, and under the tone of
         reasoning, concealing sentiments almost disclosed' ('Siddons', p. 53).
36b–8a   'After a long pause when the messenger has retired. Indicates her fell purpose settled and
         about to be accomplished' (Bell, 'Siddons', p. 53).
36b–52a In Ellen Terry's notes, she says of this passage, 'She goads herself on to crime. She feels she
         has only a *woman's* strength and calls on "Spirits". The tale of the witches fired her
         imagination, and kindled her hopes. Under her lonely battlements she dreamed of future
         splendour – she did *not* realize the measure of the crime' (Manvell, 'Terry's Lady Macbeth',
         p. 160).
38b–45a 'In a low voice – a whisper of horrid determination' (Bell, 'Siddons', p. 53). When Ristori
         played the role, and began the invocation to the spirits of evil, 'she crooned forth the
         opening words, until the voice changed almost to the hiss of a serpent; anon it rose to the
         swelling diapason of an organ, her eyes became luminous with infernal fire, the stately
         figure expanded, her white hands clutched her ample bosom, as if she would there and
         then have unsexed herself, and turned "her woman's milk to gall", and it really required but
         little stretch of the imagination to conceive that the "dunnest smoke of hell" would burst
         forth and environ her there and then' (Coleman, 'Facts and Fancies', p. 232). Ellen Terry
         found it difficult to accommodate this invocation to her belief that Lady Macbeth was
         essentially affectionate towards her husband. '"Surely she called the spirits to be made

And fill me from the crown to the toe topfull
Of direst cruelty; make thick my blood,   40
Stop up th'access and passage to remorse
That no compunctious visitings of nature
Shake my fell purpose nor keep peace between
Th'effect·and it. Come to my woman's breasts   45
And take my milk for gall, you murd'ring ministers,
Wherever in your sightless substances
You wait on nature's mischief. Come, thick night,
And pall thee in the dunnest smoke of hell,
That my keen knife see not the wound it makes,   50
Nor heaven peep through the blanket of the dark,
To cry, 'Hold, hold.'

Enter MACBETH

                Great Glamis, worthy Cawdor,
Greater than both by the all-hail hereafter,
Thy letters have transported me beyond
This ignorant present, and I feel now   55
The future in the instant.

MACBETH   My dearest love,

bad", she remarked, "because she knew she was not very bad." She gave no hint of demonic possession. The speech was mere hyperbole, and consequently the strength she exhibited later had to come from within herself' (Hughes, *Shakespearean*, pp. 98–9). 'When I called on the Spirits to unsex me', she confessed, 'I acted that bit just as badly as anybody could act anything' (Hughes, *Shakespearean*, pp. 99–100).

45–52a 'Voice quite supernatural, as in a horrible dream. Chilled with horror by the slow hollow whisper of this wonderful creature' (Bell, 'Siddons', p. 53). 'The elevation of her *brows*, the full *orbs* of sight, the raised shoulders, and the hollowed hands, seemed all to endeavour to explore what yet were pronounced no possible objects of vision. Till then, I am quite sure, a figure so terrible had never bent over the pit of a theatre' (Boaden, *Siddons*, vol. II, p. 135).

52b–3 'Loud, triumphant and wild in her air' (Bell, 'Siddons', p. 54). A member of the audience recalled the 'exulting exclamation' with which Siddons greeted Macbeth: 'The effect was electrical. Her whole performance, indeed, affected me with an awe that, when I met her in society several years afterwards, I could not entirely divest myself of, on being presented to her' (Planché, *Recollections*, p. 16). At Macbeth's entry, Ellen Terry 'rushed forward to greet him with a long embrace' (Hughes, *Shakespearean*, p. 100). Judi Dench, similarly, greeted her husband 'rapturously' in Nunn's 1976 production

56b–57a Irving spoke these words averting his eyes, and 'with an affected indifference that obviously covers a guilty thought' (Hughes, *Shakespearean*, p. 100).

> Duncan comes here tonight.
> LADY MACBETH   And when goes hence?
> MACBETH Tomorrow, as he purposes.
> LADY MACBETH   O never
> Shall sun that morrow see.
> Your face, my thane, is as a book where men   60
> May read strange matters. To beguile the time,
> Look like the time, bear welcome in your eye,
> Your hand, your tongue; look like th'innocent flower,
> But be the serpent under't. He that's coming
> Must be provided for, and you shall put   65
> This night's great business into my dispatch,

57b   'The "When goes hence?" was given [by Ellen Kean] with a subtle meaning in a hoarse whisper and with a penetrating look at her husband, on whose arm she laid her hand' (Bede, *Macbeth* on the Stage', p. 21). Before this half-line, Ellen Terry notes, 'Right hand eagerly on Macbeth's breast. Action first.' and then adds that the line should be 'slow' and that she should 'smile'. And her hand should be drawn back sharply from Macbeth on the lines, 'O never / Shall sun *that* morrow see' (Manvell, 'Terry's Lady Macbeth', p. 160).

58a   These four words have been spoken in a number of different ways. Macready quickly said 'Tomorrow', as if merely stating a fact, and then 'as if aware that his wife guessed his thought but saw his want of resolution to do the deed, continues with a lower tone and slow and conscious manner: "as – he – purposes"' (Downer, *Macready*, p. 323). '[Salvini] paused one moment, looked furtively around, as he replied, "Tomorrow, as *he* purposes"; and when Lady Macbeth made answer, "Never shall sun that morrow see!" his face lighted up, with murder written on every line of it' (Coleman, 'Facts and Fancies', p. 227). Kean conveyed a similar impression by making a different emphasis: 'Tomorrow as he . . . *purposes*', which was probably more subtle. Irving introduced a significant pause: 'Tomorrow – as he *purposes*', at which Ellen Terry 'drew back and touched her left shoulder with her right arm to denote inspiration: "Ah," she breathed, "never shall sun *that* morrow see"' (Hughes, *Shakespearean*, p. 100).

58b–9 '"O, never." A long pause, turned from him, her eye steadfast. Strong dwelling emphasis on "never" [which she appears to have repeated], with deep downward inflection, "never shall sun that morrow see!" Low, very slow, sustained voice, her eye and her mind occupied steadfastly in the contemplation of her horrid purpose, pronunciation almost syllabic, note unvaried. Her self-collected solemn energy, her fixed posture, her determined eye and full deep voice of fixed resolve never should be forgot' (Bell, 'Siddons', p. 54).

61b–8 'Alongside the "beguiling" speech, when Lady Macbeth begins to tempt her husband to murder, Ellen Terry suggests [in her notes]: "Smile at him. Bright. Quick! Aflame! Alert". Then she adds: "*He* can't face things and *talk* of 'em, but he can *do* them. *She* can talk and plan but she'd not be able *to do* so easily"' (Manvell, 'Terry's Lady Macbeth', p. 160).

Which shall to all our nights and days to come
Give solely sovereign sway and masterdom.
MACBETH We will speak further –
LADY MACBETH   Only look up clear;
To alter favour ever is to fear.   70
Leave all the rest to me.

Exeunt

'

67 Charles Kean's Promptbook indicates 'Music' here, presumably in preparation for the entrance of Duncan at the beginning of the next scene.

67–8 'Voice changes to assurance and gratulation' (Bell, 'Siddons', p. 54).

71 'Leading him out, cajoling him, her hand on his shoulder clapping him. This vulgar [gesture] gives a mean conception of Macbeth, unlike the high mental working by which he is turned to her ambitious purpose' (Bell, 'Siddons', p. 54). Ristori slowly pushed her husband from the stage, 'her hands on his shoulders, her eyes on his, her head nodding slowly at him, and a smile of determination on her face' (*Times*, 5 July 1882). Irving and Ellen Terry 'went out with arms around each other's necks, she full of spirit, he dejectedly' (Hughes, *Shakespearean*, p. 100).

ACT I, SCENE 6

Hautboys, and Torches. Enter King [DUNCAN], MALCOLM,
DONALDBAIN, BANQUO, LENNOX, MACDUFF, ROSS, ANGUS, *and*
Attendants

Tree cut the whole scene.

Setting   Phelps made 'the first attempt we have seen to reproduce some of the local features of the "pleasant site" [*sic*] – the steep, wall-crowned hill, and the clear river rushing beneath' (*Lloyd's Weekly London News*, quoted in Phelps and Forbes-Robertson, *Phelps*, p. 100). In the background of Charles Kean's set there was a mountainous landscape with some large broken columns (Promptbook). Irving had this scene played by moonlight. His designer, Craven, had created 'a massive built-up castle, rough-textured to repesent stone. As Duncan and his followers approached the cavernous gate, they climbed a great sloping bridge, which suggested that the castle was indeed situated on a rocky summit. Retainers lined the ramp, lighting the scene with torches; women bowed as Lady Macbeth swept down to meet the King, "welcoming the gentle Duncan to that murderous keep with words of poisonous honey dripping from her great, red, cruel mouth".' The entire scene was accompanied by '"serene and beautiful music"' (Hughes, *Shakespearean*, p. 100).

0 SD   *Enter* . . . Charles Kean's Promptbook here says, 'Seyton discovered looking across the ramparts off. Hears the March and exit into the castle to announce the approach of the King.' Macklin's manuscript notes show that he intended Duncan to 'be preceeded [*sic*] in the scene without by fife, tabor, Pipe, Trumpet & all the union of domestic and royal music – and a great number of Pages and Retainers of Macbeth's Train – and when Lady Macbeth comes on she should be attended by a Train of Ladies.' Macready's treatment of the entry was even more elaborate. The scene began with a royal march and two processions: 'First come a seneschal and four officers who go up to the castle gates, right of center; next two chamberlains with torches; Duncan, Malcolm, Donaldbain; then Macduff, Banquo and Fleance in a group; and six lords . . . to fill up the gaps. During Banquo's description of the castle, a counterprocession begins to enter through the gates. This is led by Seyton, followed by eight servants with torches, eight ladies who stand at either side of the gate and curtsey to Lady Macbeth who sweeps down stage, right of center, and bows low before the King – a crowded scene, made colorful and glittering by torchlight' (Downer, *Macready*,

DUNCAN This castle hath a pleasant seat; the air
Nimbly and sweetly recommends itself
Unto our gentle senses.
BANQUO   This guest of summer,
The temple-haunting martlet, does approve
By his loved mansionry that the heaven's breath   5
Smells wooingly here. No jutty, frieze,
Buttress, nor coign of vantage but this bird
Hath made his pendent bed and procreant cradle;
Where they most breed and haunt, I have observed
The air is delicate.   10

Enter LADY [MACBETH]

DUNCAN See, see, our honoured hostess. – The love
That follows us sometime is our trouble,
Which still we thank as love. Herein I teach you
How you shall bid God yield us for your pains
And thank us for your trouble.
LADY MACBETH   All our service,   15
In every point twice done and then done double,

p. 323). Fontane recorded that in Phelps's *Macbeth*, 'Whenever troops were announced or represented as crossing the stage, such as when Duncan arrived in Macbeth's castle, one heard splendidly appropriate music scored for drums and violins (representing the bagpipe)' (*London Theatre*, p. 81). Glen Byam Shaw introduced a simpler procession, preceded by trumpets, consisting of Duncan and his nobles and servants. 'His company fills the grim setting with color and life' (Mullin, *Macbeth Onstage*, p. 25).

3–10 Banquo's 'temple-haunting martlet' speech in Nunn's 1976 production was 'a genially paternal lesson for Fleance, and the "positive" value of the image lost nothing by being expressed lightly' (*Shakespeare Survey*, vol. XXX, 1977, p. 178).

6a 'Enter from Castle Seyton, 10 attendants, Lady M, 6 ladies' (Charles Kean, Promptbook).

10 SD 'Lady M. kneels at Duncan's feet, kisses robe' (Nunn, Promptbook).

15b–21a 'Dignified and simple. Beautifully spoken, quite musical in her tones and in the pronunciation, soothing and satisfying to the ear' (Bell, 'Siddons', p. 55). Ristori, playing in an Italian translation, showed 'much subtlety in the art which makes the spirit of the fox apparent in the manner of these humble and graceful solicitations. It is not overacted. There is a false tone in her voice, a false expression playing faintly now and then across her face, always intensest when the spoken words are humblest; they are courtesies with which women lead men to their death, exciting no suspicion in their victims' (Morley, *Journal*, p. 187).

Were poor and single business to contend
Against those honours deep and broad wherewith
Your majesty loads our house. For those of old,
And the late dignities heaped up to them,   20
We rest your hermits.

DUNCAN   Where's the Thane of Cawdor?
We coursed him at the heels and had a purpose
To be his purveyor, but he rides well,
And his great love, sharp as his spur, hath holp him
To his home before us. Fair and noble hostess,   25
We are your guest tonight.

LADY MACBETH   Your servants ever
Have theirs, themselves, and what is theirs in count
To make their audit at your highness' pleasure,
Still to return your own.

DUNCAN   Give me your hand;
Conduct me to mine host: we love him highly   30
And shall continue our graces towards him.
By your leave, hostess.

                                             Exeunt

19b–21a   Cut by Nunn.

32 SD   *Exeunt* '[Siddons] bows gracefully to the king, when she gives him the *pas* in entering. Then
          graciously and sweetly to the nobles before she follows the king' (Bell, 'Siddons', p. 55).
          Macready introduced a 'lively march' as Duncan and his retinue went off. There was also
          'distant thunder kept up at intervals' (Promptbook). At the exit, Seyton remained behind in
          Glen Byam Shaw's production. He was described by Shaw as 'the head manservant of the
          Macbeth household. He is trusted, absolutely, by his employer', and later became Third
          Murderer (Mullin, *Macbeth Onstage*, p. 25). In Nunn's 1976 staging 'Duncan dismissed
          Macduff, who was supporting him ("By your leave") and took [Lady Macbeth's] arm
          ("Hostess") so that she could lead him to his death.' Then Macbeth entered rapidly from the
          other side of the stage and began 'If it were done . . . then 'twere well it were done *quickly*'
          very fast, 'neatly underlining their *combined* handling of the situation' (*Shakespeare
          Survey*, vol. XXX, 1977, p. 178).

ACT I, SCENE 7

Hautboys. Torches. Enter a Sewer, and divers Servants with dishes and service over the stage. Then enter MACBETH

MACBETH If it were done when 'tis done, then 'twere well
It were done quickly. If th'assassination
Could trammel up the consequence and catch
With his surcease, success, that but this blow
Might be the be-all and the end-all – here,   5
But here, upon this bank and shoal of time,
We'd jump the life to come. But in these cases,
We still have judgement here that we but teach
Bloody instructions, which being taught, return
To plague th'inventor. This even-handed justice   10
Commends th'ingredience of our poisoned chalice
To our own lips. He's here in double trust:
First, as I am his kinsman and his subject,
Strong both against the deed; then, as his host,
Who should against his murderer shut the door,   15
Not bear the knife myself. Besides, this Duncan

Setting Macklin notes in his manuscript that 'There should be table & chairs, Macbeth should sit
down sometimes in his soliloquy – then start up, traverse – it would diversifie the actor's
position – & better mark his Perturbation. He should be discovered in deep rumination – &
perplexity either sitting or standing – not walking on – the scene must be a chamber.' As the
scene opened, Macready arranged for 'a sewer and eight servants' to cross the stage,
'bearing alternately torches and gold and silver dishes containing boar's heads, haunches of
venison' (Downer, *Macready*, p. 324). Phelps introduced a similar procession of servants.

1–28a 'In his soliloquies [Garrick] happily avoids that absurd method of speaking solitary
meditation to the audience; he appears really alone' (Gentleman, *Censor*, vol. II, p. 483).
'Kemble speaks this, as if he had never seen his sister, like *speech* to be recited. None of
that hesitation and working of the mind which in Mrs Siddons seems to inspire the words as
the natural expression of the emotion' (Bell, 'Siddons', p. 55).

2b–4a ('If th'assassination . . . success') Cut by Garrick.

16b–20 Writing to a correspondent who had objected to his pausing after 'angels', Garrick replied, 'I

>Hath borne his faculties so meek, hath been
>So clear in his great office, that his virtues
>Will plead like angels, trumpet-tongued against
>The deep damnation of his taking-off.   20
>And pity, like a naked newborn babe
>Striding the blast, or heaven's cherubin horsed
>Upon the sightless couriers of the air,
>Shall blow the horrid deed in every eye,
>That tears shall drown the wind. I have no spur   25
>To prick the sides of my intent, but only
>Vaulting ambition which o'erleaps itself
>And falls on th'other –

Enter LADY [MACBETH]

>   How now? What news?
>LADY MACBETH He has almost supped. Why have you left the
>   chamber?
>MACBETH Hath he asked for me?
>LADY MACBETH   Know you not, he has?   30
>MACBETH We will proceed no further in this business.
>   He hath honoured me of late, and I have bought

really think yᵉ force of those Exquisite four Lines and a half would be Partly lost for want of a small Aspiration after *Angels* – the epithet may agree with Either of yᵉ Substantives, but I think it more Elegant to give it to the *Virtues*, and yᵉ Sense is yᵉ Same, for if his *Virtues*, are like *Angels*, they are *trumpet-tongued*, and may be spoke justly either way' (Garrick, *Letters*, vol. I, p. 351).

27–8a   John Coleman recalls that Macready's 'sudden transitions (always re-echoed with thunders of applause by the groundlings) [became] more irritating . . . For example, after rising to heaven on the words –

>   Vaulting ambition, which o'erleaps itself
>   And falls on the other –

he dropped to earth with a growl of – "How now, what news?"' ('Facts and Fancies', p. 223).

31   'With what a trembling hand, confessing irresolution of purpose, did [Kemble] grasp his contemptuous wife, and decline to proceed "further in this business", while his eye yet seemed to gloat and glisten at the visionary crown' (Hunt, *Dramatic Essays*, p. 232). Kemble appears to have revised his interpretation of this line. According to Westland Marston he spoke it 'with such a sigh of relief and thankfulness, it seemed to bear away with it a crushing load and to leave him renewed and hopeful' (*Actors*, vol. I, pp. 75–6).

31–5a   'Here again Mrs Siddons appears with all her inimitable expression of emotion. The sudden

Golden opinions from all sorts of people,
Which would be worn now in their newest gloss,
Not cast aside so soon.
LADY MACBETH   Was the hope drunk   35
Wherein you dressed yourself? Hath it slept since?
And wakes it now to look so green and pale
At what it did so freely? From this time,
Such I account thy love. Art thou afeard
To be the same in thine own act and valour,   40
As thou art in desire? Wouldst thou have that
Which thou esteem'st the ornament of life,
And live a coward in thine own esteem,
Letting I dare not wait upon I would,
Like the poor cat i'th'adage?
MACBETH   Prithee, peace.   45
I dare do all that may become a man;
Who dares do more is none.
LADY MACBETH   What beast was't then
That made you break this enterprise to me?
When you durst do it, then you were a man.
And to be more than what you were, you would   50
Be so much more the man. Nor time, nor place
Did then adhere, and yet you would make both.
They have made themselves and that their fitness now
Does unmake you. I have given suck and know

change from animated hope and surprise to disappointment, depression, contempt, and rekindling resentment, is beyond any powers but hers' (Bell, 'Siddons', pp. 55–6).

35b–6a 'Very cold, distant and contemptuous' (Bell, 'Siddons', p. 56).
54b–82 'To Lady Macbeth's first taunts, [Olivier] remained obstinately impervious, his back turned. She drew closer, and launched into the horrible boast of her own callousness [1.7.59–61a] that is to shock him into compliance. At this Macbeth swung round to her, his back now to the audience, and laid his hand on her elbow in a gesture at once deeply affectionate and protesting. As she persisted in her self-torture, he tore himself away and moved across the stage, but his rejoinder, the last weak objection of "If we should fail" [1.7.59], showed that his defences were shaken. Lady Macbeth again moved to him and seizing him by the shoulders from behind murmured in his ear the final temptation – how easy is it then [1.7.69–72a]. He turned to her with "Bring forth men children only" [1.7.72b–4a], but it was said wryly, in almost mocking praise of her lack of scruple, and he still did not take her hand. There needed a further pause for reflection, the growing confidence of "Will it not be

How tender 'tis to love the babe that milks me: 55
I would, while it was smiling in my face,
Have plucked my nipple from his boneless gums
And dashed the brains out, had I so sworn
As you have done to this.

MACBETH   If we should fail?

LADY MACBETH   We fail?

But screw your courage to the sticking-place,   60
And we'll not fail. When Duncan is asleep,
Whereto the rather shall his day's hard journey
Soundly invite him, his two chamberlains
Will I with wine and wassail so convince

received . . .?" [1.7.74b–7a] before with "I am settled" [1.7.79b] he was her own again' (David, 'Tragic Curve', p. 128).

54b   '[Siddons] has been at a distant part of the stage. She now comes close to him – an entire change of manner, looks for some time in his face, then speaks' (Bell, 'Siddons', p. 56).

54b–9a   'This really beautiful and interesting actress [Siddons] did not at all shrink from standing before us the true and perfect image of the greatest of all natural and moral depravations – a *fiend-like woman*' (Boaden, *Siddons*, vol. II, p. 137). Ristori 'goes through the described situation as if she were actually involved in it; that is to say, she *does* hold the imaginary infant to her bosom, she *does* pluck it away, she *does* dash it to the ground with all accuracy, suiting the gesticulation to the course of the words' (*Times*, 6 July 1857). In the notes in her copy of the play, Terry writes here, 'Only an exaggeration, as she is in a fury', and adds, 'She loved her babies and she could not kill the man who looked like her Father (*Woman*)' (Manvell, 'Terry as Lady Macbeth', p. 160).

59b   ('We fail?') '[Siddons expressed] not surprise, strong downward inflection, bowing with her hands down, the palms upward. Then voice of strong assurance, "When Duncan", &c. This spoken near to him, and in a low earnest whisper of discovery she discloses her plan' (Bell, 'Siddons', p. 57). Apparently Siddons spoke the words not as a rhetorical question but as a statement. Ellen Terry, on the other hand, spoke them as 'a cry of defiance' (Hughes, *Shakespearean*, p. 103).

61b–72a   As the plan develops to blame the murder on the sleeping chamberlains, Terry wrote in her personal notes, 'Now see, here is a beautiful plan which your wifie has thought all out (the Hell-cat)' (Hughes, *Shakespearean*, p. 103). 'She mesmerized him with slow-ly-playing with his hands . . . Caressing him with hands and voice, rousing him sexually, she lured him back to the necessary action . . . Her motto for the role was "Be damned CHARMING"' (Shattuck, *American Stage*, vol. II, p. 181). Lillie Langtry was praised for 'the wonderfully winning way in which she crept into Macbeth's arms while whispering to him her plan for the assassination . . . It fairly thrilled the audience' (Sprague, *Actors*, p. 236).

That memory, the warder of the brain,   65
Shall be a fume, and the receipt of reason
A limbeck only. When in swinish sleep
Their drenchèd natures lies as in a death,
What cannot you and I perform upon
Th'unguarded Duncan? What not put upon   70
His spongy officers, who shall bear the guilt
Of our great quell?
MACBETH   Bring forth men-children only,
For thy undaunted mettle should compose
Nothing but males. Will it not be received,
When we have marked with blood those sleepy two   75
Of his own chamber, and used their very daggers,
That they have done't?
LADY MACBETH   Who dares receive it other,
As we shall make our griefs and clamour roar
Upon his death?
MACBETH   I am settled and bend up
Each corporal agent to this terrible feat.   80
Away, and mock the time with fairest show,
False face must hide what the false heart doth know.

                                                            Exeunt

67b–72a '[Siddons] pauses as if trying the effect on him. Then renews her plan more earnestly, low
still, but with increasing confidence. Throughout this scene she feels her way, observes the
wavering of his mind; suits her earnestness and whole manner to it. With contempt,
affection, reason, the conviction of her well-concerted plan, the assurance of success which
her wonderful tones inspire, she turns him to her purpose with an art in which the player
shares largely in the poet's praise' (Bell, 'Siddons', p. 57).

77b 'Pause. Look of great confidence, much dignity of mien. In "dares" great and imperial
dignity' (Bell, 'Siddons', p. 57).

79b–82 In these lines, Macready whirled upon Lady Macbeth, 'seizes her right arm and hastens her
off . . . The music begins quietly, increasing to a crescendo as they leave the stage' (Downer,
Macready, p. 324). As Macbeth said these words, Ristori's face 'brightens with exultation at
a purpose all accomplished . . . He is in her hands, and she, with a gentle familiarity
persuading yet compelling, urges him on' (Morley, *Journal*, p. 188).

82 Tree added an episode here in which Duncan was escorted to bed. 'His train includes a
harper, and there is singing which turns to a hymn as the King blesses the kneeling
company' (Crosse, *Playgoing*, p. 39). Benthall inserted a similar episode here in which
Duncan, secretly observed by the Macbeths, took off his crown and handed it to Malcolm.
'The boy laughed as he jokingly made as if to try it on before his brother' (Williamson, *Old
Vic 2*, p. 169).

ACT 2, SCENE I

Enter BANQUO, *and* FLEANCE, *with a Torch[-bearer] before him*

Setting   Macklin comments that, in previous productions of this scene, 'the Servant comes on with
two candles, he goes off & leaves his master in the dark that is a breach of manners even to
absurdity. To remedy this the scene must lie in a Hall, or antichamber [*sic*] in which there
must be a Table in the appartment [*sic*] and when the Servant goes off he must leave the
candles on the Table, on which I think Macbeth must put them out' (manuscript notes;
Appleton, *Macklin*, pp. 171–2). In the event, Macklin staged the scene in 'the inward
quadrangle of an old Gothic castle' (*Morning Chronicle*, 29 October 1773). Macready set it
in a courtyard with a gateway in the centre at the rear surmounted by a heavy tower. There
were two smaller doorways at the front, one on the left leading to Duncan's bedchamber,
the other on the right leading to Macbeth's (Downer, *Macready*, pp. 324–5). A sketch in
Macready's Promptbook shows that there was also a flight of stairs on each side of the stage
leading up to a gallery where there was a set of six doors, presumably leading to
bedchambers. Theodore Fontane describes Phelps's treatment of this scene in some detail:
'We see a wide hall. *The murder does not take place at the back of this, but very close to
the audience.* There are bed-chambers on either side of the hall: we see a few doors ajar.
On the left, right down by the orchestra pit (from which the few fiddlers have left, moreover,
so as not to distract us with their weary faces) is the bedchamber of Macbeth and his lady.
Opposite, and just as close to the audience, is that of King Duncan. After Macbeth has
opened the little door and entered the king's room, the stage is empty for a good
half-minute. Then at last Lady Macbeth darts out of her room [2.2.1]. After the first two
lines . . . she breaks off with "Hark! Peace!" and steps towards the door through which
Macbeth disappeared a minute ago. She opens it a little, and *through the narrow crack a
ray of pale light falls on the stage.* This is the moment when she whispers the fearful words,
"He is about it." [2.2.4]. Everything combines to produce a profound sensation of horror'
(*London Theatre*, p. 84). Charles Kean also set the scene in a castle courtyard. There was a
roofed gallery at the back above a Roman archway, and a round tower on either side of the
gallery, each with a door (Promptbook). Irving's set was 'built in the style wherein Norman
architecture began to put on decoration, but fully retained its rounded masses and its
rugged strength. The rude entrance-hall in the rear . . . faces the spectators. Above the
passage leading to it are murky arcaded galleries. On the right is a staircase. On the left is a

BANQUO How goes the night, boy?
FLEANCE The moon is down; I have not heard the clock.
BANQUO And she goes down at twelve.
FLEANCE   I take't, 'tis later, sir.
BANQUO Hold, take my sword. – There's husbandry in heaven,
    Their candles are all out. – Take thee that too.   5
    A heavy summons lies like lead upon me,
    And yet I would not sleep; merciful powers,
    Restrain in me the cursèd thoughts that nature
    Gives way to in repose.

        Enter MACBETH, *and a Servant with a torch*

                Give me my sword –
Who's there?   10

round tower-like structure suggestive of a spiral stairway. Against this Lady Macbeth leans her back while the murder is in progress. The passage past it is the way Macbeth is marshalled by the dagger which he sees before him. The place is comparatively dark. The revellers have settled to their slumbers' (Liverpool *Daily Post*, 31 December 1888). Immediately before this scene, Tree introduced the Witches who danced in the empty courtyard and vanished to the sound of thunder 'as if they have entered to renew their spell before Banquo and Fleance come' (Mullin, 'Images of Death', in Tardiff, *Criticism*, p. 178). In his production, stone steps rose to a large, heavy, iron-bolted door with steps arching up on either side of it. Beneath the arches were dark, cave-like spaces from which people entered in response to the alarum bell (2.3.74a) which hung nearby. 'Around stands the grey, empty courtyard, grimly looming in the darkness, with only little slits of light here and there betraying the light within. All through the awful scene, this door, now closed, now ajar with the light streaming through, holds one's imagination captive . . . At the side of the courtyard . . . is a little turret with a tiny side entrance leading up its winding stair. It is huddled against this little side entrance that . . . Macbeth sees his air-drawn dagger, while far above Lady Macbeth glides softly, silently to the great, lonely door – pushes it noiselessly ajar, slips in and as noiselessly shuts it again. It is from the little turret that Macbeth himself advances later on. He reaches the great door, stands trembling for a moment as that gaunt door shuts upon him. A moment after a muffled, gurgling groan tells one what it hides' (*Daily Chronicle*, 6 September 1911).

0 SD   *Enter* . . . In his manuscript notes Macklin says, 'Banquo should begin the Second Act by coming out of the lower door P[rompt] S[ide] – as coming from the King, with a ring to Macbeth.'

4–5   Cut by Garrick.

9 SD   *Enter* . . . Macready's Servant was Seyton (Promptbook).

MACBETH A friend.

BANQUO What, sir, not yet at rest? The king's abed.
    He hath been in unusual pleasure
    And sent forth great largess to your offices.
    This diamond he greets your wife withal,   15
        [*Gives Macbeth a diamond*]
    By the name of most kind hostess, and shut up
    In measureless content.

MACBETH   Being unprepared,
    Our will became the servant to defect,
    Which else should free have wrought.

BANQUO   All's well.
    I dreamed last night of the three weïrd sisters;   20
    To you they have showed some truth.

MACBETH   I think not of them;
    Yet when we can entreat an hour to serve,
    We would spend it in some words upon that business,
    If you would grant the time.

BANQUO   At your kind'st leisure.

MACBETH If you shall cleave to my consent, when 'tis,   25
    It shall make honour for you.

BANQUO   So I lose none
    In seeking to augment it, but still keep
    My bosom franchised and allegiance clear,
    I shall be counselled.

MACBETH   Good repose the while.

BANQUO Thanks, sir; the like to you.   30
        [*Exeunt*] *Banquo*[, *Fleance, and Torch-bearer*]

MACBETH [*To Servant*] Go bid thy mistress, when my drink is ready,
    She strike upon the bell. Get thee to bed.
                                        Exit [*Servant*]

9–31   In a letter to Garrick, Arthur Murphy reminds him how he played this passage: 'You
       dissembled indeed, but dissembled with difficulty. Upon the first entrance the eye glanced
       at the door [of Duncan's bed-chamber]; the gaiety was forced, and at intervals the eye gave
       a momentary look towards the door, and turned away in a moment . . . After saying "Good
       repose the while" the eye then fixed on the door, then after a pause in a broken tone, "Go,
       bid thy mistress, &c."' (Garrick, *Correspondence*, vol. II, p. 363; Sprague, *Actors*,
       p. 236).

15a   ('This diamond') 'Nay more', Nunn.

Is this a dagger which I see before me,
The handle toward my hand? Come, let me clutch thee:
I have thee not, and yet I see thee still.   35
Art thou not, fatal vision, sensible
To feeling as to sight? Or art thou but
A dagger of the mind, a false creation,

33–61   'Garrick's attitude, his consternation, and his pause, while his soul appeared in his
countenance, and the accents that followed, astonished the spectators. The sequel was a
climax of terror, till at last he finds it to be the effect of a disordered imagination, and his
conscience forces him to say,

It is the bloody business which informs

Thus to mine eyes'

(Murphy, *Garrick*, vol. 1, p. 81).

A German visitor records that 'a certain foreigner in his box, though understanding not a
word of English, was so moved by Garrick's mere gesture in reaching out for the imaginary
dagger . . . that he collapsed in a swoon' (Kelly, *German Visitors*, p. 40). Macklin first took
the dagger to be real, but then, suspecting that it was the product of his 'heat-oppressèd
brain' (line 39), he closed his eyes, turned his head away, and held his forehead in his hand.
At 'Thou marshall'st me the way that I was going' (line 42), he again believed it was real, but
rejected the idea at 'Mine eyes are made the fools o'th'other senses' (line 44), only to be
convinced of its reality at 'on thy blade and dudgeon gouts of blood' (line 46). Finally, in the
following line ('There's no such thing') he rejected it as a hallucination, and drew his own
dagger (*Morning Chronicle*, 30 October 1773). Kemble's interpretation was simpler. After
'Get thee to bed' (line 32), he yawned and stretched his arms but, on seeing the dagger, he
started suddenly and, from then onwards, was convinced of its existence; 'he followed it
with his eyes steadily in all its evolutions through the air, and walked after it composedly to
Duncan's door' (*Times*, 19 September 1811). Edmund Kean regarded the dagger 'with a
delirious and fascinated gaze; it grew more and more distinct to his disordered fancy; and at
length he saw this "painting of his fear" palpable and distinct, imbrued with blood, and
slowly guiding his halting footsteps to the door of Duncan's chamber. Bewildered, terrified,
brain-sick, he shrank from a belief in its reality, yet returned to it with a struggling conviction
until it obtained full possession of him' (Hawkins, *Kean*, p. 272). Macready slowly sensed
the presence of the dagger of the mind wavering before him in the air. 'He does not start at
once as if it were "tangible to the eye". Rather he keeps his eye constantly on the painting of
his fear, recoiling and advancing to the dread object of his struggling excitement, and finally
drawing his own dagger' (Downer, *Macready*, p. 325). Phelps, 'instead of at once starting at
the ideal dagger, as if he was fully convinced of its appearance . . . kept his eye fixed on the
"painting of his fear", till the brain-sick, bewildered imagination made it real; shrinking from
its belief, and returning to it with a struggling conviction, until it obtained full possession of
him' (*Lloyd's Weekly London News*, quoted in Phelps and Forbes-Robertson, *Phelps*, p. 101).

Proceeding from the heat-oppressèd brain?
I see thee yet, in form as palpable   40
As this which now I draw.
Thou marshall'st me the way that I was going,
And such an instrument I was to use.
Mine eyes are made the fools o'th'other senses,
Or else worth all the rest. I see thee still,   45
And on thy blade and dudgeon gouts of blood,
Which was not so before. There's no such thing:

'When Charles Kean began "Is this a dagger . . ." the words were spoken under his breath up to "Thou marshall'st me", when his voice was raised, and he spoke loudly to the end of the sentence. Before "There's no such thing", there was another pause; and when he spoke it was as though it was in anger with himself at giving way to childish fancies' (Bede, '*Macbeth* on the Stage', p. 21). Irving, 'alone after bidding Banquo goodnight, . . . looked towards Duncan's door, evidently intending immediate murder. The invisible dagger stopped him in his tracks: if this apparently supernatural weapon marshalled him the way that he was going, he realized with a start, perhaps it pointed the way to danger. Then, with a hollow laugh, he pulled himself together: "There's no such thing." Irving wrote, "Fear, which takes hold of him, he refuses to acknowledge"' (Hughes, *Shakespearean*, pp. 103–4). 'Macbeth [Olivier] is still giving last instructions to the servant. The man is still beside him when he sees the spectral dagger and checks at it like a pointer. With a terrible effort he withdraws his gaze for a moment and dismisses the servant; then with a swift and horrid compulsion swings round again. The first part of the dagger speech was spoken with a sort of broken quiet, only the sudden shrillness of "Mine eyes are made the fools o'th'other senses" [line 44] and "There's no such thing" [line 47] revealing the intolerable tension that strains the speaker . . . Olivier dismissed the influence of evil in its physical manifestation only to be more strongly seized by it in his mind. The second part of the speech sank to a drugged whisper and, speaking, Macbeth moved, as in a dream, towards Duncan's room, but with his face turned away from it. Tarquin's strides were only dimly reflected in his dragging pace, and it was the already trodden stones behind him that Macbeth, with deprecating hand, implored to silence. It was this scene above all that brought the audience under the enchantment' (David, 'Tragic Curve', pp. 128–9).

42   In his manuscript notes, Macklin says that he should drop the dagger on this line and take it up again after 'There's no such thing' (line 47b).

43   A correspondent disagreed with Garrick's emphasis on the word 'was' and suggested that he should rather stress 'use', to which Garrick replied, 'I think, Sir, that both yᵉ words *Was* and *Use* should be equally, tho' slightly, impress'd as I have mark'd 'em – if you please to consider the passage, You will find, they are both Emphatical – The Vision represents what *was* to be *done* – not – what is, doing, or what had been done – but in Many Passages like this – the Propriety will depend wholly upon yᵉ Manner of yᵉ Actor' (*Letters*, vol. I, p. 351).

It is the bloody business which informs
Thus to mine eyes. Now o'er the one half-world
Nature seems dead, and wicked dreams abuse   50
The curtained sleep. Witchcraft celebrates
Pale Hecate's off'rings, and withered murder,
Alarumed by his sentinel, the wolf,
Whose howl's his watch, thus with his stealthy pace,
With Tarquin's ravishing strides, towards his design   55
Moves like a ghost. Thou sure and firm-set earth,
Hear not my steps, which way they walk, for fear
Thy very stones prate of my whereabout,
And take the present horror from the time,
Which now suits with it. Whiles I threat, he lives;   60
Words to the heat of deeds too cold breath gives.
                    A bell rings
I go, and it is done. The bell invites me.
Hear it not, Duncan, for it is a knell
That summons thee to heaven or to hell.   *Exit*

60b–1   Cut by Garrick.

   61   Cut by Nunn.

61 SD   *A bell rings* Kemble introduced the sound of a clock striking two, rather than the ringing of a
        bell as in the original stage direction. 'That it was so, is proved afterwards in the perturbed
        sleep of Lady Macbeth [5.1.30–1]. It is more awful and alarming, thus to startle silence by a
        deep-toned summoner, than to be brought back into petty life by the tinkle of a table-bell'
        (Boaden, *Kemble*, vol. I, p. 415).

63 SD   *Exit* Macready was so intent on communicating Macbeth's reluctance to enter Duncan's bed
        chamber that 'when his body was actually off the stage, his left foot and leg remained
        trembling in sight, it seemed, fully half a minute' (Coleman, 'Facts and Fancies', p. 223). 'In
        contrast with the erect, martial figure that entered in the first act, this change was the moral
        of the play made visible' (Marston, *Actors*, vol. I, pp. 76–7). At his exit, 'the thunder, which
        had been low and muttering . . . now bursts with fury, and sheets of rain are heard to beat
        upon the castle walls' (Downer, *Macready*, p. 326). At the peal of thunder, Forrest 'starts
        back, gasps at the audience, slowly recovers, and disappears in the midst of the applauses
        of galleries and orchestra' (Forster, *Dramatic Essays*, p. 32). In his later performances, the
        witches appeared above the battlements, as if coming 'to preside and exult over' the crime
        (Sprague, *Actors*, p. 241). As Phelps made his exit at the end of this scene there was a loud
        peal of thunder which, according to Fontane, seemed to be 'directly over our heads'
        (*London Theatre*, p. 81). Irving, as he went into the chamber, gave the impression that his
        feet were feeling for the ground, 'as if he were walking with difficulty a step at a time on a
        reeling deck' (Sprague, *Actors*, p. 241).

ACT 2, SCENE 2

Enter LADY [MACBETH]

LADY MACBETH That which hath made them drunk, hath made me
       bold;
    What hath quenched them, hath given me fire.
       [An owl shrieks]
                                        Hark, peace!
    It was the owl that shrieked, the fatal bellman
    Which gives the stern'st good-night. He is about it.

Macready opened the scene with 'very loud thunder and sounds of storm' (Promptbook). In Tree's production, 'the witches laughed in the distance at all sorts of unexpected moments where no such laugh is indicated in the text' (*Manchester Guardian*, 6 September 1911).

1   'With a ghastly horrid smile' (Bell, 'Siddons', p. 58). Whereas Irving went off at the end of the previous scene 'a very abyss of moral teror and sickened horror', Terry, like Siddons, entered 'with a horrible smile' (Hughes, *Shakespearean*, p. 104). Before saying this line, Mary Merrall, in the 1928 modern dress production, drank a stiff whisky (Kennedy, *Looking*, p. 112).

2b–4   Phelps's Lady Macbeth 'darts out of her chamber. After her first two lines . . . she stops herself with "Hark, peace!" and steps towards the door through which Macbeth disappeared a minute ago. She opens it a little, and *through the narrow crack a ray of pale light falls on the stage*. This is the moment when she whispers the fearful words, "He is about it."' (Fontane, *London Theatre*, p. 84).

4b   J. H. Siddons tells of how as a boy he stood off stage and watched Kemble putting the blood on his hands: 'The whispered words, "He is about it", drew my attention to the half-opened door in the act of listening – her ear so close that I could absolutely feel her breath. The words, I have said, were whispered – but what a whisper was hers! Distinctly audible in every part of the house, it served the purpose of the loudest tones' (J. H. Siddons, *Memoirs*, p. 17). 'The quality that emerges from records of [Siddons in] this scene is that of intense terror. Lady Macbeth's uncertainty of the success of her husband's attempt is mirrored, as an early reviewer [for the *Public Advertiser*, 14 February 1785] found, in "her almost smothered functions of voice and gesture" and in her "tip-toe tread &c. at Duncan's door"' (Donohue, 'Kemble and Mrs Siddons', p. 81).

> The doors are open, and the surfeited grooms   5
> Do mock their charge with snores. I have drugged their
>   possets,
> That death and nature do contend about them,
> Whether they live, or die.

Enter MACBETH [*with two bloody daggers*]

MACBETH   Who's there? What ho?

---

8 SD   *Enter* . . . Murphy recalls that, when Garrick re-entered with the bloody daggers in his hand, 'he was absolutely scared out of his senses; he looked like a ghastly spectacle, and his complexion grew whiter every moment' (*Garrick*, vol. I, p. 82). He carried a dagger in each hand, as did Phelps, 'the daggers clicking like castanets' (Sprague, *Actors*, p. 242). Davies, Garrick's prompter, says that he had 'wiped the paint from his face to look more ghastly' (*Miscellanies*, vol. II, p. 144). Of Edmund Kean's performance when Macbeth returns from the murder, Hazlitt says, 'As a lesson of common humanity, it was heartrending. The hesitation, the bewildered look, the coming to himself when he sees his hands bloody; the manner in which his voice clung to his throat, and choked his utterance, his agony and tears, the force of nature overcome by passion – beggared description' (*Dramatic Essays*, p. 33). 'As Lady Macbeth waits his entrance in breathless suspense, [Forrest's] back appears at the door of Duncan's chamber, and with outstretched hands holding the bloody daggers, his face still gazing at the door, Mr Forrest moves over the stage with an elaborately noiseless step, until a touch from the hand of Miss Huddart at the opposite side gives him the opportunity, after a violent start, of throwing his body into one tremendous convulsion – which he does forthwith, to the great delight of the injudicious' (Forster, *Dramatic Essays*, p. 35). John Coleman recalls that Salvini's costume in the murder scene 'was so *bizarre* as to somewhat distract one's attention. It was a bright green corded abomination, trimmed with fur like a woman's modern dolman, with the sleeves of so vivid a hue that it was impossible to distinguish the blood on his hands from his blood-red sleeves. Despite this drawback the scene was acted both by himself and Signora Piamonte in strict accordance with the true and terrible spirit of its tragic horror' ('Facts and Fancies', p. 227). Tree returned 'with staring eyes and gaping red hands from Duncan's room. "He catches sight of hand – never takes eyes off *hand*", says the Promptbook. All the while the siren shrieks; thunder and lightning crash intermittently' (Mullin, 'Images of Death', in Tardiff, *Criticism*, p. 180). The 'wide-eyed terror' of Ian McKellen, the Macbeth in the 1976 RSC production, 'was heightened by the daggers rattling in his fist like old bones' (Williams, *Text and Performance*, p. 42).

8b–60   Immediately after the murder, '[Garrick's] distraction of mind and agonizing horrors were finely contrasted with [Mrs Pritchard's] seeming apathy, tranquility and confidence. The beginning of the scene after the murder was conducted in terrifying whispers. Their looks

LADY MACBETH Alack, I am afraid they have awaked,
    And 'tis not done; th'attempt and not the deed   10
    Confounds us. Hark! I laid their daggers ready,
    He could not miss 'em. Had he not resembled
    My father as he slept, I had done't. My husband?
MACBETH I have done the deed. Didst thou not hear a noise?
LADY MACBETH I heard the owl scream and the crickets cry.   15
    Did not you speak?
MACBETH When?
LADY MACBETH Now.
MACBETH As I descended?

and action supplied the place of words. You heard what they spoke, but you learned more from the agitation of mind displayed in their action and deportment. The poet here gives only an outline to the consummate actor' (Davies, *Miscellanies*, vol. II, pp. 148–9). This episode was generally thought to be Edmund Kean's finest. He crept back from Duncan's murder 'with the stealthy pace of fear, as if every faculty were for the time unstrung. When his timid eye first rested on Lady Macbeth, his frame was convulsed and wound up to the highest pitch of terror; even upon recognising her, he is but half-assured; in broken, half-smothered tones, forced upon him by violent exertion and evident pain, he slowly stammers – "I have done the deed." It was so terribly true to nature, that every heart and mind was electrified by the shock' (Finlay, *Miscellanies*, p. 248). Of Macready's re-entry after the murder, it was said, 'The crouching form and stealthy, felon-like step of the self-abased murderer, as he quitted the scene, made . . a picture not to be forgotten. In contrast to the martial figure that entered in the first act, this change was the moral of the play made visible' (Marston, *Actors*, vol. I, pp. 76–7). Irving returned from the murder, reeling and tottering, 'His body sways as if already hanging on a gibbet' (Sprague, *Actors*, p. 243).

9   '[Siddons expressed] the finest agony; tossing of the arms' (Bell, 'Siddons', p. 59).

12b–13a   '[Siddons] throws a degree of proud and filial tenderness into this speech . . . which is new and of great effect' (Doran, *Servants*, vol. III, p. 173). Terry, on the other hand, spoke the words in a tone of 'impatient contempt' for her own weakness (Hughes, *Shakespearean*, p. 104).

13b   '[Siddons creates the impression of] agonised suspense, as if speechless with uncertainty whether discovered' (Bell, 'Siddons', p. 59).

14a   'Macbeth [Kemble] speaks all this like some horrid secret – a whisper in the dark' (Bell, 'Siddons', p. 59). 'The involuntary hesitation which impeded [Kean's] utterance as with broken accents he gasped, "I have done the deed"; the guilty and utter stupefaction of the senses with which, pale and trembling, he gazed upon his quivering, blood-stained hands . . . impoverished description' (Hawkins, *Kean*, vol. I, p. 273).

LADY MACBETH Ay.   20
MACBETH Hark, who lies i'th'second chamber?
LADY MACBETH Donaldbain.
MACBETH This is a sorry sight.
LADY MACBETH A foolish thought, to say a sorry sight.
MACBETH There's one did laugh in's sleep, and one cried, 'Murder!',   25
        That they did wake each other; I stood, and heard them,
        But they did say their prayers and addressed them
        Again to sleep.
LADY MACBETH   There are two lodged together.
MACBETH One cried 'God bless us!' and 'Amen' the other,
        As they had seen me with these hangman's hands.   30
        List'ning their fear, I could not say 'Amen'
        When they did say 'God bless us.'
LADY MACBETH Consider it not so deeply.
MACBETH But wherefore could not I pronounce 'Amen'?
        I had most need of blessing and 'Amen'   35
        Stuck in my throat.
LADY MACBETH   These deeds must not be thought
        After these ways; so, it will make us mad.
MACBETH Methought I heard a voice cry, 'Sleep no more:
        Macbeth does murder sleep', the innocent sleep,
        Sleep that knits up the ravelled sleeve of care,
        The death of each day's life, sore labour's bath,   40
        Balm of hurt minds, great nature's second course,
        Chief nourisher in life's feast.
LADY MACBETH   What do you mean?

25   'Mrs Siddons here displays her wonderful power and knowledge of nature. As if her inhuman strength of spirit overcome by the contagion of his remorse and terror. Her arms about her neck and bosom, shuddering' (Bell, 'Siddons', p. 59).

33   In her notes, Terry writes here, 'Watching him she thinks – "Why he is quite ill! Come. Come. The danger's *past now* – Consider it not so *deeply*." This last not stern and angry, but with some feminine consideration mixed with alarm. He's been a good fellow – he has not *failed* – don't press him too far – bear with him – humour him' (Manvell, 'Terry as Lady Macbeth', p. 161).

36b–7   '[Siddons's] horror changes to agony and alarm at his derangement, uncertain what to do; calling up the resources of her spirit' (Bell, 'Siddons', p. 60).

38   Terry comments here in her notes, 'The most awful line in the play, if one realizes what it means to his guilt-burdened mind. Poor wretch, he does not sleep after this' (Manvell, 'Terry as Lady Macbeth', p. 161).

MACBETH Still it cried, 'Sleep no more' to all the house;
'Glamis hath murdered sleep', and therefore Cawdor   45
Shall sleep no more: Macbeth shall sleep no more.
LADY MACBETH Who was it, that thus cried? Why, worthy thane,
You do unbend your noble strength to think
So brain-sickly of things. Go get some water
And wash this filthy witness from your hand.   50
Why did you bring these daggers from the place?
They must lie there. Go carry them and smear
The sleepy grooms with blood.
MACBETH   I'll go no more.
I am afraid to think what I have done;
Look on't again, I dare not.
LADY MACBETH   Infirm of purpose!   55
Give me the daggers. The sleeping and the dead

47a   '[Siddons gives a] strong emphasis on *who*. Speaks forcibly into his ear, looks at him steadfastly' (Bell, 'Siddons', p. 60). Terry asked the question 'with practical common sense' (Hughes, *Shakespearean*, p. 104).

47b–53a   Beside these lines, Terry comments, 'Upon my soul, you should be ashamed. You want shaking' (Manvell, 'Terry as Lady Macbeth', p. 161).

49b–50   '[Siddons] comes near [Kemble], attempts to call back his wandering thoughts to ideas of common life' (Bell, 'Siddons', p. 60). Sprague comments, 'I gather that it was in the act of attempting to lead Macbeth [Forrest] away, so that he might rid himself of the evidence of guilt, that Lady Macbeth first noticed the daggers' (*Actors*, p. 243).

51   'Now only at leisure to observe the daggers' (Bell, 'Siddons', p. 60). Terry here notes, 'Angry. Nothing else for it. I must do it myself' (Manvell, 'Terry as Lady Macbeth', p. 161).

55a   At this line, Macready rushed to the right-hand side of the stage, as far as possible from Duncan's door (Downer, *Macready*, p. 326). 'Mcb shakes and daggers chink against each other' (Nunn, Promptbook).

56a   Mrs Pritchard, Garrick's Lady Macbeth, seized the daggers, as did Mrs Siddons (Davies, *Garrick*, vol. II, pp. 183–4; Bell, 'Siddons', p. 60). This line, says Boaden, 'excited a general start from those around me' (*Siddons*, vol. II, p. 137). 'After seizing the daggers from Macbeth [Forrest], [Miss Huddart] moved hurriedly towards the chamber of Duncan, but as she approached the entrance, as if suddenly controlled by some vision of the awful scene that awaited her there, she paused for an instant, and then passed slowly in. This was a stroke of genius' (Forster, 'Forrest as Macbeth', in Forster and Lewes, *Essays*, p. 37). Irene Worth, in the 1962 RSC production, said 'Give me the daggers' 'with nothing of the usual, obvious drama, but with a rapid, quiet simplicity which spoke eloquently for self-reliance and its limitations' (*Shakespeare Survey*, vol. XVI, 1963, p. 150).

Are but as pictures; 'tis the eye of childhood
That fears a painted devil. If he do bleed,
I'll gild the faces of the grooms withal,
For it must seem their guilt.   *Exit*

Knock within

MACBETH   Whence is that knocking?   60
How is't with me, when every noise appals me?
What hands are here? Ha: they pluck out mine eyes.
Will all great Neptune's ocean wash this blood
Clean from my hand? No: this my hand will rather
The multitudinous seas incarnadine,   65
Making the green one red.

Enter LADY [MACBETH]

58b-9   'As stealing out [Siddons] turns to him stooping, and with the finger pointed to him with malignant energy says, "If he do bleed &c."' (Bell, 'Siddons', p. 60). Terry said these lines quite differently, whispering them to herself, as 'she clung with outstretched arms to the tower wall' (Hughes, *Shakespearean*, p. 104).

60 SD   *Exit* Lillie Langtry made her exit up a winding staircase to Duncan's chamber. She 'dashes up the stair as if fearing her resolution may fail her. When she reappears, breathless, panting, overcome with the struggle against herself, she leans against a pillar and says "I shame to wear a heart so white," not as a reproach to Macbeth, but as an apology for her repugnance to the sight of blood' (Sprague, *Actors*, p. 244).

62   'Mcb . . . looks at hands in front of his face, "they" try to strangle him' (Nunn, Promptbook).

63-6   Garrick said 'in a tone of wild despair, "Will all . . . Making the *Green* – ONE RED"' (Murphy, *Garrick*, vol. I, p. 82).

66 SD   *Enter* . . . 'Upon her return from the chamber of slaughter . . . from the peculiar character of her lip [Siddons] gave an expression of *contempt* more striking than any she had hitherto displayed' (Boaden, *Siddons*, vol. II, p. 137). 'Kemble plays well here; stands motionless; his bloody hands near his face; his eye fixed, agony in his brow; quite rooted to the spot. [Siddons] at first directs him with an assured and confident air. Then alarm steals on her, increasing to agony lest his reason be quite gone and the discovery be inevitable. Strikes him on the shoulder, pulls him from his fixed posture, forces him away, he talking as he goes' (Bell, 'Siddons', p. 61). Terry entered 'red handed, picked up [Irving's] cloak with her fingertips, and led the way offstage, but finding him oblivious of danger, she came back to *push* him *pull* him off the stage'. He seemed scarcely aware of the knocking (Hughes, *Shakespearean*, p. 104). Violet Vanbrugh, Tree's Lady Macbeth, came out of Duncan's bedchamber 'like one of the Furies, with her eyes blazing, her bloody hands high above her head, the fingers pointing down at Macbeth' (Mullin, 'Images of Death', in Tardiff, *Criticism*, p. 180).

LADY MACBETH My hands are of your colour, but I shame
        To wear a heart so white.
                    Knock [*within*]
                            I hear a knocking
        At the south entry. Retire we to our chamber;
        A little water clears us of this deed.   70
        How easy is it then! Your constancy
        Hath left you unattended.
                    Knock [*within*]
                            Hark, more knocking.
        Get on your night-gown, lest occasion call us
        And show us to be watchers. Be not lost
        So poorly in your thoughts.   75
MACBETH To know my deed, 'twere best not know my self.
                    Knock [*within*]
        Wake Duncan with thy knocking: I would thou couldst.
                                                Exeunt

---

67 'There is a wild – but not a loud – defiance in her tone when [Ristori] shows him her own
    hands red with the blood of the grooms' (Morley, *Journal*, p. 188).

77 'Macready's final waking to the full conviction of the gulf between the past and the present
    was one of his grandest moments. I still vividly recall the terrible agony of his cry –
                Wake Duncan with thy knocking; I would thou could'st!
    as, with his face averted from his wife, and his arms outstretched, as it were, to the
    irrecoverable past, she dragged him from the stage' (Marston, *Actors*, vol. I, pp. 77–8). In
    Charles Kean's production, the Macbeths final exit 'was made sorrowfully, she regarding
    him as though pitying his suffering' (Bede, '*Macbeth* on the Stage', p. 21). Lady Macbeth
    'pushes Mcb. using her D[own] S[tage] shoulder, neither of them using bloody hands'
    (Nunn, Promptbook).

ACT 2, SCENE 3

Enter a PORTER. *Knocking within*

PORTER Here's a knocking indeed: if a man were porter of hell-
gate, he should have old turning the key. (*Knock*) Knock, knock,
knock. Who's there i'th'name of Beelzebub? Here's a farmer
that hanged himself on th'expectation of plenty. Come in time
– have napkins enough about you, here you'll sweat for't.   5
(*Knock*) Knock, knock. Who's there in th'other devil's name?
Faith, here's an equivocator that could swear in both the scales
against either scale, who committed treason enough for God's
sake, yet could not equivocate to heaven. O, come in, equivocator. (*Knock*) Knock, knock, knock. Who's there? Faith,   10
here's an English tailor come hither for stealing out of a French
hose. Come in, tailor, here you may roast your goose. (*Knock*)
Knock, knock. Never at quiet: what are you? But this place is
too cold for hell. I'll devil-porter it no further: I had thought to
have let in some of all professions that go the primrose way   15
to th'everlasting bonfire. (*Knock*) Anon, anon.   I pray you,
remember the porter. [*Opens door*]

0 SD *Enter . . .* In Davenant's alteration of the play, the Porter was omitted. Garrick, Kemble,
Macready, and Charles Kean also left out the Porter and in their versions the gate was
opened by Seyton or another servant (Promptbooks; Stone, 'Handling', p. 621). The first
part of the Porter's monologue was restored for a time by Phelps who later substituted
Seyton. The Officer who replaced the Porter in Macready's staging enters 'as tho' just risen
from sleep – his plaid trailing on the stage after him, hanging from his left shoulder – He
pauses . . . and then goes to C[entre] D[oor] at back, and unlocks that, and another door
beyond it, during the knocks – then reenters with Macduff and Lennox' (Promptbook).
Irving and Forbes-Robertson kept the Porter. The German version, translated by Schiller and
Goethe and performed in Weimar in 1880, has a sober Porter who speaks in verse and
enters 'singing a *Morgenlied*, welcoming the sun as it dispels the gloom of night and evil'
(Williams, *German Stage*, pp. 96–7).
4–5 ('Come . . . sweat for't') Cut by Forbes-Robertson.
7–10 ('Faith . . . Who's there?') Cut by Forbes-Robertson.

Enter MACDUFF *and* LENNOX

MACDUFF Was it so late, friend, ere you went to bed,
        That you do lie so late?
PORTER Faith, sir, we were carousing till the second cock, and drink,   20
    sir, is a great provoker of three things.
MACDUFF What three things does drink especially provoke?
PORTER Marry, sir, nose-painting, sleep, and urine. Lechery, sir, it
    provokes, and unprovokes: it provokes the desire, but it takes
    away the performance. Therefore much drink may be said to be   25
    an equivocator with lechery: it makes him, and it mars him; it
    sets him on, and it takes him off; it persuades him and dis-
    heartens him, makes him stand to and not stand to. In con-
    clusion, equivocates him in a sleep, and giving him the lie,
    leaves him.   30
MACDUFF I believe drink gave thee the lie last night.
PORTER That it did, sir, i'the very throat on me, but I requited him
    for his lie, and, I think, being too strong for him, though he
    took up my legs sometime, yet I made a shift to cast him.

Enter MACBETH

MACDUFF Is thy master stirring?   35
        Our knocking has awaked him: here he comes.
                                                    [*Exit Porter*]
LENNOX Good morrow, noble sir.
MACBETH   Good morrow, both.
MACDUFF Is the king stirring, worthy thane?
MACBETH   Not yet.

---

17 SD *Enter* . . . The Macduff in Glen Byam Shaw's production, Keith Michell, 'was not only
        young – twenty-six years old – with make-up that stressed his youth, he was also impressive
        physically. His six foot four inches towered over the others; a fur hat added to his height;
        and his great cloak made his broad-shouldered frame appear even larger' (Mullin, '*Macbeth*
        Onstage', p. 27).

20–34 ('and drink . . . to cast him') Cut by Garrick (who substituted 46–53a) and Forbes-Robertson.

32–4 ('but I . . . cast him') Cut by Nunn.

34 SD *Enter* . . . For this entrance Macready wore 'an enormous nightrobe' (Downer, *Macready*,
        p. 327). 'I could scarcely believe my eyes, when Macready entered in a fashionable
        flowered chintz dressing-gown, perhaps the one he usually wears, loosely thrown over his
        steel armour, which was seen glittering at every movement of his body, and in this curious
        costume drew his sword to kill the chamberlains who were sleeping near the King'
        (Puckler-Muskau, 'Macready's Macbeth' in Nagler, *Source Book* p. 475).

MACDUFF He did command me to call timely on him;
     I have almost slipped the hour.
MACBETH   I'll bring you to him.   40
MACDUFF I know this is a joyful trouble to you, but yet 'tis one.
MACBETH The labour we delight in physics pain. This is the door.
MACDUFF I'll make so bold to call, for 'tis my limited service.   *Exit*
LENNOX Goes the king hence today?
MACBETH He does – he did appoint so.   45
LENNOX The night has been unruly: where we lay,
     Our chimneys were blown down, and, as they say,
     Lamentings heard i'th'air, strange screams of death
     And prophesying with accents terrible
     Of dire combustion and confused events,   50
     New hatched to th'woeful time. The obscure bird
     Clamoured the livelong night. Some say, the earth
     Was feverous and did shake.
MACBETH   'Twas a rough night.
LENNOX My young remembrance cannot parallel
     A fellow to it.   55

Enter MACDUFF

42b Charles Kemble, playing Macbeth in New York in 1833, was praised for 'his manner of ushering Macduff into the chamber, and his shrinking away so guilty-like on uttering "this is the door", as if afraid to encounter again the image of his slaughtered monarch' (*New York Evening Post*, 19 February 1833; Sprague, *Actors*, p. 245).

46–53a Substituted by Garrick for 20–34.

46–55 'We can never forget the rueful horror of [Kemble's] look; which by strong exertion he endeavours to conceal, when on the morning succeeding the murder he receives Lennox and Macduff in the antechamber of Duncan. His efforts to appear composed, his endeavours to assume the attitude and appearance of one listening to Lennox's account of the external terrors of the night, while in fact he is expecting the alarm to arise within the royal apartment, formed a most astonishing piece of playing ... When Macbeth felt himself obliged to turn towards Lennox and reply to what he had been saying, you saw him, like a man awaking from a fit of absence, endeavour to recollect at least the general tenor of what had been said, and it was some time ere he could bring out the general reply, "Twas a rough night"' (Scott, 'Kemble', p. 219). Earlier, Garrick had been admired for his 'masterly dissimulation' during this episode, 'through which a consciousness of guilt was suffered to betray itself' (Stone and Kahrl, *Garrick*, p. 555). Antony Sher 'slipped easily into the black humour of the play: "'Twas a rough night," he explains, the morning after he's bumped off the king' (*Observer*, 21 November 1999).

MACDUFF O horror, horror, horror,
            Tongue nor heart cannot conceive, nor name thee.
MACBETH *and* LENNOX What's the matter?
MACDUFF Confusion now hath made his masterpiece:
            Most sacrilegious murder hath broke ope   60
            The Lord's anointed temple and stole thence
            The life o'th'building.
MACBETH What is't you say, the life?
LENNOX Mean you his majesty?
MACDUFF Approach the chamber and destroy your sight   65
            With a new Gorgon. Do not bid me speak:
            See and then speak yourselves.
                                    Exeunt Macbeth and Lennox
                        Awake, awake!
            Ring the alarum bell! Murder and treason!
            Banquo and Donaldbain! Malcolm, awake,
            Shake off this downy sleep, death's counterfeit,   70
            And look on death itself. Up, up, and see
            The great doom's image. Malcolm, Banquo,
            As from your graves rise up and walk like sprites
            To countenance this horror.

                    Bell rings. Enter LADY [MACBETH]

55 SD   *Enter* . . . In Phelps's staging, Macduff 'rushes back onto the stage, completely
        distracted . . . He rattles and staggers around the ancient castle, seizes the bell-rope and
        waves his sword about him, continually calling the sleepers from their rest' (Fontane,
        London Theatre, p. 84).
71b–2a ('Up, up . . . image') Cut by Nunn.
73b–4a Cut by Nunn.
74 SD   *Bell rings.* When the alarm bell rang out in Macready's production ('a solemn, measured
        tolling'), Macduff rushed about from door to door, beating at them violently with the hilt of
        his sword. 'Banquo, Fleance and Ross enter from doors at the left of the gallery, Malcolm,
        Donaldbain and the physician from doors at the right of the gallery. They descend to the
        courtyard, followed by lords who remain on the stairway. Four officers enter from under
        the stairs at the right . . . Six soldiers enter from the center door . . . Behind them are eight
        servants, some without caps, some with their sheathed swords in their hands, some
        fastening on weapons, plaids or portions of their dress. The claymores drawn and glittering
        in the half-light add to the ominousness of the scene. Meeting Banquo, Macduff exclaims,
        "Our royal master's murdered!" and the crowd takes up the cry, "Murdered!"' (Downer,
        Macready, pp. 327–8). Phelps also rapidly filled the stage at this point with 'nobles, knights,

LADY MACBETH   What's the business
                    That such a hideous trumpet calls to parley   75
                    The sleepers of the house? Speak, speak.
MACDUFF   O gentle lady,
                    'Tis not for you to hear what I can speak.
                    The repetition in a woman's ear
                    Would murder as it fell.–

squires, pages, and vassals, armed with every species of ancient weapons picked up on the spur of the moment . . . [They] rushed tumultuously upon the stage, as from every portion of the huge and garrisoned castle' (Phelps and Forbes-Robertson, *Phelps*, p. 99). The darkness was broken by the light from the torches carried by some of those who were running to answer the alarm (Allen, *Phelps*, p. 234) 'In the foreground, Lady Macbeth stands motionless, her pale face sunk in her bare shoulders, overwhelmed by her own crime *and grown old in a single hour*' (Fontane, *London Theatre*, p. 86). In Charles Kean's production 'crowds of half-dressed men, demented women and children, soldiers with unsheathed weapons, and retainers with torches, streamed on and filled the stage in the twinkling of an eye. Wild tumult and commotion were everywhere, while in the centre of the seething crowd, with pale face and flashing eyes, the murderer held aloft his blood-stained sword!' (Coleman, 'Facts and Fancies', p. 226). Irving notes in his study-book, 'Torches, swords etc . . . some putting clothes on . . . all pale . . . horns outside . . . raw-bodied men and women' (Hughes, *Shakespearean*, p. 105). 'The still figures of the murderers commanded attention, standing at opposite sides of the court while an excited crowd swirled around them. "This scene shd look a strange and wild affair", Ellen Terry wrote, "half torch light – half day-light & frightened half dressed people huddled together"' (Hughes, *Shakespearean*, pp. 104–5). In Glen Byam Shaw's production a similar effect was created. '"The Alarum bell crashes out and half-naked figures stand about in the Courtyard confused and terrified." The promptbook calls for more than a score of actors to fill the stage from every entrance and at every level' (Mullin, *'Macbeth* at Stratford', p. 272).

74 SD *Enter* . . . Davenant kept Lady Macbeth in this scene, but by Garrick's time it had become customary to omit her in order to avoid her fainting at line 111. Davies was told (*Miscellanies*, vol. II, p. 152), that 'many years since . . . an experiment was hazarded, whether the spectators would bear Lady Macbeth's surprise and fainting; but, however characteristical such behaviour might be, persons of a certain class were so merry upon the occasion, that it was not thought proper to venture the Lady's appearance any more. Mr Garrick thought, that even so favourite an actress as Mrs Pritchard would not, in that situation, escape derision from the gentlemen in the upper regions.' Kemble followed Garrick in omitting Lady Macbeth here, but Macready brought her back when the role was played by Helen Faucit. Phelps also included her, but Charles Kean left her out again (Promptbooks).

74b–9 Cut by Garrick, Kemble, and Charles Kean.

Enter BANQUO

                                O Banquo, Banquo,
Our royal master's murdered.

LADY MACBETH   Woe, alas.   80
       What, in our house?

BANQUO   Too cruel, anywhere.
Dear Duff, I prithee contradict thyself
And say it is not so.

Enter MACBETH *and* LENNOX

MACBETH Had I but died an hour before this chance,
       I had lived a blessèd time, for from this instant,   85
       There's nothing serious in mortality.
       All is but toys; renown and grace is dead,
       The wine of life is drawn, and the mere lees
       Is left this vault to brag of.

Enter MALCOLM *and* DONALDBAIN

DONALDBAIN What is amiss?

MACBETH   You are, and do not know't.   90
       The spring, the head, the fountain of your blood
       Is stopped, the very source of it is stopped.

MACDUFF Your royal father's murdered.

MALCOLM   O, by whom?

LENNOX Those of his chamber, as it seemed, had done't.
       Their hands and faces were all badged with blood,   95
       So were their daggers which, unwiped, we found
       Upon their pillows. They stared and were distracted;
       No man's life was to be trusted with them.

MACBETH O, yet I do repent me of my fury

84–127   After the discovery of the murder, 'the guilty Macbeth [Garrick], though struggling to assume
          the appearance of innocence and deep concern, dares not meet the eye of any person. The
          rest walk up and down as if sighing and lamenting; only Macduff and the sons of Duncan
          seem, by their looks, to point out the murderer' (Davies, *Miscellanies*, vol. II, p. 158).

89 SD   *Enter* . . . In Charles Kean's staging, Malcolm enters without Donaldbain who is absent from
          the whole scene (Promptbook). The two principals in Nunn's 1976 production 'caressed with
          false sympathy the newly orphaned Donaldbain' (Williams, *Text and Performance*, p. 42).

99–111a   Lady Macbeth [Ristori] 'does not know how her husband has dealt with the grooms, and
          listens with intense and real anxiety till he has told her as well as all the rest that he has
          killed them' (Morley, *Journal*, p. 188). Ellen Terry's note on this passage is 'Play here not the

That I did kill them.

MACDUFF   Wherefore did you so?   100

MACBETH Who can be wise, amazed, temp'rate, and furious,
Loyal and neutral, in a moment? No man.
Th'expedition of my violent love
Outran the pauser, reason. Here lay Duncan,
His silver skin laced with his golden blood   105
And his gashed stabs looked like a breach in nature,
For ruin's wasteful entrance. There the murderers,
Steeped in the colours of their trade; their daggers
Unmannerly breeched with gore. Who could refrain,
That had a heart to love and in that heart   110
Courage to make's love known?

LADY MACBETH   Help me hence, ho.

MACDUFF Look to the lady.

[*Exit Lady Macbeth, helped*]

MALCOLM [*To Donaldbain*] Why do we hold our tongues, that
most may claim
This argument for ours?

loud-voiced commanding Queen but the frightened "innocent flower" . . . She stands dead still listening . . . to Macbeth's explanation. Strung up, past pitch, she gives in at the *end* of his speech when she finds he is safely through his story, and *then she faints, really . . . she relaxes when all seems safe* and they swallow her husband's masterly explanation. Faints after pent-up agony and anxiety, *from relief'* (Manvell, 'Terry's Lady Macbeth', p. 161). Ellen Terry stood behind Banquo, 'nervously assenting by unconscious nods and gestures and inarticulate lip-movements to her lord's story, until her woman's strength fails her . . . and she falls and is raised and carried out with her fair head thrown back over a thane's shoulder, and her red hair streaming in the torchlight' (Liverpool *Daily Post*, 31 December 1888). Vivien Leigh in Glen Byam Shaw's production fainted because she could not stand the strain. 'Immediately the focus, if not the suspicion, centres on her. Her husband goes to her at once & as she recovers they are face to face with the knowledge of their guilt & surrounded by those strained, white faces peering at them out of the darkness' (Byam Shaw, Notebook, in Mullin, '*Macbeth* at Stratford', p. 276). In the 1976 RSC production, Duncan's body was brought onto the stage during this speech and it was the sight of this that made Lady Macbeth faint.

112 SD *Exit* . . . When in Tree's staging Lady Macbeth had fainted, a girl brought her water and, as she went off, the rest went with her, leaving Lennox, Macduff, and Banquo to salute Macbeth with drawn swords (Mullin, 'Images of Death', in Tardiff, *Criticism*, p. 180).

113–22a Cut by Phelps.

DONALDBAIN [*To Malcolm*]   What should be spoken here,
　　　　Where our fate hid in an auger hole may rush   115
　　　　And seize us? Let's away. Our tears are not yet brewed.
MALCOLM [*To Donaldbain*] Nor our strong sorrow upon the foot
　　　　of motion.
BANQUO Look to the lady,
　　　　And when we have our naked frailties hid
　　　　That suffer in exposure, let us meet   120
　　　　And question this most bloody piece of work
　　　　To know it further. Fears and scruples shake us:
　　　　In the great hand of God I stand and thence
　　　　Against the undivulged pretence I fight
　　　　Of treasonous malice.
MACDUFF　　　　　　　　And so do I.
ALL　　　　　　　　　　　　So all.   125
MACBETH Let's briefly put on manly readiness
　　　　And meet i'th'hall together.
ALL　　　　　　　　　　Well contented.
　　　　　　　　Exeunt [all but Malcolm and Donaldbain]
MALCOLM What will you do? Let's not consort with them.
　　　　To show an unfelt sorrow is an office
　　　　Which the false man does easy. I'll to England.   130
DONALDBAIN To Ireland, I. Our separated fortune
　　　　Shall keep us both the safer. Where we are,
　　　　There's daggers in men's smiles; the nea'er in blood,
　　　　The nearer bloody.

114b–16a	('What should . . . seize us') Cut by Forbes-Robertson.
117	Malcolm and Donaldbain made an exit here in Irving's production. This line cut by Forbes-Robertson.
125 SP	('All') 'Banquo' (Nunn).
125b	In Forrest's Promptbook there is the stage direction, 'all swords raised as if in oath', an arrangement also used by Macready.
126–7a	Forbes-Robertson gave this line and a half to Macduff.
127 SP	('All') 'Lennox' (Nunn).
128–39	Phelps, Charles Kean, and Irving cut this dialogue. In Glen Byam Shaw's production, as Malcolm and Donaldbain speak, the audience sees, but they do not, a dark figure which stands watching them from the top of the stairs. Turning to go, 'they get to the arch, they see Macbeth, and they run off' (Mullin, *Macbeth Onstage*, p. 27).
132b–4a	('Where . . . bloody') Cut by Forbes-Robertson.

MALCOLM   This murderous shaft that's shot
                    Hath not yet lighted, and our safest way   135
                    Is to avoid the aim. Therefore to horse,
                    And let us not be dainty of leave-taking,
                    But shift away. There's warrant in that theft
                    Which steals itself when there's no mercy left.

                                                        Exeunt

134b–5a ('This murderous . . . lighted') Cut by Nunn.
138b–9 ('There's . . . left') Cut by Forbes-Robertson.
139 SD *Exeunt* Wolfit returned here 'with the intention of liquidating Malcolm and Donaldbain and was disappointed by their escape, indicated by the clattering of horses' hooves without' (Crosse, *Playgoing*, p. 148). Towards the end of the scene Glen Byam Shaw introduced 'a lament . . . played as though on bagpipes or chanter in the distance. It is for the dead King, and continues to the end of the scene' (Mullin, *Macbeth Onstage*, p. 28).

ACT 2, SCENE 4

Enter ROSS, *with an* OLD MAN

OLD MAN Threescore and ten I can remember well;
                Within the volume of which time, I have seen
                Hours dreadful and things strange, but this sore night
                Hath trifled former knowings.
ROSS   Ha, good father,
                Thou seest the heavens, as troubled with man's act,   5
                Threatens his bloody stage. By th'clock 'tis day
                And yet dark night strangles the travelling lamp.
                Is't night's predominance, or the day's shame,
                That darkness does the face of earth entomb
                When living light should kiss it?
OLD MAN   'Tis unnatural,   10
                Even like the deed that's done. On Tuesday last,
                A falcon tow'ring in her pride of place
                Was by a mousing owl hawked at and killed.
ROSS And Duncan's horses, a thing most strange and certain,
                Beauteous and swift, the minions of their race,   15
                Turned wild in nature, broke their stalls, flung out,
                Contending 'gainst obedience as they would
                Make war with mankind.
OLD MAN   'Tis said, they eat each other.
ROSS They did so, to th'amazement of mine eyes
                That looked upon't.

Garrick here added a scene taken from Davenant's alteration of the text in which the three
witches and a chorus of witches prophesy that Macbeth will commit more murders. They all
take part in a dance and sing a chorus, and the scene concludes with a peal of thunder.
Kemble cut the whole of 2.4 but retained Davenant's additional scene. Macready and
Charles Kean also retained this additional scene and cut the first twenty lines of 2.4,
eliminating the Old Man, but kept the dialogue between Macduff and Ross (Promptbooks).
Phelps omitted the first twenty lines and the final couplet. Irving, Forbes-Robertson, and
Tree cut the whole scene.

19b–20   ('to th'amazement . . . Macduff') Cut by Nunn.

Enter MACDUFF

        Here comes the good Macduff. 20
   How goes the world, sir, now?
MACDUFF   Why, see you not?
ROSS Is't known who did this more than bloody deed?
MACDUFF Those that Macbeth hath slain.
ROSS   Alas the day,
   What good could they pretend?
MACDUFF   They were suborned.
   Malcolm and Donaldbain, the king's two sons, 25
   Are stol'n away and fled, which puts upon them
   Suspicion of the deed.
ROSS   'Gainst nature still.
   Thriftless ambition that will ravin up
   Thine own life's means. Then 'tis most like
   The sovereignty will fall upon Macbeth. 30
MACDUFF He is already named and gone to Scone
   To be invested.
ROSS Where is Duncan's body?
MACDUFF   Carried to Colmkill,
   The sacred storehouse of his predecessors
   And guardian of their bones.
ROSS   Will you to Scone? 35
MACDUFF No, cousin, I'll to Fife.
ROSS   Well, I will thither.
MACDUFF Well may you see things well done there. Adieu,
   Lest our old robes sit easier than our new.
ROSS Farewell, father.
OLD MAN God's benison go with you, and with those 40
   That would make good of bad, and friends of foes.

             Exeunt

30 At the end of this line, in Benthall's production, the cry 'Macbeth – King of Scotland' was
  given by a crowd off stage (Williamson, *Old Vic 2*, p. 19).
39–41 Cut by Garrick.

ACT 3, SCENE 1

Enter BANQUO [*dressed for riding*]

BANQUO Thou hast it now, King, Cawdor, Glamis, all,
         As the weïrd women promised, and I fear
         Thou played'st most foully for't; yet it was said
         It should not stand in thy posterity,
         But that myself should be the root and father   5
         Of many kings. If there come truth from them –
         As upon thee, Macbeth, their speeches shine –
         Why by the verities on thee made good,
         May they not be my oracles as well
         And set me up in hope? But hush, no more.   10

Sennet sounded. Enter MACBETH *as* King, LADY [MACBETH *as* Queen],
        LENNOX, ROSS, *Lords, and Attendants*

Between 2.4 and 3.1 Nunn added the ceremony of Macbeth's coronation. He wore the white
robe formerly worn by Duncan.

Setting   The scene was set by Irving in Duncan's palace at Forres (Hughes, *Shakespearean*, p. 106).

10 SD   *Enter . . .* In the autumn of 1785, Siddons wore a costume of 'violet-coloured satting [*sic*],
richly trimmed with gold fringe and sable. The petticoat was of gold tissue, ornamented in
like manner; her head-dress consisted of plumage, interwoven with jewels. Her stomacher
was also richly studded with gems' (*Morning Herald and Daily Advertiser*, 31 October 1785).
For a production in Dublin in 1802, she wore 'a white floor-length undergown over which is
draped a black gown trimmed with gold, cut above the knees in front and falling gradually
into a train; the high-waisted, white cincture is matched by a white tiara and a separate
crown with a simple white veil attached behind' (Donoghue, 'Kemble's *Macbeth*', p. 73).
Macready arranged for the centre doors at the back to be opened by Seyton and 'a new
royal procession enters to cut short [Banquo's] soliloquy: six lords, two officers, Seyton,
Lennox and Ross, Macbeth and Lady Macbeth, the physician (who seems to go with the
crown), and eight ladies' (Downer, *Macready*, p. 329). He wore a crown and a crimson
tunic over a white shirt. Ellen Kean wore a dress of a similar design to her first, but 'richer in
material, each portion of dress embroidered in gold' (Promptbook). According to
John Coleman, Salvini wore 'white silver lama [*sic*], the material affected by fairies and

MACBETH Here's our chief guest.
LADY MACBETH   If he had been forgotten,
    It had been as a gap in our great feast
    And all thing unbecoming.
MACBETH Tonight we hold a solemn supper, sir,
    And I'll request your presence.
BANQUO   Let your highness   15
    Command upon me, to the which my duties
    Are with a most indissoluble tie
    Forever knit.

burlesque princes in the pantomime. A delicately-jewelled filigree waistbelt vainly attempted to restrain the rebellious region which obstinately persisted in asserting itself' ('Facts and Fancies', p. 227). Irving entered in his royal robes made of 'heavy, bullion-gold damask, hand embroidered with maroon-coloured silk, with sleeves of light blue silk' (Jones, 'Stage Costume', in Foulkes, *Victorian Stage*, p. 66). He appeared 'nervy, careworn, sleepless' (Hughes, *Shakespearean*, p. 106). Mrs Patrick Campbell, playing opposite Forbes-Robertson, wore 'a gorgeous robe of golden tissue, glittering with multi-coloured jewelled embroideries, and with various strange birds wrought upon the golden background' (Dent, *Campbell*, p. 162). Violet Vanbrugh, Tree's Lady Macbeth, wore 'a dress of gold cloth with a tunic of the same material over it, embroidered with a border of green and scarlet. From her shoulders hung a train of scarlet cloth fastened with brooches of gold and rubies, and she wore a bright green scarf. From her crown floated a long black veil, and there were many huge barbaric jewels hung about her dress' (*Westminster Gazette*, 8 September 1911). Fabia Drake, directed by Komisarjevsky, wore 'a considerable amount of ironmongery . . . Her crown . . . was made of saucepan scourers . . . Her breasts were covered by what appeared to be saucepan lids' (Beauman, *Royal Shakespeare*, p. 132).

11b–13 Cut by Garrick.

14 Kemble brought Fleance on with Banquo at the beginning of the scene, as did Macready, who at this point stroked the boy's hair, a gesture to which the critic in *John Bull* objected: 'We have now to notice the actor's fondling of *Fleance*, as inferring a cat-like propensity to play with his victim, very foreign from *Macbeth's* nature' (26 May 1839; Sprague, *Actors*, p. 248). When acting with Phelps, Helen Faucit took over this business from Macbeth, on which Henry Morley commented, 'We have seen Miss Faucit praised for representation of smooth treachery in the tender playing of her fingers about the head of the child Fleance while Macbeth is sending father and child into the toils set for them. Miss Faucit knows her Shakespeare better than that. The fingers of the woman who has been a mother, and has murder on her soul, wander sadly and tenderly over the type of her lost innocence' (*Journal*, p. 291).

MACBETH Ride you this afternoon?

BANQUO Ay, my good lord.   20

MACBETH We should have else desired your good advice
Which still hath been both grave and prosperous
In this day's council: but we'll take tomorrow.
Is't far you ride?

BANQUO As far, my lord, as will fill up the time   25
'Twixt this and supper. Go not my horse the better,
I must become a borrower of the night
For a dark hour, or twain.

MACBETH Fail not our feast.

BANQUO My lord, I will not.   30

MACBETH We hear our bloody cousins are bestowed
In England and in Ireland, not confessing
Their cruel parricide, filling their hearers
With strange invention. But of that tomorrow,
When therewithal we shall have cause of state   35
Craving us jointly. Hie you to horse; adieu,
Till you return at night. Goes Fleance with you?

BANQUO Ay, my good lord; our time does call upon's.

MACBETH I wish your horses swift and sure of foot,
And so I do commend you to their backs.   40
Farewell.
                                                               Exit Banquo
Let every man be master of his time
Till seven at night; to make society
The sweeter welcome, we will keep ourself
Till supper-time alone. While then, God be with you.   45
                           Exeunt [all but Macbeth and a Servant]
Sirrah, a word with you: attend those men
Our pleasure?

SERVANT They are, my lord, without the palace gate.

MACBETH Bring them before us.
                                                               Exit Servant
                           To be thus is nothing,
But to be safely thus. Our fears in Banquo   50
Stick deep, and in his royalty of nature

---

22   Cut by Nunn.

31–6a   ('We hear . . . jointly') Cut by Garrick.

35–6a   ('When . . . jointly') Cut by Forbes-Robertson.

45 SD   Nunn's Servant was Seyton.

Reigns that which would be feared. 'Tis much he dares,
And to that dauntless temper of his mind,
He hath a wisdom that doth guide his valour
To act in safety. There is none but he,   55
Whose being I do fear; and under him
My genius is rebuked, as it is said
Mark Antony's was by Caesar. He chid the sisters
When first they put the name of king upon me
And bade them speak to him. Then prophet-like,   60
They hailed him father to a line of kings.
Upon my head they placed a fruitless crown
And put a barren sceptre in my gripe,
Thence to be wrenched with an unlineal hand,
No son of mine succeeding. If't be so,   65
For Banquo's issue have I filed my mind;
For them, the gracious Duncan have I murdered,
Put rancours in the vessel of my peace
Only for them, and mine eternal jewel
Given to the common enemy of man,   70
To make them kings, the seeds of Banquo kings.
Rather than so, come Fate into the list,
And champion me to th'utterance. Who's there?

            Enter Servant and two MURDERERS

[*To Servant*] Now go to the door and stay there till we call.
                                                Exit Servant
Was it not yesterday we spoke together?   75

<hr />

52b–8a   ('Tis much . . . Caesar') Cut by Phelps and Forbes-Robertson.
  68–70   Cut by Forbes-Robertson.
  73 SD   *Enter* . . . In Macready's production, 'the two murderers whom Macbeth hires to murder
          Banquo, are not, as on our [German] stage, ragged ruffians, – by the side of whom the King,
          in his regal ornaments and the immediate vicinity of his Court, exhibits a ridiculous contrast,
          and who could never find access to a palace in such a dress, but of decent appearance and
          behaviour, – villains, but not beggars' (Puckler-Muskau, 'Macready's Macbeth' in Nagler,
          Source Book, p. 474). Nunn's Servant was Seyton.
75–139   Irving severely reduced the dialogue with the murderers. Olivier expressed contempt for
          them, 'powerfully shot across by overtones of self-contempt' (*Times*, 8 June 1955). Ian
          McKellen was 'at his most briskly administrative' with the murderers, 'busy with papers, as
          he blackened Banquo; then he suddenly turned a beady eye upon them to make the
          distinctions about dogs and men; once the business of the meeting was over, a dismissive

MURDERERS It was, so please your highness.

MACBETH Well then, now have you considered of my speeches? Know, that it was he in the times past which held you so under fortune, which you thought had been our innocent self. This I made good to you in our last conference; passed in probation   80
with you how you were borne in hand, how crossed; the instruments, who wrought with them, and all things else that might to half a soul and to a notion crazed say, 'Thus did Banquo.'

FIRST MURDERER You made it known to us.

MACBETH I did so, and went further, which is now our point of   85
second meeting. Do you find your patience so predominant in your nature, that you can let this go? Are you so gospelled, to pray for this good man and for his issue, whose heavy hand hath bowed you to the grave and beggared yours forever?

FIRST MURDERER We are men, my liege.   90

MACBETH Ay, in the catalogue ye go for men,
As hounds, and greyhounds, mongrels, spaniels, curs,
Shoughs, water-rugs, and demi-wolves are clept
All by the name of dogs. The valued file
Distinguishes the swift, the slow, the subtle,   95
The housekeeper, the hunter, every one
According to the gift which bounteous nature
Hath in him closed, whereby he does receive
Particular addition from the bill
That writes them all alike. And so of men.   100
Now, if you have a station in the file
Not i'th'worst rank of manhood, say't,
And I will put that business in your bosoms,
Whose execution takes your enemy off,
Grapples you to the heart and love of us   105
Who wear our health but sickly in his life,

---

jerk of the head to Seyton to get rid of them contrasted with the affable "abide within" to them' (*Shakespeare Survey*, vol. xxx, 1977, p. 178).

78–86   ('Know that . . . second meeting') Cut by Garrick, Macready, Phelps, and Charles Kean.

79–87   ('This I . . . let this go?') Cut by Forbes-Robertson.

90–107a Cut by Macready, Phelps, Charles Kean, and Forbes-Robertson.
During Olivier's dialogue with the murderers, they appeared 'half scared, half-fascinated by the now evil magnetism of the King'. They 'shrank back each time he approached them in a swirl of robes, while he, pacing the stage between and around them, continuously spun a web of bewildering words about their understandings' (David, 'Tragic Curve', p. 129).

105–7a Cut by Nunn.

        Which in his death were perfect.
SECOND MURDERER   I am one, my liege,
        Whom the vile blows and buffets of the world
        Hath so incensed that I am reckless what I do
        To spite the world.
FIRST MURDERER   And I another,   110
        So weary with disasters, tugged with fortune,
        That I would set my life on any chance
        To mend it or be rid on't.
MACBETH   Both of you know
        Banquo was your enemy.
MURDERERS   True, my lord.
MACBETH So is he mine, and in such bloody distance   115
        That every minute of his being thrusts
        Against my near'st of life; and though I could
        With barefaced power sweep him from my sight
        And bid my will avouch it, yet I must not,
        For certain friends that are both his and mine,   120
        Whose loves I may not drop, but wail his fall
        Who I myself struck down. And thence it is
        That I to your assistance do make love,
        Masking the business from the common eye
        For sundry weighty reasons.
SECOND MURDERER   We shall, my lord,   125
        Perform what you command us.
FIRST MURDERER   Though our lives –
MACBETH Your spirits shine through you. Within this hour at most,
        I will advise you where to plant yourselves,
        Acquaint you with the perfect spy o'th'time,
        The moment on't, for't must be done tonight,   130
        And something from the palace: always thought,
        That I require a clearness. And with him,
        To leave no rubs nor botches in the work,
        Fleance, his son that keeps him company,

111–13a   Cut by Nunn.

120–4   Cut by Garrick and Forbes-Robertson.

131–3   Cut by Forbes-Robertson.

134–7a   'Speaking of Fleance [Irving's] voice became "white and flute-like . . . giving for the fraction of a moment a picture of youth and innocence". Then it deepened with a veiled menace that was simply appalling' (Hughes, *Shakespearean*, p. 106).

Whose absence is no less material to me   135
Than is his father's, must embrace the fate
Of that dark hour. Resolve yourselves apart,
I'll come to you anon.
MURDERERS   We are resolved, my lord.
MACBETH I'll call upon you straight; abide within.
                                              [*Exeunt Murderers*]
It is concluded. Banquo, thy soul's flight,   140
If it find heaven, must find it out tonight.   *Exit*

135–6a   Cut by Garrick.
  138b   During Salvini's performance in New York in 1881, the murderers at this point 'tried with
         fawning servility, to seize the hem of [Macbeth's] regal robe, and thereupon he repulsed
         them with a deportment of imperial disdain and a momentary shudder' (Winter,
         Shakespeare on the Stage, p. 488; Sprague, *Actors*, p. 249).
   139   Cut by Garrick.

ACT 3, SCENE 2

Enter [LADY MACBETH], *and a* SERVANT

LADY MACBETH Is Banquo gone from court?
SERVANT Ay, madam, but returns again tonight.
LADY MACBETH Say to the king, I would attend his leisure
      For a few words.
SERVANT   Madam, I will.   *Exit*
LADY MACBETH   Nought's had, all's spent
      Where our desire is got without content.   5
      'Tis safer to be that which we destroy
      Than by destruction dwell in doubtful joy.

Enter MACBETH

      How now, my lord, why do you keep alone,

0 SD *Enter* . . . Macready's, Charles Kean's, and Nunn's Servant was Seyton (Promptbook), the
      only servant who remains loyal to Macbeth until the end of the play.
  1 [Siddons] spoke this line with 'great dignity and solemnity of voice; nothing of the joy of
      gratified ambition' (Bell, 'Siddons', p. 61).
4b–7 Ellen Terry's manuscript note in her edition of the play reads 'Hands to head. Albert Dürer's
      Melancholy. Express here (when *alone*) a "rooted sorrow" . . . She sees clearer now, knows
      she has missed what she had hoped to gain. I sometimes think she is rather stupid!!'
      (Manvell, 'Terry's Lady Macbeth', p. 161).
7 SD *Enter* . . . 'I can see [Kemble] now, standing in the doorway in the centre of the scene. The
      kingly crown appeared a burden and a torture to him. How terribly clear it was, before he
      uttered a word, that his mind was "full of scorpions" – that he acutely felt – "Better be with
      the dead"' (Planché, *Recollections*, p. 15).
8–12 In her 'Remarks on the Character of Lady Macbeth', Siddons says of these lines, 'She knows,
      by her own woeful experience, the torment which [Macbeth] undergoes, and endeavours to
      alleviate his sufferings . . . Far from her former habits of reproach and contemptuous
      taunting, you perceive that she now listens to his complaints with sympathizing feelings'
      (Campbell, *Siddons*, vol. II, p. 23). Bell observes that Siddons's tone was 'very plaintive.
      This is one of the passages in which her intense love of her husband should animate every
      word' ('Siddons', p. 62). In Lewis Casson's 1926 production, 'the guilty couple, richly robed

          Of sorriest fancies your companions making,
          Using those thoughts which should indeed have died   10
          With them they think on? Things without all remedy
          Should be without regard; what's done, is done.
MACBETH We have scorched the snake, not killed it;
          She'll close, and be herself, whilst our poor malice
          Remains in danger of her former tooth.   15
          But let the frame of things disjoint, both the worlds suffer,
          Ere we will eat our meal in fear, and sleep
          In the affliction of these terrible dreams
          That shake us nightly. Better be with the dead
          Whom we, to gain our peace, have sent to peace,   20
          Than on the torture of the mind to lie
          In restless ecstasy. Duncan is in his grave.
          After life's fitful fever, he sleeps well;
          Treason has done his worst; nor steel nor poison,
          Malice domestic, foreign levy, nothing   25
          Can touch him further.
LADY MACBETH Come on. Gentle my lord,
          Sleek o'er your rugged looks, be bright and jovial
          Among your guests tonight.
MACBETH   So shall I, love,
          And so I pray be you. Let your remembrance   30
          Apply to Banquo, present him eminence
          Both with eye and tongue; unsafe the while, that we
          Must lave our honours in these flattering streams
          And make our faces vizards to our hearts,
          Disguising what they are.
LADY MACBETH   You must leave this.   35
MACBETH O, full of scorpions is my mind, dear wife!

and newly-crowned, cower in the deepening dark with their guilt growing grimmer and bloodier in their own minds . . . With despair growing in their hearts, they huddle together in the dusk, with the shouts and acclamations of their adherents still sounding in their ears' (*Observer*, 26 December 1926).

16–26　'The contrast between the innocent sleep of his victims, and the fearful and wretched watchings of their murderer, uttered [by Edmund Kean] in a voice broken by terror, inward torment, and hopeless despair, were among the most masterly performances that perhaps the English stage has ever witnessed' (*Times*, 7 November 1814).

23　'"After life's fitful fever, *he* sleeps well" was Macready's way of saying it' (Marston, *Recent Actors*, vol. 1, p. 78).

32b–4a　('unsafe . . . And') Cut by Forbes-Robertson.

                 Thou know'st that Banquo and his Fleance lives.
LADY MACBETH But in them Nature's copy's not eterne.
MACBETH There's comfort yet, they are assailable;
                 Then be thou jocund: ere the bat hath flown   40
                 His cloistered flight, ere to black Hecate's summons
                 The shard-born beetle with his drowsy hums
                 Hath rung night's yawning peal, there shall be done
                 A deed of dreadful note.
LADY MACBETH   What's to be done?
MACBETH Be innocent of the knowledge, dearest chuck,   45
                 Till thou applaud the deed. Come, seeling night,
                 Scarf up the tender eye of pitiful day
                 And with thy bloody and invisible hand
                 Cancel and tear to pieces that great bond
                 Which keeps me pale. Light thickens,   50
                 And the crow makes wing to th'rooky wood;
                 Good things of day begin to droop and drowse,

38 Through the way she said this single line, Siddons made Lady Macbeth responsible for
    suggesting that Banquo and Fleance should be murdered. She revealed, says Bell, 'a flash of
    her former spirit and energy' ('Siddons', p. 62). Helen Faucit, a very feminine Lady
    Macbeth, made it clear that the idea did not occur to her (Morley, *Journal*, p. 291). Ellen
    Terry's reaction was also entirely innocent. 'She paraphrases the line with a characteristic
    touch of mischief: "Don't trouble so, for they cannot live for ever – that fellow Banquo may
    die any day – *why not*! and the boy may have whooping cough in such a climate as this –
    we keep all the whisky to ourselves – I lock up the cupboard every night"' (Manvell, 'Terry's
    Lady Macbeth', p. 161). In his own annotated copy of the play, Irving wrote, 'She doesn't
    understand – & he goes off abruptly' (Sprague, *Actors*, pp. 249–50).

40a 'A note of resentment against crime's awful necessities creeps into [Olivier's] ironic "Then be
    thou jocund"' (*Times*, 8 June 1955).

45b–50 'If in [Macready's] early bewilderment at the prophecies of the witches there was something
    of the sensitivity of Hamlet, there is now a smack of Richard III about him. His voice is
    decided and firm, his manner hard, composed, and full of the terror of almost abstract Evil'
    (Downer, *Macready*, p. 330).

46b–50a ('Come . . . pale') Cut by Forbes-Robertson.

50b–3 According to Leigh Hunt, Macready said these words 'as merely intimating a fact – a note of
    time – pointing with his hand as he did it, and as he might have pointed to a clock.' The
    speech was delivered 'with too much rapidity and indifference . . . Mr Macready seems
    afraid of the poetry of some of his greatest parts, as if it would hurt the effect of his
    naturalness and his more familiar passages' (*Dramatic Essays*, p. 211).

Whiles night's black agents to their preys do rouse.
Thou marvell'st at my words, but hold thee still;
Things bad begun, make strong themselves by ill.   55
So prithee, go with me.

Exeunt

56   Garrick cut this half line, as did Irving who left Terry to sit alone. Her own note at this point
is, 'Nervous clutch at his sleeve. Henry goes out first. *Sit still*. I think and try to find the
meaning of his words. Anxious. Uncertain and rather ill' (Manvell, 'Terry's Lady Macbeth',
p. 161).

ACT 3, SCENE 3

Enter three MURDERERS

FIRST MURDERER But who did bid thee join with us?

THIRD MURDERER   Macbeth.

SECOND MURDERER He needs not our mistrust, since he delivers
Our offices and what we have to do
To the direction just.

FIRST MURDERER [*To Third Murderer*] Then stand with us.
The west yet glimmers with some streaks of day;   5
Now spurs the lated traveller apace
To gain the timely inn, and near approaches
The subject of our watch.

THIRD MURDERER   Hark, I hear horses.

BANQUO (*Within*) Give us a light there, ho!

SECOND MURDERER   Then 'tis he; the rest
That are within the note of expectation   10
Already are i'th'court.

FIRST MURDERER   His horses go about.

THIRD MURDERER Almost a mile; but he does usually,
So all men do, from hence to th'palace gate
Make it their walk.

Enter BANQUO *and* FLEANCE, *with a torch*

SECOND MURDERER A light, a light!   15

THIRD MURDERER 'Tis he.

Whole scene cut by Irving, Forbes-Robertson, and Tree.

Setting In Charles Kean's staging, the exterior of a castle partially screened by trees; cloudy sky
(Promptbook).

0 SD *Enter* . . . In some productions, including Nunn's, the Third Murderer was Seyton, the
servant who supports Macbeth almost to the end of the play.

1–4 Cut by Phelps.

2b–4a ('since he . . . just') Cut by Nunn.

7b–8a ('and near . . . watch') Cut by Nunn.

15–18 Cut by Garrick.

FIRST MURDERER Stand to't.
BANQUO It will be rain tonight.
FIRST MURDERER   Let it come down.
            [*The Murderers attack. First Murderer strikes out the light*]
BANQUO O, treachery!
            Fly, good Fleance, fly, fly, fly!   20
            Thou mayst revenge – O slave!   [*Dies. Fleance escapes*]
THIRD MURDERER Who did strike out the light?
FIRST MURDERER   Was't not the way?
THIRD MURDERER There's but one down; the son is fled.
SECOND MURDERER We have lost best half of our affair.
FIRST MURDERER Well, let's away, and say how much is done.   25
                                    Exeunt[*, with Banquo's body*]

19–21 Spoken 'within' (Garrick)
21 SD *Dies. Fleance escapes* In Davenant's alteration of the play, Banquo and Fleance make an
       exit here, followed by the murderers. Then there is the sound of a swordfight 'within', and
       Fleance runs across the stage and escapes. Garrick followed this arrangement.
22–5   Cut by Garrick.

ACT 3, SCENE 4

Banquet prepared. [*Two thrones are placed on stage.*] *Enter* MACBETH [*as King*], LADY [MACBETH *as Queen*], ROSS, LENNOX, LORDS, *and Attendants.* [*Lady Macbeth sits*]

Setting   For this scene the stage has been arranged in a variety of different ways. In the notes he made in preparation for his production, Macklin says, 'The shape of the Table should be a horse-shoe, the whole scope of the stage – a man & a woman all round, the Queen can then come to Macbeth down centre of the stage – Macbeth can address and prepare better for the Ghost' (Appleton, *Macklin*, p. 172). Kemble used four playing areas: 'a platform with two thrones somewhere near the centre of the stage; the banqueting tables stage right; an open area downstage centre, used by the two chief characters; and the area next to the left proscenium door, where the murderer makes his entrance. Kemble, in order to "mingle with society and play the humble host", moves right to where his company have just seated themselves, while Mrs Siddons as hostess "keeps her state" upon the throne' (Donohue, 'Kemble and Mrs Siddons', p. 82). Fanny Kemble, who played Lady Macbeth opposite Macready, explains, 'From time immemorial, the banquet scene . . . has been arranged after one invariable fashion: the royal dais and throne, with the steps leading up to it, holds the middle of the stage, sufficiently far back to allow of two long tables, at which the guests are seated on each side, in front of it, leaving between them ample space for Macbeth's scene with Banquo's ghost, and Lady Macbeth's repeated rapid descents from the dais and returns to it, in her vehement expostulations with him, and her courteous invitations to the occupants of both the tables to "feed and regard him not". Accustomed to this arrangement of the stage, which I never saw different anywhere in all my life for this scene, I was much astonished and annoyed to find, at my first rehearsal, a long banqueting table set immediately at the foot of the steps in front of the dais, which rendered all but impossible my rapid rushing down to the front of the stage, in my terrified and indignant appeals to Macbeth, and my sweeping back to my place, addressing on my way compliments to the tables on either side . . . All my remonstrances were, however, in vain. Mr Macready persisted in his determination to have the stage arranged solely with reference to himself' (*Later Life*, vol. III, pp. 379–80). Her description is confirmed by a sketch drawn in Macready's Promptbook. The tables were 'piled high with the most splendid fruits, and gorgeous dish-covers glitter[ed] in endless perspective. Servants, gathered at the centre table, move to left and right to serve the banqueters and music adds to the high festivity of the beginning' (Downer, *Macready*, p. 331). In Phelps's production, 'the new royal couple have taken their places on a dais on the left of the stage, and look out over the guests who sit at six or eight tables, making two lines with a free passage down the middle. The whole stage is full and one has the impression of a real banquet to which numerous thanes have been invited. Between the first and second rows of tables, opposite the king's throne and in the exact centre of the stage, is a separate seat – a place of honour prepared for Banquo. He appears standing there, before he sits down in the seat. His face is deathly pale but unwounded' (Fontane, *London Theatre*, p. 86). Phelps's Promptbook shows that more than forty actors were on the stage and that there was a trap in front of Banquo's chair. In Charles Kean's revival, 'the banquet was prepared on the upper half of the stage, under a sloping timber roof, supported on either side by a row of Saxon pillars. At the back of the hall was an opening in the wall, half way up, admitting to a small minstrels' gallery, in which were seven bards with harps. A long table was laid along the back of the stage, with two side tables in advance of the round pillars. In the front of these was a semicircular arch, supported by two round pillars, at a short distance R. and L. of the centre of the stage. Much of the business of the scene was done by the Keans between these pillars and the footlights. The only lights for the banquet were torches stuck in the pillars (Bede, 'Macbeth on the Stage', p. 21). A plan drawn in Charles Kean's Promptbook more or less confirms this description except that the torches are held by servants. In his farewell address on retiring from the Princess's Theatre, Kean recalled that 'fault was . . . found with my removal of the gorgeous banquet and its gold and silver vessels, together with the massive candelabra (Such as no Highlander of the eleventh century ever gazed upon), and with the substitution of the more appropriate feast of coarse fare, served upon rude tables, and lighted by simple pine torches. I was admonished that such diminution of regal pomp impaired the strength of *Macbeth's* motive for the crime of murder, the object being less dazzling and attractive. Until that hour I had never believed that the Scottish Thane had an eye to Duncan's plate' (Nagler, *Source Book*, p. 489). Before the action of the scene began, Irving arranged for '"a rough soldiery [to] enter, hang up shields and drink; then a procession is formed . . . of a score of attendants and a number of cooks to set the table, each man bearing viands or furniture for the table." Cattermole's designs for costumes, weapons, "wine-cups, ivory cups, salt-cellars, Anglo-Saxon wine-pots, besides cakes in the form of castles" were based upon painstaking research' (Hughes, *Shakespearean*, p. 108). The music played for Salvini's banquet scene, recalls John Coleman, was 'a Scotch jig, usually associated with the highland fling. The half empty stage was sparsely peopled by pale, squalid guests, attired in tawdry costumes of all periods and all nations' ('Facts and Fancies' p. 228). The banquet in Tree's production was preceded by a torch dance. The *Academy* complained that he had rejected the traditional idea of one long table for the banquet and substituted a number of small tables, 'after the custom of the modern supper-room'. As a result, half the guests had their

MACBETH You know your own degrees, sit down; at first and last,
the hearty welcome.

[*The Lords sit*]

LORDS Thanks to your majesty.

MACBETH Our self will mingle with society and play the humble
host; our hostess keeps her state, but in best time we will   5
require her welcome.

LADY MACBETH Pronounce it for me, sir, to all our friends, for
my heart speaks they are welcome.

Enter FIRST MURDERER

MACBETH See, they encounter thee with their hearts' thanks.
Both sides are even; here I'll sit i'th'midst.   10
Be large in mirth, anon we'll drink a measure
The table round. [*To First Murderer*] There's blood upon
thy face.

FIRST MURDERER 'Tis Banquo's then.

MACBETH 'Tis better thee without, than he within.
Is he dispatched?   15

FIRST MURDERER My lord, his throat is cut; that I did for him.

MACBETH Thou art the best o'th'cut-throats,
Yet he's good that did the like for Fleance;

backs to the audience. Moreover, at Tree's stage banquets, 'there is never anything to eat'
(9 September 1911). In Glen Byam Shaw's staging there was a dais with two thrones in the
centre at the back of the stage and the guests sat at a long table downstage centre with their
backs to the audience. The set was lighted by torches fixed to the walls (Mullin, *Macbeth
Onstage*, p. 115). In Nunn's 1976 staging at the Other Place, the actors carried the crates on
which they had been sitting onto the stage and sat there in a circle where they passed round
a large loving-cup. At the Swan in 1999 the banquet table was small and held only six or
eight guests.

1–2 'Who, that has once seen this exhibition, will ever forget Mrs Siddons in the banqueting
scene? The lofty courtesy with which she receives her guests, and the haughty, hurried and
apprehensive manner in which she dismisses them' (*Bell's Weekly Messenger*, 5 July 1812).

12b On one occasion, Garrick hissed this line with such intensity that 'the actor playing the first
murderer was completely thrown. Instead of growling "'Tis Banquo's then", his hand flew
involuntarily to his face and the words that came out were "Is there, by God?"' (McIntyre,
Garrick, p. 84).

12b–32a During Macbeth's conversation with the murderers, Siddons showed 'a growing uneasiness'
until (line 32b) 'at last she rises and speaks' (Bell, 'Siddons', p. 62).

14 Cut by Forbes-Robertson.

If thou didst it, thou art the nonpareil.

FIRST MURDERER Most royal sir, Fleance is scaped.   20

MACBETH Then comes my fit again: I had else been perfect;
        Whole as the marble, founded as the rock,
        As broad and general as the casing air:
        But now I am cabined, cribbed, confined, bound in
        To saucy doubts and fears. But Banquo's safe?   25

FIRST MURDERER Ay, my good lord: safe in a ditch he bides,
        With twenty trenchèd gashes on his head,
        The least a death to nature.

MACBETH   Thanks for that.
        There the grown serpent lies; the worm that's fled
        Hath nature that in time will venom breed,   30
        No teeth for th'present. Get thee gone; tomorrow
        We'll hear ourselves again.

                             Exit [First] Murderer

LADY MACBETH   My royal lord,
        You do not give the cheer; the feast is sold
        That is not often vouched while 'tis a-making,
        'Tis given with welcome. To feed were best at home: 35
        From thence, the sauce to meat is ceremony,
        Meeting were bare without it.

      Enter the Ghost of Banquo and sits in Macbeth's place

---

19   Cut by Forbes-Robertson.

29–31a   ('There . . . present') Cut by Forbes-Robertson.

31b–2a   ('Get thee . . . again') Cut by Nunn.

33b–7a   ('the feast . . . without it') Cut by Nunn.

37 SD   *Enter . . .* The Folio stage direction suggests that the Ghost simply walked on, but it is
        possible that in the early performances it came up through a trap. Davenant simply
        reproduced the Folio entry direction, but notes for its exit 'the Ghost descends', i.e. through
        a trap. For its second appearance in Davenant's version the Ghost 'rises at [Macbeth's] feet',
        presumably through a trap, but later simply 'exits'. For both of the Ghost's entrances,
        Garrick arranged for him to come up through a trap, but he made his second exit walking
        backwards (*St James's Chronicle*, 15–18 May 1773). In Kemble's 1794 production, 'an
        alteration was made respecting the ghost of *Banquo*, whose visible appearance to *Macbeth*
        was now omitted'. In other words, Banquo did not appear at all in this scene, and the ghost
        became a creation of Macbeth's guilty imagination. Although this alteration was 'generally
        approved' (Oulton, *History*, p. 142), nevertheless in his revival of 1811, Kemble reintroduced
        the ghost, much to the disapproval of the *Times* critic (19 September) who protested against
        '*Banquo* coming in with his throat cut and shaking his head like a Mandarin'.

MACBETH   Sweet remembrancer!
          Now good digestion wait on appetite,
          And health on both.

Macready arranged for the entrance of the Ghost to be screened by the servants: 'By this time [line 36], 4 of the attendants, with wine jugs, meet here, as tho' designedly, in front of the cauldron trap C[entre] – the other 4 join them, with empty goblets, which those with the jugs fill – and when Banquo up and seated – they go to the guests L[eft] and R[ight]' (Promptbook). At line 37 the Promptbook notes 'Banquo rises up Cauldron trap', and at 43a 'Banquo is up and seated; – the attendants divide.' It was only when Macbeth prepared to sit down that both he and the audience actually saw Banquo sitting in Macbeth's place. Banquo then 'slowly turns his chalky face towards the King, revealing a crimson gash across his throat' (Downer, *Macready*, p. 331; Sprague, *Actors*, pp. 257–8). At line 37a Phelps's Promptbook says 'the Lords form a Group to mask Trap'; then at line 43 'Banquo rises on Trap and sits on Chair. Lords open C[entre] for Mac. to go to Chair.' In Charles Kean's production in 1853, one of the pillars in the arch which supported the roof of the banqueting hall became transparent and the Ghost appeared inside it. 'The lights on the stage remained unaffected, but the lime light, then in its infancy, threw a ghastly sepulchral glare upon the blood-boltered Banquo'. Salvini's ghost 'scrambled up from under a table, tumbled down again, and re-appeared from a front trap, jerked up like a Harlequin' (Coleman, 'Facts and Fancies', pp. 226, 228). In Irving's first production, the Ghost was represented by 'a shadowy, transparent, greenish silhouette' which most critics disliked, and in his second production he reverted to tradition: 'The ghost first rose through a trick chair . . . and later emerged from the crowd. It departed "positively crouching down in order to ecape notice", according to William Archer, who complained, "a spectre that dares not hold its head up is certainly not a credit to its class".' Later 'the visible apparition was replaced by a shaft of blue limelight' (Hughes, *Shakespearean*, p. 107). Forbes-Robertson arranged for the actor playing Banquo to 'stalk in by the open door like an ordinary guest, save that he is arrayed in a bluish and somewhat spectral costume in contrast with which the bloody gash on his face shows up vividly. Simple as it is, this is probably as good a way as any other' (*Times*, 19 September 1898). When the Ghost appeared in Macbeth's chair, Macbeth (Tree) fled in terror, pursued by the Ghost, who walked behind a special scrim which rendered him alternately visible and invisible. Lady Macbeth 'steps between the Ghost and Macbeth, drags her husband to the throne and gives him wine. The Ghost disappears' (Mullin, 'Images of Death', in Tardiff, *Criticism*, p. 177). Komisarjevsky in 1933 eliminated the supernatural element from the play entirely, and what Macbeth took to be Banquo's ghost was actually his own shadow on the wall, an indication of his guilty conscience (Crosse, *Playgoing*, p. 97). Both the entrances of the Ghost in Glen Byam Shaw's staging were accompanied

LENNOX   May't please your highness, sit.
MACBETH Here had we now our country's honour roofed,   40
            Were the graced person of our Banquo present,
            Who may I rather challenge for unkindness
            Than pity for mischance.
ROSS   His absence, sir,
            Lays blame upon his promise. Please't your highness
            To grace us with your royal company?   45
MACBETH The table's full.
LENNOX   Here is a place reserved, sir.
MACBETH Where?
LENNOX Here, my good lord. What is't that moves your highness?
MACBETH Which of you have done this?
LORDS   What, my good lord?
MACBETH Thou canst not say I did it; never shake   50
            Thy gory locks at me!
ROSS Gentlemen, rise, his highness is not well.
                    [*Lady Macbeth joins the Lords*]
LADY MACBETH Sit, worthy friends. My lord is often thus,
            And hath been from his youth. Pray you, keep seat.
            The fit is momentary; upon a thought   55
            He will again be well. If much you note him
            You shall offend him and extend his passion.
            Feed, and regard him not. [*To Macbeth*] Are you a man?

by 'strange music'. In an interview, Peter Hall, who directed *Macbeth* in 1967, remarked that some directors try to hide the entrance of the Ghost, but 'the excitement for the audience is that they see him first, and *then* Macbeth sees him' (Tardiff, *Criticism*, p. 270).

39   Forbes-Robertson brought the Ghost on here.

44b–5 Siddons's 'secret uneasiness' during these lines was, says Bell, 'very fine. Suppressed but agitating her whole frame' ('Siddons', p. 62).

53   Ellen Terry, in her notes, comments 'with *great* – quick-decision. *Then* except for pausing, entirely hide all emotion – Smile' (Manvell, 'Terry as Lady Macbeth' p. 161).

53–8 'Mrs Pritchard [Garrick's Lady Macbeth] shewed admirable art in endeavouring to hide Macbeth's frenzy from the observation of the guests, by drawing their attention to conviviality. She smiled on one, whispered to another, and distantly saluted a third; in short she practiced every possible artifice to hide the transaction that passed between her husband and the vision his disturbed imagination had raised. Her reproving and angry looks, which glanced towards Macbeth, at the same time were mixed with marks of inward vexation and uneasiness. When, at last, as if unable to support her feelings any longer, she

MACBETH Ay, and a bold one, that dare look on that
      Which might appal the devil.
LADY MACBETH   O proper stuff!   60
      This is the very painting of your fear;
      This is the air-drawn dagger which you said
      Led you to Duncan. O, these flaws and starts,
      Impostors to true fear, would well become
      A woman's story at a winter's fire   65
      Authorised by her grandam. Shame itself!
      Why do you make such faces? When all's done
      You look but on a stool.
MACBETH Prithee, see there! Behold, look, lo! How say you?
      [*To Ghost*] Why, what care I? If thou canst nod, speak too.   70
      If charnel-houses and our graves must send
      Those that we bury back, our monuments
      Shall be the maws of kites.
                      [*Exit Ghost of Banquo*]
LADY MACBETH   What, quite unmanned in folly?

rose from her seat, and seized his arm, and, with a half-whisper of terror, said "*Are you a man!*" she assumed a look of such anger, indignation, and contempt, as cannot be surpassed' (Davies, *Miscellanies*, vol. II, pp. 166–7). In her 'Remarks on Lady Macbeth', Siddons recalls Mrs Pritchard's treatment of this episode. Lady Macbeth, she writes, 'entertains her guests with frightful smiles, with over-acted attention, and with fitful graciousness; painfully, yet incessantly, labouring to divert their attention from her husband' (Campbell, *Siddons*, vol. II, p. 27). Ellen Terry, 'with an effort that drained her last emotional reserves . . . put up a brilliant facade, moving among the guests, smiling and gracious, calming them down' (Hughes, *Shakespearean*, p. 109).

60b–8a 'When [Siddons] addresses her husband, and commands him to recollect himself . . . she throws into the character such an irony and sarcasm, such a proud and disdainful raillery, that Macbeth seems himself even to doubt his senses' (*Bell's Weekly Messenger*, 5 July 1812). Bell describes her at this point as 'peevish and scornful' ('Siddons', p. 63).

67a Cut by Garrick.

68 Siddons said this half line into Kemble's ear, 'as if to bring him back to objects of common life. Her anxiety makes you creep with apprehension; uncertain how to act. Her emotion keeps you breathless' (Bell, 'Siddons', p. 63). Mirren in Nunn's production actually sat on the empty stool in an attempt to bring Macbeth to his senses (Williams, *Text and Performance*, p. 44).

74a Kemble spoke this half line with striking simplicity. 'He could hit the merely natural, when no other considerations called upon him for a more elevated style of utterance' (Boaden, *Kemble*, vol. I, p. 177).

MACBETH If I stand here, I saw him.
LADY MACBETH   Fie, for shame.
MACBETH Blood hath been shed ere now, i'th'olden time,   75
    Ere humane statute purged the gentle weal;
    Ay, and since too, murders have been performed
    Too terrible for the ear. The time has been
    That when the brains were out, the man would die,
    And there an end. But now they rise again   80
    With twenty mortal murders on their crowns
    And push us from our stools. This is more strange
    Than such a murder is.
LADY MACBETH   My worthy lord,
    Your noble friends do lack you.
MACBETH   I do forget –
    Do not muse at me, my most worthy friends.   85
    I have a strange infirmity which is nothing
    To those that know me. Come, love and health to all,
    Then I'll sit down. Give me some wine; fill full!

        Enter Ghost [of Banquo]

    I drink to th'general joy o'th'whole table,

75–8a ('Blood . . . ear') Cut by Nunn.
76   Cut by Forbes-Robertson.
78b–80a As Macbeth said these lines, Ristori 'drinks from a large bowl of wine; the cup is in her hand when she tries to recall her husband to the guests; she does not lay it down until after the next appearance of the spectre. On the night of Duncan's murder she had made addition to her courage by the help of wine. She feels it sinking now' (Morley, *Journal*, p. 189).
80b–2a Olivier said the word 'push' with a convulsive shoving gesture.
83b–4a Ellen Terry, in her notes, says that these lines should be spoken 'not severe but with playful amazement. Are you blind or deaf? Don't you see your noble friends do lack you?' (Manvell, 'Terry as Lady Macbeth', p. 161).
88 SD *Enter . . .* Macready's Promptbook notes 'Banquo re-enters R[ight] and stands in the middle of the attendts on R[ight].' 'To make sure whether his mind has deceived him or not, *Macbeth* [Phelps] *has positioned himself by the raised chair of Banquo, grasping the back of it*, and speaks the name of the murdered man a second time. But instead of rising again from below, Banquo steps softly but swiftly from the wings and positions himself in front of the first table immediately next to the footlights. Now for the first time one sees the deep gash in his throat' (Fontane, *London Theatre*, p. 86). In Poel's production, the second ghost at the banquet was the ghost of Duncan. 'Macbeth's reaction to it is stronger than to the first apparition. See also "Take any shape but *that*" (line 102), and "Can such things be?"

> And to our dear friend Banquo, whom we miss.   90
> Would he were here! To all, and him we thirst,
> And all to all.
> LORDS   Our duties and the pledge.
> MACBETH Avaunt and quit my sight! Let the earth hide thee!

[line 110]' (Speaight, *Poel*, p. 188). On the second appearance of the Ghost, Paul Rogers, in Benthall's 1956 production, leapt up onto the table as draperies crashed down and the guests scattered (Griffin, *Quarterly*, p. 516). Glen Byam Shaw placed the ghost at the back of the stage between the two empty thrones: 'Macbeth [Olivier] turns to sit and sees the Ghost. The cup falls from his hand. He backs away from the Ghost. Lady Macbeth goes to him, soothing, trying to reassure her guests. Macbeth pushes her aside, and, shouting, he rushes at the Ghost, leaping on the table amidst the clatter of tableware, shouting at it, sweeping his scarlet cloak up in front of him to hide from it. As if by magic the Ghost sinks from sight [through a trap]' (Mullin, *Macbeth Onstage*, pp. 114–15). Banquo's ghost was not visible on his first entrance in the RSC's 1999 production but created considerable surprise at his second entrance when he did appear (*Times*, 18 November 1999).

91b–2a According to Nunn's Promptbook, Lady Macbeth here begins clapping; 'all men join in as Mcb. drinks. Mcb. drains cup, all clapping, then throws cup in air.'

92a Forbes-Robertson brought on the Ghost here.

93a A passage in Beaumont's *Knight of the Burning Pestle* (c. 1607) may refer to a piece of stage business used at this point in the earliest performances of *Macbeth*. Jasper, who is made up to look like his own ghost, threatens the Merchant:

> When thou art at thy Table with thy friends,
> Merry in heart, and fild with swelling wine,
> I'll come in midst of all thy pride and mirth,
> Invisible to all men but thy self,
> And whisper such a sad tale in thine ear
> Shall make thee let the Cup fall from thy hand,
> And stand as mute and pale as Death itself.
>
> Act 5, ll. 22–8

Macbeth, having presumably raised his glass to toast the guests (lines 89–92a), keeps it in his hand until he sees the ghost (line 93), and then lets it fall to the ground. In his *Essay on Acting*, Garrick, who must have used a similar gesture, advises, 'the Glass of Wine in his [Macbeth's] hand should not be dash'd to the Ground, but it should fall *gently* from him, and he should not discover the least Consciousness of having such a Vessel in his Hand'. During a performance at Brighton in 1809, Siddons narrowly escaped injury: 'Charles Kemble, who was the Macbeth, threw the cup from him with such violence, that it broke the arm of a glass chandelier, which stood very near to Mrs Siddons' face. The great actress,

> Thy bones are marrowless, thy blood is cold;
> Thou hast no speculation in those eyes   95
> Which thou dost glare with.
> LADY MACBETH   Think of this, good peers,
> But as a thing of custom. 'Tis no other,
> Only it spoils the pleasure of the time.
> MACBETH What man dare, I dare;

nevertheless, "sat as if she had been made of marble"' (Sprague, *Actors*, p. 262). Tree dropped the cup, stabbed at the Ghost and 'then has fit on steps' (Mullin, 'Images of Death', in Tardiff, *Criticism*, p. 177).

96b–8   According to Terry's own notes, these lines were to be said 'sweetly but with a ghastly mouth – the *mouth* tells all – the pain and the effort and the madness' (Manvell, 'Terry as Lady Macbeth', p. 161).

99–107a   In a letter to Garrick, a correspondent remarked, 'You recollect a degree of resolution, and advancing on the Ghost, pronounce the passage in a firm tone of voice. I apprehend the whole situation supposes a fixed, immovable attitude of horror and amazement' (Garrick, *Correspondence*, vol. 1, p. 134). Garrick replied, 'My notions . . . are I fear the opposite to Your Opinion – Should Macbeth sink into pusillanimity, I imagine that it would hurt ye Character . . . The first appearance of ye Spirit overpow'rs him more than ye 2d – but before it vanishes at first, Macbeth gains strength – *If thou can'st nod, Speak too* – Must be spoke with terror, but with a recovering Mind – and in the next Speech with him – He cannot pronounce *Avaunt & quit my Sight*! without a Stronger Exertion of his Powers under the Circumstance of Horror – the *Why so – being gone* – &c means, in my opinion, – I am returning to my Senses, wch were before Mad & inflam'd with what I have Seen – I make a great difference between a Mind sunk by Guilt into Cowardice, & one rising with Horror to Acts of Madness and desperation; which last I take to be the case of Macbeth – I certainly (as you say) recollect a degree of Resolution – but I never advance an *inch*, for notwithstanding my Agitation, my feet are immovable' (*Letters*, vol. 1, p. 351). Kemble 'chid and scolded the ghost out, and rose in vehemence and courage as he went on' (Bell, 'Siddons', p. 64). Macready 'made an original and admirable effect. Instead of intimidating the ghost into a retreat, he fell back, sank in his chair, covered his face with his hands, then looked again, perceived the ghost had disappeared and, upon being relieved from the fearful vision, recovered once more the spring of his soul and body' (*Morning Herald*, 10 June 1820, quoted in Macready, *Reminiscences*, vol. 1, p. 214). 'Quailing before the ghost, [Irving] flung down his coronet as though repudiating the fruits of his crime. Crying "Unreal mock'ry hence!" he crouched beside his wife's chair and covered his face with his cloak' (Hughes, *Shakespearean*, p. 108). Edwin Booth in New York in 1929 'raved at the vision, daring it to meet him sword to sword; until, when the guests had shrunk away, he stood

Approach thou like the rugged Russian bear,   100
The armed rhinoceros, or th'Hyrcan tiger,
Take any shape but that, and my firm nerves
Shall never tremble. Or be alive again,
And dare me to the desert with thy sword;
If trembling I inhabit then, protest me   105
The baby of a girl. Hence horrible shadow,
Unreal mock'ry hence.
                                      [*Exit Ghost of Banquo*]
                        Why so, being gone,
I am a man again. – Pray you, sit still.
LADY MACBETH You have displaced the mirth, broke the good meeting
With most admired disorder.
MACBETH   Can such things be,   110
And overcome us like a summer's cloud,
Without our special wonder? You make me strange
Even to the disposition that I owe,
When now I think you can behold such sights
And keep the natural ruby of your cheeks,   115
When mine is blanched with fear.
ROSS   What sights, my lord?
LADY MACBETH I pray you speak not; he grows worse and worse.
Question enrages him. At once, good night.
Stand not upon the order of your going,
But go at once.

sobbing, quaking in his wife's arms with the hysteria of a child terrified at night' (*New York Herald Tribune*, 3 November 1929).

114–16a Of Ristori's performance at this point, Morley writes, 'Her spirit has been on the rack, but she has kept down every cry, no eye has seen the torture she has borne; from this last wrench she flinches bodily, and we see now that her strength begins to fail. Those words of Macbeth mark the turning point in Madame Ristori's personation of the lady's character. She meets them with the action of an eager, startled hush [line 117]' (Morley, *Journal*, pp. 189–90).

116a Charles Kean here threw himself on a bench (Promptbook).

117–20a '[Siddons] descends in great eagerness; voice almost choked with anxiety to prevent their questioning; alarm, hurry, rapid and convulsive as if afraid he should tell of the murder of Duncan' (Bell, 'Siddons', p. 64). Similarly, Terry said the lines with 'voice choked. Alarm. Hurry. Convulsive fear', but nevertheless managed to smile as the guests left (Manvell, 'Terry as Lady Macbeth', p. 161).

LENNOX	Good night, and better health	120
	Attend his majesty.	
LADY MACBETH	A kind good night to all.	

[Exeunt] Lords [and Attendants]

MACBETH It will have blood they say: blood will have blood.
　　　Stones have been known to move and trees to speak.
　　　Augures, and understood relations, have
　　　By maggot-pies, and choughs, and rooks brought forth　　　125
　　　The secret'st man of blood. What is the night?

121b　Helen Faucit bowed low as she said goodnight to the guests. 'For a moment or two she
　　　remains in that position, and when she rises she is a broken woman. There has settled over
　　　her bent head the gloomy shadow of an immovable cloud. She has seen that her husband's
　　　malady is incurable; that his guilt has enveloped him in an impenetrable curse. She is
　　　simply hopeless. She staggers and is faint. She totters to a table, sits down at it, rests her
　　　forehead on her hand, touches the crown, takes off with a melancholy, not quite absent, air
　　　this gilded symbol of her irretrievable wretchedness, presses her agonised brow the more
　　　freely for its absence, lets it hang listlessly in her hand as she marches faintly, yet with
　　　persistent dignity, after her husband from the scene of her fearful change. She is the last to
　　　leave' (*Liverpool Post*, December 1870; quoted in Martin, *Faucit*, p. 312). 'After the banquet,
　　　[Dench's] hysterical "go at once!" instantly gave way to an attempt at graciousness ("A kind
　　　goodnight"); there they sat, she bleakly smiling and he waving goodbye in the aftermath of
　　　a foaming fit, both total wrecks, a marvellous image of the hollow kingship they risked so
　　　much to gain. But then she collapsed; he dragged her up at "young in deed" [line 144] and
　　　pulled her away, firmly replacing her as the more resolute of the two' (*Shakespeare Survey*,
　　　vol. xxx, 1977, p. 178).

122–41　'When [Ristori] is alone with her husband, and he in his wild pacing up and down comes
　　　suddenly upon her still face, over which a new expression is now creeping, he recoils as
　　　from another spectre. After that she replies to his questions in the tone of one wearily
　　　disregardful of their import. As Macbeth continues talking . . . she watches him with a
　　　face of which the expression becomes more and more spectral' (Morley, *Journal*, p. 190).
　　　Terry writes that, when the two of them are left alone, 'she is now beginning to know him
　　　well and is thoroughly frightened at him. I think she feels pretty frail – and that her *reason*
　　　here begins to be shaken. Now – she knows him. *Now Lady* Macbeth shall sleep no more –
　　　for she is at last – *frightened!*' (Manvell, 'Terry as Lady Macbeth', p. 161). She said later, 'I
　　　do believe that at the end of that Banquet, that poor wretched creature was brought
　　　through agony and sin to repentance, and was forgiven' (Hughes, *Shakespearean*,
　　　p. 109).

LADY MACBETH Almost at odds with morning, which is which.
MACBETH How sayst thou that Macduff denies his person
        At our great bidding?
LADY MACBETH   Did you send to him, sir?
MACBETH I hear it by the way, but I will send.   130
        There's not a one of them but in his house
        I keep a servant feed. I will tomorrow –
        And betimes I will – to the weïrd sisters.
        More shall they speak. For now I am bent to know
        By the worst means, the worst; for mine own good,   135
        All causes shall give way. I am in blood
        Stepped in so far that should I wade no more,
        Returning were as tedious as go o'er.
        Strange things I have in head that will to hand,
        Which must be acted ere they may be scanned.   140
LADY MACBETH You lack the season of all natures, sleep.
MACBETH Come, we'll to sleep. My strange and self-abuse

127   '[Siddons] very sorrowful. Quite exhausted' (Bell, 'Siddons', p. 65).
136b–8   Antony Sher spoke these lines 'with an ironic chuckle' (*Times*, 18 November 1999).
139–40   Cut by Garrick, Forbes-Robertson, and Nunn.
141   '[Siddons] feeble now, and as if preparing for her last sickness and final doom' (Bell,
        'Siddons', p. 65). Ristori's interpretation of this line was apparently similar to Siddons's :
        'There is a weariness of soul and body in her voice and manner, and with a weary step she
        quits the stage with him' (Morley, *Journal*, p. 190). Irving 'paused, in ascending the
        steps by which he was to leave the stage, and looked back once more, fascinated at the
        Ghost's chair' (Winter, *Stage*, p. 485; Sprague, *Actors*, p. 264). 'Fresh shuddering came
        over [Booth] as they passed the spot where his eyes had shaped the murdered man.
        Then [Ristori] stepped quickly to the other side of him, as if to interpose between him
        and his visions, but with an awful glance over her own shoulder, as if even her firmness
        had begun to give way to fear of the unseen' (*New York Herald Tribune*, 3 November
        1929).
142a   Tree 'picks up his cloak, then a torch and . . . is about to leave when he sees the Ghost again,
        suspended above the heads of the audience in the stalls. Lady Macbeth takes his left hand
        in her right. He looks round again. He comes to throne – he looks at throne. Lady M. opens
        arras at back. She takes his hand and pulls him through' (Promptook, quoted by Mullin,
        'Images of Death', in Tardiff, *Criticism*, p. 181). In Nunn's production Macbeth stands up
        here. Lady Macbeth also stands but then falls. Macbeth picks her up and goes off holding
        her (Promptbook).

> Is the initiate fear that wants hard use;
> We are yet but young in deed.

Exeunt

144   Terry comments, 'Young in deed. *He* to go off full of vigour, *blood – more blood*!! *She*, left behind – dazed – turn weary – faint – and stagger to the throne – Alone – *Isolation- On* the throne – Crown on her lap. Laugh? Dark. *Curtain*' (Manvell, 'Terry as Lady Macbeth', p. 161).

144 SD   *Exeunt* 'Helen Faucit led her Macbeth off, "never once looking at him, turning aside her head, as if in dread of meeting his glance"' (Sprague, *Actors*, p. 264). 'Irving adopted a piece of melodramatic claptrap to bring down the curtain: "Macbeth takes a torch from behind a pillar, but suddenly, in a paroxysm, hurls it blazing to the ground. He shrouds his face in his robe as he leans rapidly forward and rests against a pillar. The Queen as swiftly kneels behind him, and remains clinging to his skirts, with an upturned face full of tragical solicitude." The tableau marked the end of the act' (Hughes, *Shakespearean*, p. 109). Salvini, in Boston, gave a start of 'extreme terror . . . when in going out with his wife her mantle fell against him' (*Boston Daily Advertiser*, 22 April 1881). Macbeth and his wife made their exits 'giggling with nervous exhaustion' in Gregory Doran's production. 'As they did so, the empty chairs topple over as if struck by an invisible hand, and the table tips backwards – to show the three witches hanging from it, grimacing like triumphant misericords' (*Observer*, 21 November 1999). The witches were now ready on the stage to begin the next scene.

ACT 3, SCENE 5

Thunder. Enter the three WITCHES, *meeting* HECATE

FIRST WITCH Why how now, Hecate, you look angerly?
HECATE Have I not reason, beldams, as you are,
      Saucy and over-bold? How did you dare
      To trade and traffic with Macbeth
      In riddles and affairs of death?   5
      And I the mistress of your charms,
      The close contriver of all harms,
      Was never called to bear my part

Irving, Forbes-Robertson, Tree, and Nunn cut this scene. Most editors believe that this scene and parts of 4.1 were not written by Shakespeare but were added to the original text sometime before the printing of the First Folio, though precisely when is not known. The reasons given are that Hecate is a new character whose entrance has not been prepared for, that her speech is in iambic octosyllabics and not trochaic like those of the witches, and that the scene contributes nothing of significance to the play. Moreover, both scenes call for the performance of songs that appear in *The Witch*, a play of uncertain date written by Thomas Middleton. It is, of course, possible that the Middleton passages were included with Shakespeare's approval. In an interview, Peter Hall (who directed *Macbeth* in 1967) defended his inclusion of the Hecate scenes on the grounds that 'the verse is odd and mesmeric; it seems to me deliberately primitive, drawing on folk tradition of riddles, spells, incantations, nursery rhymes . . . The whole scene has been questioned because of its style, but I would say that's no justification for writing it off. It's a deliberate and theatrically exciting contrast.' He explains that Hecate 'gives metaphorical presence to God, or, rather, anti-God. This is essential to the dramatic action . . . The real old women release supernatural evil through the actions of Macbeth' (Tardiff, *Criticism*, p. 269.). According to Hall's Promptbook, however, he cut Hecate from his production. The question of authenticity is discussed in detail by Brooke (pp. 53–5), and Braunmuller (pp. 255–9).

0   Charles Kean's Promptbook here notes, 'Put lights down and pull above and below for gauzes and opaque cloth' in readiness for the entry of the witches.

0 SD   *Enter* . . . Macready's Promptbook notes 'Hecate rises up centre Trap in front, on a set piece – which is lowered when she steps out on the stage – The 3 witches kneel to her.'

Or show the glory of our art?
And which is worse, all you have done   10
Hath been but for a wayward son,
Spiteful and wrathful, who, as others do,
Loves for his own ends, not for you.
But make amends now. Get you gone,
And at the pit of Acheron   15
Meet me i'th'morning. Thither he
Will come to know his destiny.
Your vessels and your spells provide,
Your charms and every thing beside.
I am for th'air. This night I'll spend   20
Unto a dismal and a fatal end.
Great business must be wrought ere noon.
Upon the corner of the moon
There hangs a vap'rous drop profound;
I'll catch it ere it come to ground;   25
And that distilled by magic sleights,
Shall raise such artificial sprites
As by the strength of their illusion
Shall draw him on to his confusion.
He shall spurn fate, scorn death, and bear   30
His hopes 'bove wisdom, grace, and fear.
And you all know, security
Is mortals' chiefest enemy.
            Music, and a song[, '*Come away, come away*', *within*]

10–13   Cut by Charles Kean.
30–3   Cut by Charles Kean.
33 SD   *Music, and a song* In Davenant's version of the play, the stage direction *Machine descends*
        at this point indicates that Hecate is about to make an exit 'flying'. The full text of the song,
        of which this is the first line, is in Thomas Middleton's *The Witch*, Act 3, Scene 3, though this
        does not necessarily mean that Middleton wrote the entire scene. It is incorporated into the
        text of Brooke's edition (pp. 162–3), and reproduced in an Appendix by Braunmuller
        (p. 269). Garrick kept Hecate on the stage and she sang the song together with the witches.
        Towards the end of the song, he added the stage direction, '*Symphony, whilst* Hecate *places
        herself in the machine.*' The 'machine' enabled Hecate to make a flying exit (Burnim,
        Director, p. 120). In Kemble's and Macready's staging the 'Come away' song was sung by a
        chorus which, in Macready's production, consisted of '8 1st sopranos, 8 2nd sopranos, 8
        tenors, 8 altos and 8 basses'. They stood 'at the extreme back of the flies – every person

Hark, I am called: my little spirit, see,
Sits in a foggy cloud, and stays for me.   [*Exit*]   35
FIRST WITCH Come, let's make haste; she'll soon be back again.

Exeunt

sang with his face turned to the wall, but as loudly as possible'. During the final verse they stood 'at a greater distance – in the painting room with the door open which closed grad[ual]ly towards the end' (Promptbook). 'At the end of the song, Hecate steps into her car, which immediately begins a slow rise. When it is two feet from the stage floor, the cloudings that fill the stage are drawn off, displaying a bird's-eye view of the country with a transparent winding river softly glowing in the moonlight' (Downer, *Macready*, p. 333; Promptbook). The landscape was presumably designed to illustrate the words of the song:

> Over Woods, high Rocks, and Mountains,
> Over misty Hills and Fountains,
> Over Steeples, Towres, and Turrets,
> We flie by night 'mongst Troops of spirits.
>
> (Braunmuller, p. 269)

Phelps arranged for Hecate to enter and exit from below, by a trap. The 'Come away' chorus was accompanied by an orchestra (Weiner, 'Phelps' *Macbeth*', p. 130). Charles Kean also concluded the scene with part of the 'Come away' song, performed by a chorus of witches who then vanished, as they had appeared, by means of a gauze and opaque cloth (Promptbook). The scene then changed to a lake with an island in the middle and a full moon. This was the much-advertised 'Distant View of Iona by Moonlight'. Irving transposed the song to the end of 4.1.

ACT 3, SCENE 6

Enter LENNOX *and another* LORD

LENNOX My former speeches have but hit your thoughts
　　　　Which can interpret further; only I say
　　　　Things have been strangely borne. The gracious Duncan
　　　　Was pitied of Macbeth; marry, he was dead.
　　　　And the right-valiant Banquo walked too late,　　　　　　　5
　　　　Whom you may say, if't please you, Fleance killed,
　　　　For Fleance fled. Men must not walk too late.
　　　　Who cannot want the thought how monstrous
　　　　It was for Malcolm and for Donaldbain
　　　　To kill their gracious father? Damnèd fact,　　　　　　　　10
　　　　How it did grieve Macbeth! Did he not straight
　　　　In pious rage the two delinquents tear,
　　　　That were the slaves of drink and thralls of sleep?
　　　　Was not that nobly done? Ay, and wisely too,
　　　　For 'twould have angered any heart alive　　　　　　　　　15
　　　　To hear the men deny't. So that I say,
　　　　He has borne all things well, and I do think
　　　　That had he Duncan's sons under his key –
　　　　As, an't please heaven, he shall not – they should find
　　　　What 'twere to kill a father. So should Fleance.　　　　　20
　　　　But peace, for from broad words, and 'cause he failed
　　　　His presence at the tyrant's feast, I hear
　　　　Macduff lives in disgrace. Sir, can you tell
　　　　Where he bestows himself?
LORD　　　　　　　　　　　　　　　The son of Duncan,
　　　　From whom this tyrant holds the due of birth,　　　　　　25
　　　　Lives in the English court and is received

The whole scene cut by Garrick, Kemble, Macready, Phelps, Charles Kean, Irving, Forbes-Robertson, and Tree.

　0 SD　*Enter* . . . In Nunn's production the Lord was Angus.
　24b　('son of Duncan') 'noble Malcolm' (Nunn).
　25　Cut by Nunn.

Of the most pious Edward with such grace,
That the malevolence of fortune nothing
Takes from his high respect. Thither Macduff
Is gone to pray the holy king upon his aid   30
To wake Northumberland and warlike Siward,
That by the help of these, with him above
To ratify the work, we may again
Give to our tables meat, sleep to our nights,
Free from our feasts and banquets bloody knives,   35
Do faithful homage and receive free honours,
All which we pine for now. And this report
Hath so exasperate their king that he
Prepares for some attempt of war.
LENNOX Sent he to Macduff?   40
LORD He did. And with an absolute, 'Sir, not I',
The cloudy messenger turns me his back
And hums, as who should say, 'You'll rue the time
That clogs me with this answer.'
LENNOX   And that well might
Advise him to a caution t'hold what distance   45
His wisdom can provide. Some holy angel
Fly to the court of England and unfold
His message ere he come, that a swift blessing
May soon return to this our suffering country
Under a hand accursed.
LORD   I'll send my prayers with him. 50

                                        Exeunt

27b–9a   ('with such . . . respect') Cut by Nunn.
  31–2   Cut by Nunn.
   33a   ('To ratify the work') 'That by his help' (Nunn).

ACT 4, SCENE I

Thunder. Enter the three WITCHES [*with a cauldron*]

Setting   The opening stage direction in the 1773 edition, based on Garrick's production, reads 'SCENE *a dark Cave: in the middle, a great Cauldron burning. Thunder. Enter the three Witches . . . They march round the cauldron, and throw in the several Ingredients, as for the Preparation of their Charm*' (p. 46). In the preliminary notes Macklin made for this scene, he writes, 'there must be high Rocks all round so as to form the stage into a deep Cave, & down the back must be a winding way for Macbeth to come and meet the witches' (Appleton, *Macklin*, p. 172). Phelps opened the scene with 'Lights, thunder and music.' He turned up the house lights and brought down a gauze (Promptbook). Charles Kean's set was a cave cut in a rock, seen through a jagged opening in the rock which served as a false proscenium. The cauldron in Irving's 1888 production was a hollow in the rock. 'Every device was used to intensify the effect: there were "lurid exhalations, flashes from the nether fires, blood-dripping skies, and other meteorological eccentricities" . . . Sullivan's music attracted attention. An introduction *andante maestoso* foreshadowed a "strangely demoniacal" incantation theme' (Hughes, *Shakespearean*, pp. 109–10). Komisarjevsky placed the scene in Macbeth's bedroom and it became a nightmare in his mind. Macbeth was discovered in bed and the witches were grouped behind a transparency (Mullin, 'Komisarjevsky's *Macbeth*', p. 29). Benthall in 1954 used a huge cauldron from which the apparitions emerged. Overhead and behind the witches in Glen Byam Shaw's staging 'rough stone walls rise up to a natural arch reminiscent of the arches in Macbeth's palace'. In addition to the thunder and lightning, the bubbling sound of the boiling cauldron could be heard (Mullin, *Macbeth Onstage*, p. 154). The cauldron was small, and 'the witches, leaning over it, plucked horrible emblems from it – a severed head transfixed on a pike, a bloody foetus, a waxen crowned child – while the voices came, not altogether satisfactorily, from elsewhere' (David, 'Tragic Curve', p. 130).

0 SD   *Enter* . . . Macready arranged for the witches to be disovered, 'one at the mouth of the cavern, intently on watch, one cowering over the livid flame flickering beneath a caldron [*sic*], and the third on the opposite side of the stage, seated on a jut of stone, his arms folded, rocking to and fro in impatience. In the expectant silence not a word is spoken. Then from offstage comes a cat-call and the first witch hisses "Thrice the brinded cat hath mewed." The eyes of the other witches are instantly turned toward him: they listen intently,

FIRST WITCH Thrice the brindled cat hath mewed.
SECOND WITCH Thrice and once the hedge-pig whined.
THIRD WITCH Harpier cries, ''Tis time, 'tis time.'
FIRST WITCH Round about the cauldron go;
        In the poisoned entrails throw.   5
        Toad, that under cold stone
        Days and nights has thirty-one
        Sweltered venom sleeping got,
        Boil thou first i'th'charmèd pot.
ALL Double, double toil and trouble;   10
        Fire burn, and cauldron bubble.
SECOND WITCH Fillet of a fenny snake,
        In the cauldron boil and bake:
        Eye of newt, and toe of frog,
        Wool of bat, and tongue of dog,   15
        Adder's fork, and blind-worm's sting,
        Lizard's leg, and howlet's wing,
        For a charm of powerful trouble,
        Like a hell-broth, boil and bubble.
ALL Double, double toil and trouble,   20
        Fire burn, and cauldron bubble.
THIRD WITCH Scale of dragon, tooth of wolf,
        Witches' mummy, maw and gulf
        Of the ravined salt-sea shark,
        Root of hemlock, digged i'th'dark;   25

motionless. The witch at the caldron hears his familiar; he starts from his cowering attitude: "Thrice; and once the hedge-pig whines." Another pause, and silence. At length the third witch springs to his feet: "Harpier cries!" and then, exulting, to his fellows: "'Tis time! 'Tis time!" They join hands and circle the caldron, speaking slowly so as to make a complete turn on each repetition of "Double",

        Double, double, toil and trouble;
        Fire burn and cauldron bubble.

At these words they poke the fire under the caldron and at the end of the incantation wave their wands over it twice' (Downer, *Macready*, pp. 333–4). After the entry of the three witches, Tree arranged for 'tier upon tier of pale-gowned witches' to appear on rocky ledges, 'singing, their bodies swaying gracefully' (Mullin, 'Images of Death', in Tardiff, *Criticism*, p. 178).

10–11 In Nunn's 1976 production the witches chanted these lines to the *Dies irae* (*Shakespeare Survey*, vol. xxx, 1977, p. 177).

18–19 Cut by Nunn.

Liver of blaspheming Jew,
Gall of goat, and slips of yew,
Slivered in the moon's eclipse;
Nose of Turk, and Tartar's lips,
Finger of birth-strangled babe,   30
Ditch-delivered by a drab,
Make the gruel thick and slab.
Add thereto a tiger's chawdron
For th'ingredient of our cauldron.
ALL Double, double toil and trouble,   35
Fire burn, and cauldron bubble.
SECOND WITCH Cool it with a baboon's blood,
Then the charm is firm and good.

Enter HECATE, *and the other three Witches*

26–9   Cut by Nunn.
30–2   Cut by Forbes-Robertson.
32–4   Cut by Nunn.
38 SD   *Enter* . . . The part of Hecate in this scene, like the whole of 3.5, is thought to be a late
        addition to the play. The question is examined by Braunmuller (pp. 257–9). At the entrance
        of Hecate in Macready's staging, 'the witches turn and kneel to her, then rise, after which
        [line 43] the whole tribe of witches appear from the right and form four concentric circles
        around the caldron, covering the entire stage area. As they sing [words from Davenant's
        version], the witches circle in opposite directions:
               First witch. Here's the blood of a bat. (She advances to the caldron.)
               Hecate (at the back). O! Put in that, put in that.
               Second witch. Here's a lizard's brain. (Advances towards the caldron)
               Hecate. Put in a grain.
               Third witch. Here's juice of toad, here's oil of adder,
                    Which will make the charm grow madder. (Advances to the
                    caldron.)
        As each witch makes her individual contribution, the entire chorus turns and looks closely at
        the singer. Then extending their wands directly to the caldron, the Chorus sings:
               Put in all these, 'twill raise the stench.
        The third witch comes once more to the caldron, bidding them hold. They draw back their
        wands. "Here's three ounces of a red-hair'd wench," and the Chorus resumes its circling
        and counter-circling of the caldron until the second witch's thumbs announce a visitor. The
        witches divide to the right and left, close to the entrances. There is a series of heavy knocks,
        and the choral witches vanish, leaving the original three to confront Macbeth"' (Downer,
        Macready, pp. 334–5). Fontane describes Phelps's Hecate, who rose through a trap, as

HECATE O well done! I commend your pains,
             And every one shall share i'th'gains;   40
             And now about the cauldron sing
             Like elves and fairies in a ring,
             Enchanting all that you put in.
                    Music, and a song, 'Black spirits, etc.'
                    [*Exeunt Hecate and the other three Witches*]
SECOND WITCH By the pricking of my thumbs,
             Something wicked this way comes;   45
             Open locks, whoever knocks.

                    Enter MACBETH

'a well-nourished and stately lady in a Mary Stuart head-dress with a glittering brooch on it'
who was 'anything but demonic, and her song, echoed by invisible spirits, is well-nigh
laughable. The whole scene is a failure' (*London Theatre*, p. 82). Charles Kean's
Promptbook here has the stage direction 'Rock opens', and presumably Hecate entered out
of it. With the words of the song, 'Black spirits and white', 'Black and white imps enter', and,
at the next line, 'Red and grey imps enter.' Hecate came on in Irving's production, 'with an
electric star on her forehead and an off-stage chorus sang the traditional ditty from
Middleton's *The Witch* to "a fine wild melody"' (Hughes, *Shakespearean*, p. 110).
Forbes-Robertson and Nunn cut the part of Hecate.

41–3 Cut by Garrick.

43 SD *Music, and a song . . .* The full text of this song, like the one in 3.5, occurs in Thomas
       Middleton's play *The Witch* (5.2). It is incorporated into Brooke's text (pp. 170–2) and
       reprinted by Braunmuller in an appendix (p. 270). Davenant included a version of it but
       Garrick omitted it. Kemble introduced groups of children (one of whom was the child
       Edmund Kean) to represent the 'black spirits and white, / Red spirits and grey' who 'Mingle,
       mingle, mingle' as Hecate directs them in the song. In his production 'the number of people
       on stage, including Hecate and the three witches, the chorus of singing witches numbering
       fifty or sixty, the three spirits separately listed in the "Persons Represented" and the groups
       of children, must have been well near one hundred' (Donoghue, 'Kemble's *Macbeth*',
       p. 69). Forbes-Robertson and Nunn cut the song.

46 SD *Enter . . .* A correspondent to the *St James's Chronicle* (28–30 October 1773), addressing
       Garrick, writes, 'When you precipitate yourself down the Steps which lead to the Cavern,
       you have never appeared enough struck with the Solemnity of a Scene concerning which
       MACBETH could have no previous Information . . . A Pause of silent Wonder, when you
       descend, and a more earnest Enquiry into their mysterious Purposes, would not be thrown
       away on your Audience . . . The last Dress in which you played *Macbeth* was that of
       a *modern fine Gentleman*; so that when you came among the witches in the 4th. Act, you

MACBETH How now, you secret, black, and midnight hags!
          What is't you do?
ALL THE WITCHES   A deed without a name.
MACBETH I conjure you by that which you profess,
          Howe'er you come to know it, answer me.   50
          Though you untie the winds and let them fight
          Against the churches, though the yeasty waves
          Confound and swallow navigation up,
          Though bladed corn be lodged and trees blown down,
          Though castles topple on their warders' heads,   55
          Though palaces and pyramids do slope
          Their heads to their foundations, though the treasure
          Of nature's germen tumble altogether
          Even till destruction sicken: answer me
          To what I ask you.
FIRST WITCH   Speak.
SECOND WITCH   Demand.
THIRD WITCH   We'll answer.   60
FIRST WITCH Say, if thou'dst rather hear it from our mouths,
          Or from our masters'?
MACBETH   Call 'em, let me see 'em.
FIRST WITCH Pour in sow's blood, that hath eaten
          Her nine farrow; grease that's sweaten
          From the murderer's gibbet throw   65
          Into the flame.
ALL THE WITCHES   Come high or low:
          Thyself and office deftly show.

looked like a Beau, who had unfortunately slipped his foot and tumbled into a Night Celler [*sic*], where a Parcel of old Women were boiling Tripe for their Supper.' Macready wore 'a tartan skirt over a padded flannel vest' in this scene, 'but his beret had been replaced by a coronet cap with feather' (Downer, *Macready*, p. 335). Tree came on through a crack in the rocks and stood up stage on a rock, glaring at the Witches who 'crouch together stage right' (Mullin, 'Images of Death', in Tardiff, *Criticism*, p. 178). The witches' cavern in Nunn's 1976 staging 'exhibited no marvels, no doom-long line of kings ... On entering, Macbeth stood upstage of the witches with hands in pockets. They ignore him' (Promptbook).

54   Cut by Forbes-Robertson.
56–8 Cut by Forbes-Robertson.
62b   In Nunn's production the witches here 'push Mcb. down and strip off his coat'. The third witch 'ladles mixture into cup. Gives cup. He drinks and falls backwards.' Then the witches kiss him (Promptbook).

Thunder. [*Enter*] FIRST APPARITION, *an armed Head*

MACBETH Tell me, thou unknown power –
FIRST WITCH   He knows thy thought;
    Hear his speech, but say thou nought.
FIRST APPARITION Macbeth, Macbeth, Macbeth: beware Macduff,   70
    Beware the Thane of Fife. Dismiss me. Enough.   *Descends*
MACBETH Whate'er thou art, for thy good caution, thanks;
    Thou hast harped my fear aright. But one word more –
FIRST WITCH He will not be commanded. Here's another,
    More potent than the first.   75

Thunder. [*Enter*] SECOND APPARITION, *a bloody Child*

67 SD *Enter . . .* Since, according to the Folio stage directions, the apparitions made their exits through traps, they probably rose through traps as well. In Garrick's staging the apparitions rose and descended by a trap, but in Kemble's production of 1803 'the apparitions rise from the mouth of the cauldron . . . but here again the effect and the interest suffer, since, from the glare of the cauldron, it is not easy to distinguish one apparition from another' (*The Monthly Mirror*, vol. XVI, p. 414). At this point in Macready's production, 'the stage is darkened, soft music is played in the background and, as each apparition appears to predict the future history of Scotland, there is a strong flash of light, the back of the cavern splits open, and the figure is seen, brightly lighted in billowing clouds' (Downer, *Macready*, p. 335). Phelps's apparitions rose through a trap. According to Komisarjevsky's Promptbook, Macduff spoke as the first Apparition, Lady Macbeth as the second and Malcolm as the third. Before Macbeth's nightmare ended, he was grovelling on the floor of the Great Hall, 'the walls of which have become luminous with the images of Banquo and the Scottish kings' (Mullin, 'Komisarjevsky's *Macbeth*', p. 29). The Armed Head in Glen Byam Shaw's staging was Macbeth's own head cut from his body, the Bloody Child spoke in Macduff's voice and the Crowned Child spoke in Malcolm's voice (Mullin, *Macbeth Onstage*, p. 154). The three 'voices' in Nunn's 1976 production 'were spoken by the witches as they held up in turn three horrible wizened emblems which were thereafter kept clutched in Macbeth's hands till the ineffectiveness of one talisman after another had been demonstrated' (David, *Theatre*, p. 87). Here the third witch held the puppet over her, 'waving it up and down' (Promptbook). The visions in Gregory Doran's production appeared as 'tortured faces showing through membranes in the back wall' of the stage (*Financial Times*, 18 November 1999).

71, 80, 93a SDs *Descends* According to the text in the Folio, each of the three apparitions makes an exit through a trap. The cauldron also descends through a trap (104 SD).

SECOND APPARITION Macbeth, Macbeth, Macbeth.

MACBETH Had I three ears, I'd hear thee.

SECOND APPARITION Be bloody, bold, and resolute; laugh to scorn
        The power of man, for none of woman born
        Shall harm Macbeth.   *Descends*   80

MACBETH Then live, Macduff, what need I fear of thee?
        But yet I'll make assurance double sure
        And take a bond of fate: thou shalt not live,
        That I may tell pale-hearted fear it lies,
        And sleep in spite of thunder.

Thunder. [Enter] THIRD APPARITION, *a Child crowned, with a tree*
in his hand
                                What is this,   85
        That rises like the issue of a king
        And wears upon his baby-brow the round
        And top of sovereignty?

ALL THE WITCHES   Listen, but speak not to't.

THIRD APPARITION Be lion-mettled, proud, and take no care
        Who chafes, who frets, or where conspirers are.   90
        Macbeth shall never vanquished be until
        Great Birnam Wood to high Dunsinane hill
        Shall come against him.   *Descends*

MACBETH   That will never be:
        Who can impress the forest, bid the tree
        Unfix his earthbound root? Sweet bodements, good.   95
        Rebellious dead, rise never till the wood
        Of Birnam rise, and our high-placed Macbeth
        Shall live the lease of nature, pay his breath
        To time and mortal custom. Yet my heart
        Throbs to know one thing. Tell me, if your art   100

---

76 SD   Here, in Nunn's production, the third witch 'holds the puppet by Mac's right ear'
        (Promptbook).

81–5b These lines, in Glenn Byam Shaw's production, were 'interrupted by the sound of galloping
        messengers who (we learn later) bring the news that Macduff has escaped' (David, 'Tragic
        Curve', p. 127).

85 SD *Enter . . .* '2nd & 3rd W hold 3rd puppet between them. Mcb. looks at it without moving'
        (Nunn, Promptbook).

87–8a Cut by Nunn.

89–90 Cut by Nunn.

96–9a ('Rebellious . . . custom') Cut by Garrick and Forbes-Robertson.

Can tell so much, shall Banquo's issue ever
Reign in this kingdom?
ALL THE WITCHES   Seek to know no more.
MACBETH I will be satisfied. Deny me this,
And an eternal curse fall on you. Let me know.
          [*Cauldron descends.*] *Hautboys*
Why sinks that cauldron? And what noise is this?   105
FIRST WITCH Show!
SECOND WITCH Show!
THIRD WITCH Show!
ALL THE WITCHES Show his eyes and grieve his heart,
Come like shadows, so depart.   110

    [*Enter*] *a show of eight kings, and* [*the*] *last with a glass in his hand* [;
                    Banquo's Ghost following]

MACBETH Thou art too like the spirit of Banquo. Down!
Thy crown does sear mine eyeballs. And thy hair,
Thou other gold-bound brow, is like the first;
A third, is like the former. – Filthy hags,
Why do you show me this? – A fourth? Start, eyes!   115
What, will the line stretch out to th'crack of doom?
Another yet? A seventh? I'll see no more.
And yet the eighth appears, who bears a glass

---

104 SD *Cauldron descends* Macklin notes that when the cauldron sinks, 'there [should] be a great
Crash of Screaming discordant musick. – at – an eternal [curse] fall on you – and after mac
says why sinks that Cauldron, – & what noise is this? there must be a loud flourish or prelude
of music to introduce the eight visions' (Manuscript notes; see above, Introduction, p. 16).

106–8 'Each witch puts a doll onto a box' (Nunn, Promptbook).

110 SD *Enter . . .* Garrick's Promptbook shows that the procession of the kings took place behind a
transparent backscene. 'With proper lighting the hazy supernatural nature of the
transparency would have created an effective atmosphere' (Burnim, *Director*, pp. 122–3).
For this same episode Kemble arranged for the kings to move behind what Sir Walter Scott
describes as 'a screen of black crape' which 'diminished their corporeal appearance'
('Kemble', p. 227) A note in Phelps's Promptbook says 'Banquo. 8 Kings one with glass',
then, in a later hand, 'Not needed if done with profile figures'. The profile figures came up
through a slot behind a gauze. In Nunn's production the witches here blindfolded Macbeth.
"So depart" was spoken three times and a witch exited each time, leaving all three dolls on
boxes in front of McB. He sits blindfolded facing D[own] S[tage]' (Nunn, Promptbook).

112b–13 ('And thy hair . . . gold-bound brow, is') 'A second' (Garrick).

116 Cut by Garrick.

Which shows me many more. And some I see,
That two-fold balls and treble sceptres carry.   120
Horrible sight! Now I see 'tis true,
For the blood-boltered Banquo smiles upon me,
And points at them for his.
                    [*Exeunt show of kings and Banquo's Ghost*]
                              What, is this so?
FIRST WITCH   Ay, sir, all this is so. But why
Stands Macbeth thus amazedly?   125
Come, sisters, cheer we up his sprites,
And show the best of our delights.
I'll charm the air to give a sound,
While you perform your antic round
That this great king may kindly say,   130
Our duties did his welcome pay.
             Music. The Witches dance, and vanish
MACBETH   Where are they? Gone? Let this pernicious hour,
Stand aye accursèd in the calendar.
Come in, without there!

                    Enter LENNOX

LENNOX   What's your grace's will?
MACBETH   Saw you the weïrd sisters?
LENNOX   No, my lord.   135
MACBETH   Came they not by you?
LENNOX   No indeed, my lord.

119b–20   ('And some . . . carry') Cut by Garrick and Forbes-Robertson.
119b–21a   Cut by Nunn.
123a–31   Cut by Nunn.
123 SD   *Exeunt* . . . Tree arranged for the kings to rise upwards and disappear into the darkness of
           the flies. 'As the last spectres vanish, they laugh in the distance . . . The vision of Banquo and
           his heirs rising heavenwards, a vision the witches sought to conceal, suggested larger and
           holy powers surrounding their diabolical world' (Mullin, 'Images of Death', in Tardiff,
           Criticism, p. 178).
132   'Removes blindfold' (Nunn, Promptbook).
134 SD   *Enter* . . . Macready and Nunn substituted Seyton for Lennox (Promptbooks). Lennox did
           not enter in Tree's production but called 'Macbeth' from offstage and repeated the call as the
           curtain fell at the end of the scene' (Mullin, 'Images of Death', in Tardiff, *Criticism*, p. 178).
135   'picks up one doll' (Nunn, Promptbook).
136   'picks up doll' (Nunn, Promptbook).

MACBETH Infected be the air whereon they ride,
              And damned all those that trust them. I did hear
              The galloping of horse. Who was't came by?
LENNOX 'Tis two or three, my lord, that bring you word   140
              Macduff is fled to England.
MACBETH   Fled to England?
LENNOX Ay, my good lord.
MACBETH [*Aside*] Time, thou anticipat'st my dread exploits;
              The flighty purpose never is o'ertook
              Unless the deed go with it. From this moment,   145
              The very firstlings of my heart shall be
              The firstlings of my hand. And even now
              To crown my thoughts with acts, be it thought and done.
              The castle of Macduff I will surprise;
              Seize upon Fife; give to th'edge o'th'sword   150
              His wife, his babes, and all unfortunate souls
              That trace him in his line. No boasting like a fool;
              This deed I'll do before this purpose cool,
              But no more sights. – Where are these gentlemen?
              Come, bring me where they are.   155

Exeunt

145b–8 Cut by Forbes-Robertson.
147b–8 Cut by Garrick.
155 SD *Exeunt* In Irving's production, the set for Scene 1 was quickly replaced by '"an undulating,
          far-reaching, aery mountain-top landscape" with a moonlit sea in the distance. Some sixty
          witches in gauze draperies appeared, apparently flying so that they seemed to "people the
          wind". The whole preposterous charade was simply a vehicle for Sullivan's setting of
          the . . . Middleton song [transposed from 3.5.33],

> Come away, come away,
>
> Hecate, Hecate, come away!
>
> Over woods, high rocks and mountains,
>
> Over seas, our mistress' fountains.

Most critics thought the music exquisite, though *The Times* found it "loud and operatic" and
remarked that evil-tongued persons might term it "Pinaforean". Dawn was breaking, and
the witches vanished with unearthly shrieks' (Hughes, *Shakespearean*, p. 111). 'The singing
witches . . . removed by Phelps, were put back by [Charles] Kean in 1853; Irving achieved
one of the spectacular triumphs of his 1888 *Macbeth* with his "black spirits and white"
chorus . . . and it was not until 1911 that they made what seems to have been positively their
last appearance in Tree's production' (Byrne, 'Fifty Years', p. 2).

ACT 4, SCENE 2

Enter [LADY MACDUFF], *her* SON, *and* ROSS

LADY MACDUFF What had he done, to make him fly the land?
ROSS You must have patience, madam.
LADY MACDUFF   He had none;
     His flight was madness. When our actions do not,
     Our fears do make us traitors.
ROSS   You know not
     Whether it was his wisdom or his fear.   5
LADY MACDUFF Wisdom? To leave his wife, to leave his babes,
     His mansion, and his titles in a place
     From whence himself does fly? He loves us not.
     He wants the natural touch, for the poor wren,
     The most diminutive of birds, will fight,   10
     Her young ones in her nest, against the owl.
     All is the fear, and nothing is the love;
     As little is the wisdom, where the flight
     So runs against all reason.
ROSS   My dearest coz,
     I pray you school yourself. But for your husband,   15
     He is noble, wise, judicious, and best knows
     The fits o'th'season. I dare not speak much further,
     But cruel are the times when we are traitors
     And do not know ourselves, when we hold rumour
     From what we fear, yet know not what we fear,   20
     But float upon a wild and violent sea,
     Each way and none. I take my leave of you;
     Shall not be long but I'll be here again.

Kemble, Macready, Charles Kean, Irving, and Forbes-Robertson cut this scene entirely.
Phelps originally included it but later cut it as being too painful.

Setting As a contrast to the dark interiors of Macbeth's castle, Tree set this scene in an orchard
(Mullin, 'Images of Death', in Tardiff, *Criticism*, p. 177). In the 1928 modern-dress
production, Lady Macduff and her son were murdered over a cup of afternoon tea by killers
who entered through a casement window (Styan, *Revolution*, p. 150).

Things at the worst will cease, or else climb upward
To what they were before. My pretty cousin,   25
Blessing upon you.
LADY MACDUFF Fathered he is, and yet he's fatherless.
ROSS I am so much a fool, should I stay longer
It would be my disgrace and your discomfort.
I take my leave at once.   *Exit*
LADY MACDUFF   Sirrah, your father's dead,   30
And what will you do now? How will you live?
SON As birds do, mother.
LADY MACDUFF   What, with worms and flies?
SON With what I get I mean, and so do they.
LADY MACDUFF Poor bird, thou'dst never fear the net, nor lime, the
pitfall, nor the gin.   35
SON Why should I, mother? Poor birds they are not set for.
My father is not dead for all your saying.
LADY MACDUFF Yes, he is dead. How wilt thou do for a father?
SON Nay, how will you do for a husband?
LADY MACDUFF Why, I can buy me twenty at any market.   40
SON Then you'll buy 'em to sell again.
LADY MACDUFF Thou speak'st with all thy wit, and yet i'faith with
wit enough for thee.
SON Was my father a traitor, mother?
LADY MACDUFF Ay, that he was.   45
SON What is a traitor?
LADY MACDUFF Why, one that swears and lies.
SON And be all traitors, that do so?
LADY MACDUFF Every one that does so is a traitor and must be
hanged.   50
SON And must they all be hanged that swear and lie?
LADY MACDUFF Every one.
SON Who must hang them?
LADY MACDUFF Why, the honest men.
SON Then the liars and swearers are fools, for there are liars and   55
swearers enough to beat the honest men and hang up them.
LADY MACDUFF Now God help thee, poor monkey, but how wilt thou
do for a father?
SON If he were dead, you'd weep for him; if you would not, it were   60
a good sign that I should quickly have a new father.

30b–61   Cut by Davenant and Garrick.
32b–6   Cut by Nunn.
41–3   Cut by Nunn.
57–61   ('but how . . . talk'st!') Cut by Nunn.

LADY MACDUFF Poor prattler, how thou talk'st!

Enter a MESSENGER

MESSENGER Bless you, fair dame. I am not to you known,
    Though in your state of honour I am perfect;
    I doubt some danger does approach you nearly.
    If you will take a homely man's advice,   65
    Be not found here. Hence with your little ones.
    To fright you thus, methinks I am too savage;
    To do worse to you were fell cruelty,
    Which is too nigh your person. Heaven preserve you,
    I dare abide no longer.   *Exit*
LADY MACDUFF   Whither should I fly?   70
    I have done no harm. But I remember now
    I am in this earthly world where to do harm
    Is often laudable, to do good sometime
    Accounted dangerous folly. Why then, alas,
    Do I put up that womanly defence,   75
    To say I have done no harm?

Enter MURDERERS
What are these faces?

61 SD   *Enter . . .* Garrick's and Nunn's Messenger was Angus.
62–3   Cut by Nunn.
65   Cut by Nunn.
66b–9a   Cut by Garrick.
69   Nunn added SD 'knock' (Promptbook).
76b   Cut by Nunn.
76b–82   Cut by Davenant and Garrick. Garrick's cut became customary practice until Phelps restored the complete scene at Sadler's Wells in 1847 (*Athenaeum*, 2 October 1847, p. 1036). The omission of the child's death made a considerable difference to the effect of the play. Shakespeare portrays it as the last and most brutal of the atrocities committed by Macbeth. Moreover, the audience's knowledge of the child's murder hangs over the next scene (the 'England' scene) during most of which Macduff is unaware of it until its revelation towards the end of the scene motivates him into joining the rebellion against Macbeth. 'Phelps's 1847 stage directions include '"falling on her knees" for Lady Macduff, when she begins to talk with the boy (she rises at line 45, "Ay, that he was"); "Lady M. rushes and clings to her son" at the messenger's injunction, "Hence with your little ones" [66b] "1st. Murderer Snatches up young Macduff and bears him off screaming 'Murder' – &c. thro openg [*sic*] LH, at "young fry of treachery" [81a]; and, finally, "The 2nd. Murderer drags off Lady Macduff thro opening LH screaming 'Murder'. A pause then whistle" – i.e. for the change of scene'

A MURDERER Where is your husband?

LADY MACDUFF I hope in no place so unsanctified,
     Where such as thou mayst find him.

A MURDERER   He's a traitor.

SON Thou liest, thou shag-haired villain.

A MURDERER   What, you egg!   80
     Young fry of treachery!
                [*Kills him*]

SON   He has killed me, mother,
     Run away, I pray you!
           Exit [Lady Macduff] crying 'Murder'[, pursued by
                              Murderers with her Son]

(Sprague, *Actors*, pp. 267–8). The audience at Sadler's Wells objected to the murder of the boy as too painful and Phelps gave way to public opinion and removed it. It is likely that Davenant also believed it was too painful. In Tree's production, the cackling of the witches could be heard just before Lady Macduff and her son were murdered (Mullin, 'Images of Death', in Tardiff, *Criticism*, p. 178). In Glen Byam Shaw's production, Lady Macduff was accompanied by three children, one a baby. 'They are a family at peace. The nobleman [Ross] is close kin. "He kisses her," says the Promptbook, and as they speak of the children, "he goes back to the baby, saying 'my pretty cousin, Blessing upon you'" [25b–26]. Lady Macduff banters with her child. She sits in a chair; one of the boys lies down; the other, wearing a toy sword, "looks at the baby and kneels." All are at rest. Then a threat materializes in the form of an old Shepherd telling of dangers, who "is frightened himself and leaves as soon as he has given his warning". The tableau breaks . . . Almost immediately the two terrible brutes who murdered Banquo appear' (Mullin, '*Macbeth* at Stratford', p. 274). The murderers in Nunn's 1976 production were relaxed and smiling, and 'the boy, though defiant, went up to them without fear. First Murderer, still smiling, took the boy onto his lap – and thrust his dagger into his back, seen bloodied as the boy fell forward onto the stage crying "He has killed me, mother", while the Murderer, starting up, cut the Lady's throat' (David, *Theatre*, p. 89). Seyton carried off the child and the Murderer dragged Lady Macduff off (Promptbook).

ACT 4, SCENE 3

Enter MALCOLM *and* MACDUFF

MALCOLM Let us seek out some desolate shade and there
    Weep our sad bosoms empty.
MACDUFF   Let us rather
    Hold fast the mortal sword and like good men
    Bestride our downfall birthdom; each new morn,
    New widows howl, new orphans cry, new sorrows   5
    Strike heaven on the face, that it resounds

Setting   Several directors, from Garrick onwards, have made cuts in this scene, the longest in the play, partly because much of it consists of an extensive dialogue between Malcolm and Macduff which contributes little to the action, partly because, presumably, they failed to recognise the significance of the account of Edward the Confessor whose saintliness contrasts with the evil of Macbeth. The Folio text, as is customary, specifies no location for this scene, but it is implicit in the dialogue that it takes place in England. Davenant, for no apparent reason, shifted it to Birnam Wood and thereby made nonsense of Malcolm's reference to 'here from gracious England' (line 43) which he retained. Garrick brought it back to '*the* King *of* England's Palace' (*Macbeth*, 1773, p. 52). Charles Kean set it in 'The Exterior of an Anglo-Saxon city with a Roman Wall' (Promptbook). The sets and lighting for Irving's production were generally gloomy and severe, but the sunny English lane in which this scene was set came as a welcome relief. '"Good old England!" shouted a pittite, and there was a patter of applause. Sullivan reinforced the atmospheric change with a fresh and idyllic prelude during the brief interval' (Hughes, *Shakespearean*, p. 111). Like most of his predecessors, Irving cut the 'England' scene severely. Komisarjevsky brought down the drop curtain and the scene was played in front of it, 'marking in visual terms the utter separation of the sunlit world of Malcolm and the saintly Edward from the shadowy world of Macbeth' (Mullin, 'Komisarjevsky's Macbeth', p. 24). 'The England scene . . . is usually thought of as a point of brightness and sunlight', but in Glen Byam Shaw's staging, 'the sunlit backdrop was overhung with the dark shapes of huge trees that met overhead to form [a] twisted archway' (Mullin, *Macbeth Onstage*, p. 15).

3b–4a   ('and like . . . birthdom') Cut by Garrick.

As if it felt with Scotland and yelled out
Like syllable of dolour.
MALCOLM   What I believe, I'll wail;
What know, believe; and what I can redress,
As I shall find the time to friend, I will.   10
What you have spoke, it may be so perchance.
This tyrant, whose sole name blisters our tongues,
Was once thought honest; you have loved him well –
He hath not touched you yet. I am young, but something
You may discern of him through me, and wisdom   15
To offer up a weak, poor, innocent lamb
T'appease an angry god.
MACDUFF I am not treacherous.
MALCOLM   But Macbeth is.
A good and virtuous nature may recoil
In an imperial charge. But I shall crave your pardon: 20
That which you are, my thoughts cannot transpose;
Angels are bright still, though the brightest fell.
Though all things foul would wear the brows of grace,
Yet grace must still look so.
MACDUFF   I have lost my hopes.
MALCOLM Perchance even there where I did find my doubts.   25
Why in that rawness left you wife and child,
Those precious motives, those strong knots of love,
Without leave-taking? I pray you,
Let not my jealousies be your dishonours,
But mine own safeties; you may be rightly just,   30
Whatever I shall think.
MACDUFF   Bleed, bleed, poor country.
Great tyranny, lay thou thy basis sure,
For goodness dare not check thee; wear thou thy wrongs,
The title is affeered. Fare thee well, lord,
I would not be the villain that thou think'st   35

8b–10	Cut by Garrick and Charles Kean.
8b–38	Cut by Forbes-Robertson.
14b–17	('I am . . . god') Cut by Phelps and Charles Kean.
20b–4a	('But I . . . look so') Cut by Garrick, Phelps, and Charles Kean.
26–8	Cut by Garrick.
28	Cut by Nunn.
30b–1a	Cut by Nunn.
32–4a	('Great tyranny . . . affeered') Cut by Nunn.

For the whole space that's in the tyrant's grasp,
And the rich East to boot.
MALCOLM   Be not offended.
I speak not as in absolute fear of you:
I think our country sinks beneath the yoke;
It weeps, it bleeds, and each new day a gash   40
Is added to her wounds. I think withal
There would be hands uplifted in my right,
And here from gracious England have I offer
Of goodly thousands. But for all this,
When I shall tread upon the tyrant's head,   45
Or wear it on my sword, yet my poor country
Shall have more vices than it had before,
More suffer, and more sundry ways than ever,
By him that shall succeed.
MACDUFF   What should he be?
MALCOLM It is myself I mean – in whom I know   50
All the particulars of vice so grafted
That when they shall be opened, black Macbeth
Will seem as pure as snow, and the poor state
Esteem him as a lamb, being compared
With my confineless harms.
MACDUFF   Not in the legions   55
Of horrid hell can come a devil more damned
In evils to top Macbeth.
MALCOLM   I grant him bloody,
Luxurious, avaricious, false, deceitful,
Sudden, malicious, smacking of every sin
That has a name. But there's no bottom, none,   60
In my voluptuousness: your wives, your daughters,
Your matrons, and your maids could not fill up
The cistern of my lust, and my desire
All continent impediments would o'erbear

41b–4a   ('I think ... thousands') Cut by Forbes-Robertson.
48   Cut by Nunn.
49   ('By') 'Thro', Nunn.
49b–55a Cut by Garrick.
57b–76a Cut by Forbes-Robertson.
59–60a   Cut by Garrick.
61b–76a Cut by Macready, Phelps, and Charles Kean.
61b–97a ('your wives ... many ways') Cut by Garrick.

                              That did oppose my will. Better Macbeth,   65
                              Than such an one to reign.
MACDUFF   Boundless intemperance
                              In nature is a tyranny; it hath been
                              Th'untimely emptying of the happy throne
                              And fall of many kings. But fear not yet
                              To take upon you what is yours: you may   70
                              Convey your pleasures in a spacious plenty
                              And yet seem cold. The time you may so hoodwink.
                              We have willing dames enough; there cannot be
                              That vulture in you to devour so many
                              As will to greatness dedicate themselves,   75
                              Finding it so inclined.
MALCOLM   With this, there grows
                              In my most ill-composed affection such
                              A stanchless avarice that, were I king,
                              I should cut off the nobles for their lands,
                              Desire his jewels, and this other's house,   80
                              And my more-having would be as a sauce
                              To make me hunger more, that I should forge
                              Quarrels unjust against the good and loyal,
                              Destroying them for wealth.
MACDUFF   This avarice
                              Sticks deeper, grows with more pernicious root   85
                              Than summer-seeming lust, and it hath been
                              The sword of our slain kings; yet do not fear,
                              Scotland hath foisons to fill up your will
                              Of your mere own. All these are portable,
                              With other graces weighed.   90
MALCOLM But I have none. The king-becoming graces –
                              As justice, verity, temp'rance, stableness,
                              Bounty, perseverance, mercy, lowliness,
                              Devotion, patience, courage, fortitude –
                              I have no relish of them, but abound   95
                              In the division of each several crime,
                              Acting it many ways. Nay, had I power, I should
                              Pour the sweet milk of concord into hell,
                              Uproar the universal peace, confound
                              All unity on earth.

79–80   Cut by Nunn.
82b–100a   ('that I . . . on earth') Cut by Forbes-Robertson.
86b–7a   ('and it . . . kings') Cut by Nunn.

MACDUFF   O Scotland, Scotland!   100
MALCOLM If such a one be fit to govern, speak.
    I am as I have spoken.
MACDUFF   Fit to govern?
    No, not to live. O nation miserable!
    With an untitled tyrant, bloody-sceptred,
    When shalt thou see thy wholesome days again,   105
    Since that the truest issue of thy throne
    By his own interdiction stands accursed
    And does blaspheme his breed? Thy royal father
    Was a most sainted king; the queen that bore thee,
    Oft'ner upon her knees than on her feet,   110
    Died every day she lived. Fare thee well,
    These evils thou repeat'st upon thyself
    Hath banished me from Scotland. O my breast,
    Thy hope ends here.
MALCOLM   Macduff, this noble passion,
    Child of integrity, hath from my soul   115
    Wiped the black scruples, reconciled my thoughts
    To thy good truth and honour. Devilish Macbeth
    By many of these trains hath sought to win me
    Into his power, and modest wisdom plucks me
    From over-credulous haste; but God above   120
    Deal between thee and me, for even now
    I put myself to thy direction and
    Unspeak mine own detraction, here abjure
    The taints and blames I laid upon myself,
    For strangers to my nature. I am yet   125
    Unknown to woman, never was forsworn,
    Scarcely have coveted what was mine own,
    At no time broke my faith, would not betray
    The devil to his fellow, and delight
    No less in truth than life. My first false speaking   130
    Was this upon myself. What I am truly
    Is thine, and my poor country's, to command:
    Whither indeed, before thy here-approach,

108b–11a   ('Thy royal . . . lived') Cut by Forbes-Robertson.
117b–30a   ('Devilish . . . life') Cut by Forbes-Robertson.
123b–31a   ('here abjure . . . upon myself') Cut by Garrick, Phelps, and Charles Kean.
  133–7a   ('Whither . . . quarrel') Cut by Forbes-Robertson.

Old Siward with ten thousand warlike men
Already at a point was setting forth.   135
Now we'll together, and the chance of goodness
Be like our warranted quarrel. Why are you silent?
MACDUFF Such welcome and unwelcome things at once,
'Tis hard to reconcile.

Enter a DOCTOR

MALCOLM   Well, more anon. –
Comes the king forth, I pray you?   140
DOCTOR Ay, sir: there are a crew of wretched souls
That stay his cure; their malady convinces
The great assay of art, but at his touch,
Such sanctity hath heaven given his hand,
They presently amend.   *Exit*   145
MALCOLM I thank you, doctor.
MACDUFF What's the disease he means?
MALCOLM 'Tis called the Evil.
A most miraculous work in this good king,
Which often since my here-remain in England   150
I have seen him do. How he solicits heaven
Himself best knows, but strangely visited people
All swoll'n and ulcerous, pitiful to the eye,
The mere despair of surgery, he cures,
Hanging a golden stamp about their necks   155
Put on with holy prayers, and 'tis spoken
To the succeeding royalty he leaves
The healing benediction. With this strange virtue,
He hath a heavenly gift of prophecy,
And sundry blessings hang about his throne   160
That speak him full of grace.

Enter ROSS

134 ('Old Siward with') Cut by Nunn.
135 ('was') 'were', Nunn.
139 SD *Enter . . .* Charles Kean substituted Ross for the Doctor. Nunn cut the Doctor and gave his speech to Malcolm. SD 'They embrace' (Nunn, Promptbook).
139b–61a Cut by Garrick, Phelps, Charles Kean, and Forbes-Robertson.
140–1b ('Comes the king . . . Ay, sir:') 'The king comes forth today', Nunn.
142b–3a ('their malady . . . art') Cut by Nunn.
146 Cut by Nunn.
147 ('What's . . . means?') 'What's their disease?', Nunn.

MACDUFF   See who comes here.
MALCOLM My countryman, but yet I know him not.
MACDUFF My ever gentle cousin, welcome hither.
MALCOLM I know him now. Good God betimes remove
        The means that makes us strangers.
ROSS   Sir, amen.   165
MACDUFF Stands Scotland where it did?
ROSS   Alas, poor country,
        Almost afraid to know itself. It cannot
        Be called our mother, but our grave, where nothing,
        But who knows nothing, is once seen to smile;
        Where sighs, and groans, and shrieks that rend the air   170
        Are made, not marked; where violent sorrow seems
        A modern ecstasy. The deadman's knell
        Is there scarce asked for who, and good men's lives
        Expire before the flowers in their caps,
        Dying or ere they sicken.
MACDUFF   O relation   175
        Too nice, and yet too true.
MALCOLM   What's the newest grief?
ROSS That of an hour's age doth hiss the speaker;
        Each minute teems a new one.
MACDUFF   How does my wife?
ROSS Why, well.
MACDUFF   And all my children?
ROSS   Well, too.
MACDUFF The tyrant has not battered at their peace?   180
ROSS No, they were well at peace when I did leave 'em.
MACDUFF Be not a niggard of your speech: how goes't?
ROSS When I came hither to transport the tidings
        Which I have heavily borne, there ran a rumour
        Of many worthy fellows that were out,   185
        Which was to my belief witnessed the rather
        For that I saw the tyrant's power afoot.
        Now is the time of help. [*To Malcolm*] Your eye in
            Scotland
        Would create soldiers, make our women fight
        To doff their dire distresses.

162b   ('But . . . not') Cut by Nunn.
164a   ('I . . . now') Cut by Nunn.
172b–5a ('The deadman's . . . sicken') Cut by Forbes-Robertson.

MALCOLM   Be't their comfort   190
      We are coming thither. Gracious England hath
      Lent us good Siward and ten thousand men –
      An older and a better soldier none
      That Christendom gives out.
ROSS   Would I could answer
      This comfort with the like. But I have words   195
      That would be howled out in the desert air,
      Where hearing should not latch them.
MACDUFF   What concern they?
      The general cause, or is it a fee-grief
      Due to some single breast?
ROSS   No mind that's honest
      But in it shares some woe, though the main part   200
      Pertains to you alone.
MACDUFF   If it be mine,
      Keep it not from me; quickly let me have it.
ROSS Let not your ears despise my tongue forever
      Which shall possess them with the heaviest sound
      That ever yet they heard.
MACDUFF   H'm – I guess at it.   205
ROSS Your castle is surprised; your wife and babes
      Savagely slaughtered. To relate the manner
      Were on the quarry of these murdered deer
      To add the death of you.
MALCOLM   Merciful heaven –
      What, man, ne'er pull your hat upon your brows: 210
      Give sorrow words; the grief that does not speak,
      Whispers the o'erfraught heart and bids it break.
MACDUFF My children too?
ROSS   Wife, children, servants, all
      That could be found.
MACDUFF   And I must be from thence?
      My wife killed too?
ROSS   I have said.
MALCOLM   Be comforted.   215
      Let's make us med'cines of our great revenge
      To cure this deadly grief.

191b–4a ('Gracious . . . out') 'and with ten thousand men' (Nunn).
205b Garrick substituted the line, 'At once, I guess, and am afraid to know!'
210 Cut by Nunn.

MACDUFF He has no children. All my pretty ones?
           Did you say all? O hell-kite! All?
           What, all my pretty chickens and their dam
           At one fell swoop?   220
MALCOLM Dispute it like a man.
MACDUFF I shall do so;
           But I must also feel it as a man;
           I cannot but remember such things were
           That were most precious to me. Did heaven look on,   225
           And would not take their part? Sinful Macduff,
           They were all struck for thee. Naught that I am,
           Not for their own demerits but for mine,
           Fell slaughter on their souls. Heaven rest them now.
MALCOLM Be this the whetstone of your sword, let grief   230
           Convert to anger. Blunt not the heart, enrage it.
MACDUFF O, I could play the woman with mine eyes
           And braggart with my tongue. But gentle heavens,
           Cut short all intermission. Front to front
           Bring thou this fiend of Scotland and myself;   235
           Within my sword's length set him. If he scape,
           Heaven forgive him too.
MALCOLM   This tune goes manly.
           Come, go we to the king; our power is ready;
           Our lack is nothing but our leave. Macbeth
           Is ripe for shaking, and the powers above   240
           Put on their instruments. Receive what cheer you may:
           The night is long that never finds the day.
                                                          Exeunt

228b   Cut by Garrick.
 230   Cut by Garrick.
238b–43   Cut by Macready, Phelps, and Charles Kean.
240b–1a   ('and the ... instruments') Cut by Nunn.
241b–242   ('Receive ... day') Cut by Forbes-Robertson.

Enter a DOCTOR OF PHYSIC, *and a* WAITING-GENTLEWOMAN

DOCTOR I have two nights watched with you, but can perceive no
truth in your report. When was it she last walked?

GENTLEWOMAN Since his majesty went into the field, I have seen
her rise from her bed, throw her night-gown upon her, unlock
her closet, take forth paper, fold it, write upon't, read it, after- 5
wards seal it, and again return to bed, yet all this while in a
most fast sleep.

DOCTOR A great perturbation in nature, to receive at once the
benefit of sleep and do the effects of watching. In this slumbery
agitation, besides her walking and other actual performances, 10
what at any time have you heard her say?

GENTLEWOMAN That, sir, which I will not report after her.

Setting   Macready staged the scene simply: 'A room in the castle, with a small table on the left to
hold the taper that Lady Macbeth carries in, a convenient alcove at the right for the
physician and gentlewoman to hide in' (Downer, *Macready*, p. 335). Phelps set it in 'an
antechamber in Macbeth's castle in which a bedchamber was visible through an opening'
(Weiner, 'Phelps' Staging', p. 130). The scene in Irving's production was 'a massive
anteroom in Dunsinane Castle with a cloistered corridor upstage, from which a short flight
of steps descended'. Terry came along the cloister before descending the stairs (Hughes,
Shakespearean, pp. 111–12). The stage was empty in Tree's production: 'There is nothing
else in it but a bare flight of stone stairs leading right from the highest visible point of the
stage to the ground, set close against a bare stone wall, without even a balustrade, but
turning zig-zag half way down, where there is a square ledge just big enough to put a candle
on. There is no attempt even to suggest a castle, or any earthly stairs at all – just the idea of
stairs, and nothing more' (*Daily Chronicle*, 7 September 1911).

0 SD   *Enter . . .* The Doctor was replaced by Seyton in Davenant's alteration but was restored by
Garrick.

1–2a   ('I have . . . report.') Cut by Nunn.

8–10a   ('A great . . . agitation') Cut by Charles Kean.

DOCTOR You may to me, and 'tis most meet you should.

GENTLEWOMAN Neither to you, nor anyone, having no witness to
    confirm my speech.   15

Enter LADY [MACBETH], *with a taper*

13b ('and 'tis . . . should') Cut by Nunn.

15 SD *Enter* . . . In a production of 1784, Siddons wore 'a long, flowing dress over which a sleeved dressing gown is loosely thrown'. In 1785 she had changed this to 'a flowing night-dress, presumably white . . . Her hair, much dishevelled, is surmounted by no head dress at all' (Donoghue, 'Kemble's *Macbeth*', p. 73). Bell comments 'I should like [Siddons] to enter less suddenly. A slower and more interrupted step more natural. She advances rapidly to the table, sets down the light and rubs her hand, making the action of lifting up water in one hand at intervals' ('Siddons', p. 65). As Siddons was preparing in the dressing room for her first night, Sheridan, the Manager of Drury Lane, tried to persuade her not to put down the candle with which she entered, because this had not been done before. Nevertheless she persisted in doing so and thereby left both her hands free to rub together. When the scene was over, Sheridan returned to the dressing room and 'congratulated me on my obstinacy' (Campbell, *Siddons*, vol. II, p. 39). 'The actresses previous to [Siddons] seemed to consider such a perturbation as not possessing *full* power upon the frame; they therefore, rather *glided* than walked . . . Mrs Siddons seemed to conceive the fancy as having equal power over the frame, and all her actions had the wakeful vigour. She laded the water from the imaginary ewer over her hands – bent her body to listen to the sounds presented by her fancy, and hurried to resume the taper where she had left it, that she might with all speed drag her pallid husband to their chamber . . . The quantity of white drapery in which the actress was enveloped had a singular and striking effect . . . [She was] extremely majestic both in form and motion – it was, however, the majesty of the *tomb* . . . Perhaps her friend, Sir Joshua Reynolds, might have suggested the almost *shroud-like* clothing of this important scene' (Boaden, *Siddons*, vol. II, pp. 143–4). '[Siddons] looked a living statue and spoke with the solemn tone of a voice from a shrine. She stood more the *sepulchral avenger* of regicide than the *sufferer* from its convictions. Her grand voice, her fixed and marble countenance, and her silent step, gave the impression of a supernatural being, the genius of an ancient oracle – a tremendous Nemesis' (*Blackwood's Magazine*, June 1843, p. 710). 'The deathlike stare of [Siddons's] countenance, while the body was in motion, was sublime; and the anxious whispering with which she made her exit, as if beckoning her husband to bed, took the audience along with her into the silent and dreaming horror of her retirement; but we know not whether in attempting a natural monotony of gesture she did not throw too great an air of indolence over the scene in general' (Hunt, *Dramatic Criticism*, p. 72).

Faucit's performance in this scene was quite different: 'Here is no impassive statue, no monumental Nemesis. Here instead is a great lady sick to death' (*Liverpool Post*, December 1870, quoted in Martin, *Faucit*, p. 312). Macready praised Faucit, for creating 'the idea of sleep, disturbed by fearful dreams, but still it was sleep. It was to be seen even in [her] walk, which was heavy and inelastic, marking the distinction – too often overlooked – between the muffled voice and seeming-mechanical motion of the somnambulist, and the wandering mind and quick fitful gestures of the maniac' (Faucit, *Female Characters*, p. 231). Ristori's look was haggard: 'her whole aspect is spectral, her action slow and painfully nervous in its manner, her voice low, full of such weariness as follows acute and exhausting pain. Her exit, when her mind has recurred to the night of the murder, is with a ghostly repetition of the old gesture of urging Macbeth on before her' (Morley, *Journal*, p. 190). Ellen Terry wore a plain white, hooded gown as she passed through the cloister carrying the traditional lamp, and descended the stairs. The great, red braids in her hair she had worn formerly were now replaced with 'a straggle of auburn hair . . . She adopted a real somnambulist's "long-drawn, almost whining utterance, and the breaking up of words into their syllables"' (Hughes, *Shakespearean*, p. 112). In the notes in her copy of the play, she writes, 'Remember she is weak and asleep. Macbeth preyed on her mind more than the deed. *This* might be some time afterwards and grey hair would be pathetic. For both of them have gone through enough to make 'em grey.' Her actions, she comments, should be undertaken 'with trembling hands – she is very weak. Rub the Palms of hands' (Manvell, 'Terry as Lady Macbeth', p. 161). Sarah Bernhardt had bare feet and wore a clinging nightdress (*Times*, 5 July 1884). Tree's Lady Macbeth, Violet Vanbrugh, came down the long flight of stairs 'step by step, in a dark robe and mystic blue light . . . all a-dream, candle in hand. Half way she pauses to put the candle on the ledge, and still comes down, making as to wash her hands, and murmuring the immortal lines. She reaches the ground, and falls there in a wailing heap . . . Then she gets up, and as slowly as before, step by step, mounts the stairs, feeling her way by the wall. She takes her candle and, mounting still, vanishes into the dark from whence she came' (*Daily Chronicle*, 7 September 1911). 'In the sleep-walking scene, [Poel] had the brilliant idea of showing her at her dressing table, playing mechanically with her brushes and comb and going through the motions of brushing her hair . . . Later she rose and began to walk about. Poel held that the effect of the scene would be far more impressive if the audience could see her moving gradually into the rhythm of her sleep-walking instead of being already fixed in it at the moment of her first appearance' (Speaight, *Poel*, p. 188). The Lady Macbeth in Glen Byam Shaw's production, Vivien Leigh, entered from the back of the stage down a great, long corridor which, as several critics remarked, emphasised her solitude (David, 'Tragic Curve', p. 126). She wore a 'dishevelled, dark grey nightdress' and her hair, now grey, hung about her shoulders (Mullin, *Macbeth Onstage*, p. 155). Nunn's Promptbook notes 'Lady M. puts candle down, kneels, "hand washing" movements, stopping to look at them in light.'

Lo you, here she comes. This is her very guise and, upon my life, fast asleep. Observe her, stand close.

DOCTOR How came she by that light?

GENTLEWOMAN Why, it stood by her. She has light by her continually, 'tis her command.   20

DOCTOR You see her eyes are open.

GENTLEWOMAN Ay, but their sense are shut.

DOCTOR What is it she does now? Look how she rubs her hands.

GENTLEWOMAN It is an accustomed action with her, to seem thus
washing her hands; I have known her continue in this a quarter   25
of an hour.

LADY MACBETH Yet here's a spot.

DOCTOR Hark, she speaks; I will set down what comes from her to
satisfy my remembrance the more strongly.

LADY MACBETH Out, damned spot! Out, I say! One, two. Why   30
then 'tis time to do't. Hell is murky. Fie, my lord, fie, a soldier,
and afeard? What need we fear? Who knows it, when none can
call our power to account? Yet who would have thought the old
man to have had so much blood in him?

DOCTOR Do you mark that?   35

LADY MACBETH The Thane of Fife had a wife. Where is she
now? What, will these hands ne'er be clean? No more o'that
my lord, no more o'that. You mar all with this starting.

DOCTOR Go to, go to; you have known what you should not.

GENTLEWOMAN She has spoke what she should not, I am sure of   40
that. Heaven knows what she has known.

LADY MACBETH Here's the smell of the blood still; all the per-
fumes of Arabia will not sweeten this little hand. O, O, O.

17b ('Observe . . . close') Cut by Nunn.

28b–9 ('I will . . . strongly') Cut by Nunn.

30–43 Bell comments in detail on Siddons's interpretation: "One, two" ('Listening eagerly'); "'Tis time to do't" ('A strange, unnatural whisper'); "Where is she now?" ('Very melancholy tone'); "Will these hands ne'er be clean?" ('Melancholy peevishness'); "You mar all with this starting" ('Eager whisper'); "O, O, O." ('This is not a sigh. A convulsive shudder – very horrible. A tone of imbecility audible in the sigh') ('Siddons', p. 66).

42 Leigh Hunt remarks that, 'when she smelt the blood on her hand . . . [Siddons] made a face of ordinary disgust, as though the odour were offensive to the senses, not appalling to the mind' (*Autobiography*, p. 133). Ellen Terry noted of this line, 'Trembling hands . . . she is very weak' (Hughes, *Shakespearean*, p. 112). Nunn's Promptbook says, 'Lady puts hand each side of candle and looks at them, after smelling them.'

DOCTOR What a sigh is there! The heart is sorely charged.

GENTLEWOMAN I would not have such a heart in my bosom for   45
    the dignity of the whole body.

DOCTOR Well, well, well –

GENTLEWOMAN Pray God it be, sir.

DOCTOR This disease is beyond my practice; yet I have known
    those which have walked in their sleep who have died holily in   50
    their beds.

LADY MACBETH Wash your hands, put on your night-gown, look
    not so pale. I tell you yet again, Banquo's buried; he cannot
    come out on's grave.

DOCTOR Even so?   55

LADY MACBETH To bed, to bed; there's knocking at the gate.
    Come, come, come, come, give me your hand; what's done
    cannot be undone. To bed, to bed, to bed.   *Exit*

DOCTOR Will she go now to bed?

GENTLEWOMAN Directly.   60

DOCTOR Foul whisp'rings are abroad; unnatural deeds
    Do breed unnatural troubles; infected minds
    To their deaf pillows will discharge their secrets.
    More needs she the divine than the physician.
    God, God forgive us all. Look after her;   65
    Remove from her the means of all annoyance,
    And still keep eyes upon her. So, good night,

---

43   In Davenant's version, Lady Macbeth makes an exit here and the rest of the scene is cut.
    Garrick restored these lines but made one small cut (line 68).

44a ('What . . . there!') Cut by Nunn.

47–51 Cut by Forbes-Robertson.

48 Cut by Nunn.

49–51 Cut by Garrick.

58 SD *Exit* Siddons 'used, as it were, to *feel* for the light; that is, while stalking backwards, and
    keeping her eyes glaring on the house' (Magnin, *Piozziana*, p. 127). Bernhardt, 'after
    apostrophising the "damned spot" . . . falls back shrieking hysterically, and finally rushes off
    to the wings, calling out lustily the while, "To bed, to bed"' (*Times*, 5 July 1884).

61a ('Foul . . . abroad') Cut by Nunn.

61–3 Cut by Charles Kean.

61–9 Cut by Phelps.

61b–5a ('unnatural . . . us all') Cut by Forbes-Robertson.

62b–3 ('infected . . . secrets') Cut by Nunn.

67b–9 ('So . . . doctor') Cut by Charles Kean.

My mind she has mated, and amazed my sight.
I think, but dare not speak.
GENTLEWOMAN   Good night, good doctor.   70

Exeunt

---

68   Cut by Garrick and Forbes-Robertson.
68–9a   Cut by Nunn.

ACT 5, SCENE 2

Drum and colours. Enter MENTEITH, CAITHNESS, ANGUS,
LENNOX, *Soldiers*

MENTEITH The English power is near, led on by Malcolm,
       His uncle Siward, and the good Macduff.
       Revenges burn in them, for their dear causes
       Would to the bleeding and the grim alarm
       Excite the mortified man.
ANGUS   Near Birnam Wood   5
       Shall we well meet them; that way are they coming.
CAITHNESS Who knows if Donaldbain be with his brother?
LENNOX For certain, sir, he is not. I have a file
       Of all the gentry; there is Siward's son
       And many unrough youths that even now   10
       Protest their first of manhood.
MENTEITH   What does the tyrant?
CAITHNESSS Great Dunsinane he strongly fortifies.
       Some say he's mad; others that lesser hate him
       Do call it valiant fury, but for certain
       He cannot buckle his distempered cause   15
       Within the belt of rule.
ANGUS   Now does he feel
       His secret murders sticking on his hands.
       Now minutely revolts upbraid his faith-breach;
       Those he commands, move only in command,
       Nothing in love. Now does he feel his title   20
       Hang loose about him, like a giant's robe
       Upon a dwarfish thief.
MENTEITH   Who then shall blame

Whole scene cut by Garrick, Macready, Phelps, Charles Kean, Forbes-Robertson, and Tree.
Davenant replaced it with a scene between Donaldbain, Fleance, and Lennox which he had
written himself.

2–11a   Cut by Nunn.

11b–31   Nunn replaced Menteith and Caithness with Ross and Angus.

His pestered senses to recoil and start,
When all that is within him does condemn
Itself for being there?
CAITHNESS   Well, march we on   25
To give obedience where 'tis truly owed;
Meet we the med'cine of the sickly weal,
And with him pour we in our country's purge,
Each drop of us.
LENNOX   Or so much as it needs
To dew the sovereign flower and drown the weeds.   30
Make we our march towards Birnam.
                              Exeunt, marching

26–31   Cut by Nunn.

ACT 5, SCENE 3

Enter MACBETH, DOCTOR, *and Attendants*

MACBETH   Bring me no more reports, let them fly all;
　　　　　Till Birnam Wood remove to Dunsinane,
　　　　　I cannot taint with fear. What's the boy Malcolm?
　　　　　Was he not born of woman? The spirits that know
　　　　　All mortal consequences have pronounced me thus:　　5
　　　　　'Fear not, Macbeth, no man that's born of woman
　　　　　Shall e'er have power upon thee.' Then fly false thanes
　　　　　And mingle with the English epicures;
　　　　　The mind I sway by and the heart I bear
　　　　　Shall never sag with doubt nor shake with fear.　　10

Enter SERVANT

　　　　　The devil damn thee black, thou cream-faced loon.
　　　　　Where got'st thou that goose-look?
SERVANT   There is ten thousand –
MACBETH　　　　　　　　　　　　Geese, villain?
SERVANT　　　　　　　　　　　　　　　　Soldiers, sir.
MACBETH   Go prick thy face and over-red thy fear,
　　　　　Thou lily-livered boy. What soldiers, patch?　　15
　　　　　Death of thy soul, those linen cheeks of thine
　　　　　Are counsellors to fear. What soldiers, whey-face?

0 SD   *Enter* . . . Macready entered reading a letter which he immediately tore up and threw off the
　　　stage (Downer, *Macready*, p. 335).
4b–7a   ('The spirits . . . upon thee') Cut by Garrick.
9–10   Cut by Nunn.
10 SD   Nunn's Servant was a boy.
11a   ('The devil . . . black') Cut by Garrick.
16–17a   ('Death . . . fear') Cut by Nunn.
17b   'Mcb cuts boy. Boy lifts hand to face covered in blood' (Nunn, Promptbook). 'The trick by
　　　which a knife, drawn across an actor's skin, produces a stream of apparent blood was used
　　　[in Nunn's 1976 staging] . . . when Macbeth, with "Go prick thy face and over-red thy fear",

SERVANT The English force, so please you.

MACBETH Take thy face hence!

[Exit Servant]

Seyton! – I am sick at heart,

When I behold – Seyton, I say! – this push   20

Will cheer me ever or disseat me now.

I have lived long enough. My way of life

Is fall'n into the sere, the yellow leaf,

And that which should accompany old age,

As honour, love, obedience, troops of friends,   25

I must not look to have; but in their stead,

Curses, not loud but deep, mouth-honour, breath

Which the poor heart would fain deny, and dare not.

Seyton!

Enter SEYTON

SEYTON What's your gracious pleasure?

MACBETH   What news more?   30

SEYTON All is confirmed, my lord, which was reported.

MACBETH I'll fight till from my bones my flesh be hacked.

Give me my armour.

SEYTON 'Tis not needed yet.

MACBETH I'll put it on;   35

Send out more horses; skirr the country round.

Hang those that talk of fear. Give me mine armour.

How does your patient, doctor?

actually applied his dagger to the cheek of the "lily-livered boy" who reports the sighting of Malcolm's army' (David, *Theatre*, p. 89).

29 SD *Enter* . . . Charles Kean brought on the Doctor with Seyton.

37 Garrick and Macready brought the Doctor on here and not at the opening of the scene.

38a John Foster Kirk, who once played the Doctor, describes how Macready acted in this episode: 'Macready, at my entrance, left the attendants . . . and, striding across the stage with a step that seemed to shake the boards, stationed himself so near me that all the lines in his face appeared to be magnified, like those of a picture to the close gaze of a short-sighted man. In tones that sounded like thunder [he demanded], "How does your patient, doctor?" . . . On receiving my disclaimer of . . . power, he turned his back upon me . . . and strode back to have his armour buckled on, turning, in the intervals of his stormy chidings, to direct some inquiry or splenetic remark to me, and at last rushing off to meet the approaching foe' (Sprague, *Actors*, p. 273).

DOCTOR   Not so sick, my lord,
          As she is troubled with thick-coming fancies
          That keep her from her rest.
MACBETH   Cure her of that.   40
          Canst thou not minister to a mind diseased,
          Pluck from the memory a rooted sorrow,
          Raze out the written troubles of the brain,
          And with some sweet oblivious antidote
          Cleanse the stuffed bosom of that perilous stuff   45
          Which weighs upon the heart?
DOCTOR   Therein the patient
          Must minister to himself.
MACBETH Throw physic to the dogs, I'll none of it.
          Come, put mine armour on; give me my staff. –
          Seyton, send out. – Doctor, the thanes fly from me. –   50
          [*To Attendant*] Come sir, dispatch. – If thou couldst,
                doctor, cast
          The water of my land, find her disease,
          And purge it to a sound and pristine health,
          I would applaud thee to the very echo
          That should applaud again. – Pull't off, I say! –   55
          What rhubarb, cynne, or what purgative drug
          Would scour these English hence? Hear'st thou of them?
DOCTOR Ay, my good lord; your royal preparation
          Makes us hear something.
MACBETH   Bring it after me. –
          I will not be afraid of death and bane,   60
          Till Birnam Forest come to Dunsinane,
                              [*Exeunt all but Doctor*]
DOCTOR Were I from Dunsinane away and clear,
          Profit again should hardly draw me here.   *Exit*

40a   Cut by Nunn.
49b   ('give . . . staff') Cut by Nunn.
49–57   Garrick says of this passage, 'Macbeth is greatly heated & agitated with the News of the
          English Force coming upon him – His Mind runs from one thing to another – all in hurry, &
          confusion' (*Letters*, vol. II, p. 594).
51a   ('Come . . dispatch') Cut by Nunn.
59b   '[Macbeth] rise to climb on boxes' (Nunn, Promptbook).
62–3   Cut by Garrick and Forbes-Robertson.

ACT 5, SCENE 4

Drum and colours. Enter MALCOLM, SIWARD, MACDUFF, *Siward's son*, MENTEITH, CAITHNESS, ANGUS, *and* SOLDIERS, *marching*

MALCOLM Cousins, I hope the days are near at hand
      That chambers will be safe.
MENTEITH   We doubt it nothing.
SIWARD What wood is this before us?
MENTEITH   The Wood of Birnam.
MALCOLM Let every soldier hew him down a bough,
      And bear't before him; thereby shall we shadow   5
      The numbers of our host and make discovery
      Err in report of us.
A SOLDIER   It shall be done.
SIWARD We learn no other, but the confident tyrant
      Keeps still in Dunsinane and will endure
      Our setting down before't.
MALCOLM   'Tis his main hope,   10
      For where there is advantage to be given,
      Both more and less have given him the revolt,
      And none serve with him but constrainèd things
      Whose hearts are absent too.
MACDUFF   Let our just censures

Nunn cut and rearranged this scene so that it consisted of lines 8–10 followed by lines 3–7, after which Ross, Malcolm, Angus, and Lennox shouted in turn, 'Advance the war!'

0 SD   *Enter* . . . This scene, as directed by Glen Byam Shaw, 'enacted a meeting and an alliance between Malcolm's party and the Scots rebels . . . As they had done for Duncan, trumpets and drums sound, Malcolm and his English allies enter O[pposite] P[rompt Side], the Scots P[rompt] S[ide], and, meeting center stage, Malcolm "shakes hands with Angus & Lennox, then with Menteith and Caithness". Their plans concluded, they leave together, marching to "Drums and trumpets". To the same music in 5.6, they enter as a group, now grown to twenty, with their leafy screens, and then disperse in several directions to hunt out Macbeth. Finally, in the last scene, they reassemble around Malcolm, whose position at the center of the tableau marks him as Duncan's successor as surely as do his white robes, the trumpets, and the cheers of his subjects' (Mullin, '*Macbeth* at Stratford', pp. 279–80).

Attend the true event and put we on   15
Industrious soldiership.
SIWARD   The time approaches
That will with due decision make us know
What we shall say we have and what we owe;
Thoughts speculative their unsure hopes relate,
But certain issue strokes must arbitrate.   20
Towards which, advance the war.

Exeunt, marching

16b–21   Cut by Forbes-Robertson.

ACT 5, SCENE 5

Enter MACBETH, SEYTON, *and Soldiers, with drum and colours*

MACBETH   Hang out our banners on the outward walls;
        The cry is still, 'They come.' Our castle's strength
        Will laugh a siege to scorn; here let them lie
        Till famine and the ague eat them up.
        Were they not forced with those that should be ours,   5
        We might have met them dareful, beard to beard,
        And beat them backward home.
                 A cry within of women
                             What is that noise?
SEYTON   It is the cry of women, my good lord.
MACBETH   I have almost forgot the taste of fears;
        The time has been, my senses would have cooled   10
        To hear a night-shriek and my fell of hair
        Would at a dismal treatise rouse and stir

Setting   In Irving's production the scenes alternated rapidly between the ramparts of the castle and realistic exteriors. 'Crowds of supernumeraries were skilfully manipulated, troops crossing and recrossing the stage at shorter and shorter intervals to cover scene changes and speed the pace. The scale of the movement can be guessed from the fact that 165 costumes were made for soldiers (designed in batches of 10), 115 Scottish and 50 English' (Hughes, *Shakespearean*, p. 112). Malcolm's soldiers sang off stage as they fought (to music by Arthur Sullivan). 'Simulated distance made it a kind of hum, but there was a distinct tune to it. Nothing could have been more evocative of the inevitability of Macbeth's fall' (Hughes, *Shakespearean*, p. 113).

0 SD   Nunn replaced Seyton with the Doctor.

1–2   Edmund Kean 'shouted the command in a voice like thunder. Suddenly he paused, dropped his double-handled sword to the ground and, leaning on it, whispered "The cry is still they come, they come", at the same time seeming to become ashy grey with fear, for according to him Macbeth, although spoken of early in the play as "Bellona's bridegroom", and the quintessence of bravery, had become a moral coward through having steeped himself in the murder of Duncan, Banquo and Macduff's wife and children' (Kendal, *Herself*, p. 7).

5–7a   Cut by Nunn.

As life were in't. I have supped full with horrors;
Direness familiar to my slaughterous thoughts
Cannot once start me. Wherefore was that cry?   15
SEYTON The queen, my lord, is dead.
MACBETH   She should have died hereafter;
There would have been a time for such a word.
Tomorrow, and tomorrow, and tomorrow
Creeps in this petty pace from day to day
To the last syllable of recorded time;   20
And all our yesterdays have lighted fools
The way to dusty death. Out, out, brief candle,
Life's but a walking shadow, a poor player

13b Of this half-line, Agate says, 'the actor must make the audience realize that this supper-time has been the time of the interval . . . Mr Gielgud . . . came on the stage as if he had lived the interval' (*Chonicles*, p. 227).

15a 'Macbeth looks at his right hand to see it shake' (Nunn, Promptbook).

16a 'Drops his baton' (Phelps, Promptbook). 'Macbeth drops his battle axe. All express sorrow' (Charles Kean, Promptbook).

16b–17 When Kemble spoke these lines 'he seemed struck to the heart; gradually collecting himself, he sighed out, "She should have died hereafter!", then, as if with the inspiration of despair, he hurried out, distinctly and pathetically, the lines ['Tomorrow . . . signifying nothing'] . . . rising to a climax of desperation that brought down the enthusiastic cheers of the closely-packed theatre' (Macready, *Reminiscences*, vol. 1, p. 148). According to Hazlitt, Kemble's 'action in delivering the speech "Tomorrow and tomorrow" was particularly striking and expressive, as if he had stumbled by an accident on fate, and was baffled by the impenetrable obscurity of the future' (*Examiner*, 16 June 1816, p. 379). Macready began the speech 'slowly and haltingly at first, conveying the agony of his mind; then as if struck with the thought which follows, he goes rapidly through the famous passage. There is no excitement in the reading, only a withering calm, a controlled agony. His voice is chill with despair, his look blank and desolate' (Downer, *Macready*, p. 336). Irving expessed 'nothing but dull indifference in his elegy on his wife's death, emended to begin, "She *would* have died hereafter." Here Irving wrote, "she'd have died another time, if not now"; after all, he had long since ceased to care for her or for any living soul beside himself' (Hughes, *Shakespearean*, p. 113). Antony Sher, whose Macbeth was ironical and detached, concluded the speech by walking off the stage into the audience 'with a flourish of disdain' (*Observer*, 21 November 1999).

22b–7a In a letter to Garrick, a correspondent (the Rev. S. Nott) says that these lines 'pronounced by the softest voice that ever drew pity from the heart of man, I well remember to have affected me beyond expression' (*Correspondence*, vol. 1, p. 377).

That struts and frets his hour upon the stage
And then is heard no more. It is a tale   25
Told by an idiot, full of sound and fury
Signifying nothing.

Enter a MESSENGER

Thou com'st to use thy tongue: thy story quickly.
MESSENGER Gracious my lord,
I should report that which I say I saw,   30
But know not how to do't.
MACBETH   Well, say, sir.
MESSENGER As I did stand my watch upon the hill
I looked toward Birnam and anon methought
The wood began to move.
MACBETH   Liar and slave!
MESSENGER Let me endure your wrath if't be not so;   35
Within this three mile may you see it coming.
I say, a moving grove.
MACBETH   If thou speak'st false,
Upon the next tree shall thou hang alive
Till famine cling thee; if thy speech be sooth,
I care not if thou dost for me as much.   40

27 SD Nunn's Messenger was Seyton.

34b   Rowe here has the stage direction, '*Striking him*', and Garrick, on hearing that Birnam Wood
      had begun to move, struck the Messenger on the arm with his truncheon. Macklin seized
      the Messenger's arm and bent him down to the ground (Sprague, *Actors*, p. 275). Kemble
      strongly objected to the stage direction on the grounds that it was 'irreconcileable to
      Macbeth's emotions at the moment' (*Macbeth and Richard*, pp. 110–11). He himself
      'staggered' and could barely say the words 'Liar and slave!' (Macready, *Reminiscences*,
      vol. I, p. 148). 'Here Mr Forrest . . . exhibited a most lusty despair, for at the close of these
      words he lifted the unfortunate officer bodily from the ground and fairly flung him off the
      stage' (Forster, *Dramatic Essays*, p. 37). In Irving's 1888 production, three soldiers stared in
      through the door 'in a peeping attitude, with fright in their eyes' while their comrade
      delivered the news to Macbeth (Brereton, *Irving*, vol. II, p. 147). Olivier seized the
      Messenger and threw him to the floor. '[Olivier's] picking up the Birnam messenger and
      carrying him off the stage was absurd' (Crosse, *Playgoing*, p. 102).

37b–40 Macklin delivered the first part of this speech 'in a tone and look of such terrible menace as
      almost petrified the audience; while in the last line [40] he fell into such an air of
      despondency, as showed the effect of contrast in a most masterly manner' (Cooke, *Macklin*,
      pp. 285–6).

I pull in resolution and begin
To doubt th'equivocation of the fiend
That lies like truth. 'Fear not, till Birnam Wood
Do come to Dunsinane', and now a wood
Comes toward Dunsinane. Arm, arm, and out!   45
If this which he avouches does appear,
There is nor flying hence nor tarrying here.
I 'gin to be aweary of the sun
And wish th'estate o'th'world were now undone.
Ring the alarum bell! Blow wind, come wrack;   50
At least we'll die with harness on our back.

                                        Exeunt

41   '[Macbeth] grabs doll & talks to it' (Nunn, Promptbook).

42   'Puts 4 boxes from U[p] S[tage] L[eft] into C[entre] under light. Puts 5th box with sword on top. Climbs onto top & takes lamp [the light hanging from the ceiling] shines it D[own] S[tage] L[eft] at doll. Drops doll' (Nunn, Promptbook).

ACT 5, SCENE 6

Drum and colours. Enter MALCOLM, SIWARD, MACDUFF, *and their army, with boughs*

MALCOLM Now near enough; your leafy screens throw down
              And show like those you are. You, worthy uncle,
              Shall with my cousin your right noble son
              Lead our first battle. Worthy Macduff and we
              Shall take upon's what else remains to do,   5
              According to our order.
SIWARD   Fare you well.
              Do we but find the tyrant's power tonight,
              Let us be beaten if we cannot fight.
MACDUFF Make all our trumpets speak; give them all breath,
              Those clamorous harbingers of blood and death.   10

                                    Exeunt

                 Alarums continued

0 SD   *Enter . . .* In Macready's staging, 'the flats withdraw and show the entire depth of the stage, at the back a set scene of wooded hills. Malcolm appears to be alone on the stage, standing in a thicket. Four trumpets sound, one after the other, from the front to the back of the stage. At Malcolm's command, the trees suddenly disappear, becoming five officers and eighteen soldiers. At the same moment, the carpenters release a series of flaps on the set piece. The painted trees vanish and the hills are seen to be alive with (painted) soldiers' (Downer, *Macready*, p. 337). Macready was praised for his handling of this scene: 'The approach of the English army . . . really was a *moving grove*, as if Birnham [*sic*] Wood had come to Duncinane [*sic*], not as heretofore, a dozen men with small branches of laurel which did not half cover their faces' (*Theatrical Observer*, 7 November 1837). Phelps's Promptbook calls for 'Troops behind openings, covered by boughs, leaves, Laurels &c' and at the opening of the scene, 'The Troops give a loud shout and discover themselves by throwing down the boughs' (Sprague, *Actors*, p. 274). Charles Kean's Promptbook says 'Trumpet call. The Boughs are thrown, and general entrance.'

2b–10   ('You . . . death') Cut by Nunn.

10   'Flourish and shout till Macbeth on [i.e. at the opening of the next scene]' (Charles Kean, Promptbook).

ACT 5, SCENE 7

Enter MACBETH

MACBETH They have tied me to a stake; I cannot fly,
　　　　　But bear-like I must fight the course. What's he
　　　　　That was not born of woman? Such a one
　　　　　Am I to fear, or none.

　　　　　　　　　　Enter YOUNG SIWARD

YOUNG SIWARD What is thy name?　　　　　　　　　　5
MACBETH Thou'lt be afraid to hear it.
YOUNG SIWARD No, though thou call'st thyself a hotter name
　　　　　Than any is in hell.
MACBETH　　　　　　　　　My name's Macbeth.
YOUNG SIWARD The devil himself could not pronounce a title
　　　　　More hateful to mine ear.
MACBETH　　　　　　　　　　　　No, nor more fearful.　　10
YOUNG SIWARD Thou liest, abhorrèd tyrant; with my sword
　　　　　I'll prove the lie thou speak'st.
　　　　　　　　　Fight, and young Siward slain
MACBETH　　　　　　　　　　Thou wast born of woman.
　　　　　But swords I smile at, weapons laugh to scorn,
　　　　　Brandished by man that's of a woman born.
　　　　　　　　　　　　Exit [*with young Siward's body*]

　　　　　　　　Alarums. Enter MACDUFF

In Macklin's manuscript notes, he comments, 'In the last act the English must have Bows &
arrows, the Scotch broad swords, pistols and targets. The fight must be so manoeuvred as
to make the Scotch seem first to defeat the English & drive them off the stage – the English
must beat them back and totally rout the Scotch. English – Scotch – English. Macbeth must
appear in the front of the battle when the Scotch drives [*sic*] the English off.'

4 SD–14SD　*Enter . . . Exit . . .* Young Siward and his death were cut by Davenant, restored by Garrick,
　　　　　and cut again by Macready, Phelps, Charles Kean, and Nunn.

13–14　Cut by Garrick.

MACDUFF That way the noise is. Tyrant, show thy face!   15
        If thou be'st slain, and with no stroke of mine,
        My wife and children's ghosts will haunt me still.
        I cannot strike at wretched kerns whose arms
        Are hired to bear their staves; either thou, Macbeth,
        Or else my sword with an unbattered edge   20
        I sheath again undeeded. There thou shouldst be;
        By this great clatter, one of greatest note
        Seems bruited. Let me find him, Fortune,
        And more I beg not.   .   *Exit*

        Alarums. Enter MALCOLM *and* SIWARD

SIWARD This way, my lord; the castle's gently rendered.   25
        The tyrant's people on both sides do fight;
        The noble thanes do bravely in the war.
        The day almost itself professes yours,
        And little is to do.
MALCOLM   We have met with foes
        That strike beside us.
SIWARD   Enter, sir, the castle.   30
                                                          Exeunt
                        Alarum

    15a   ('That . . . is') Cut by Nunn.
 18b–23a ('whose arms . . . bruited') Cut by Garrick.
   21b–3a ('There thou . . . bruited') Cut by Forbes-Robertson and Nunn.
   23b–4 ('Let me . . . beg not') 'Fortune let me find him, more I beg not' (Nunn, Promptbook).
   25–30 Cut by Charles Kean and Nunn. Nunn replaced these lines with lines 9–10 of 5.6, spoken not
          by Macduff but Malcolm.
      27 Cut by Forbes-Robertson.

ACT 5, SCENE 8

Enter MACBETH

MACBETH Why should I play the Roman fool and die
         On mine own sword? Whiles I see lives, the gashes
         Do better upon them.

Enter MACDUFF

MACDUFF   Turn, hell-hound, turn.
MACBETH Of all men else I have avoided thee,

Setting   In Macready's production, the final duel was set 'on the ramparts of the castle, with a great
iron gate in the background' (Downer, *Macready*, p. 337). Phelps's arrangement of the final
scenes were said to have been 'spirited in the extreme. The old conventional business of a
general action – a flourish of trumpets every two or three minutes, with a single combat
between, was very properly dispensed with . . . Looking through heavy Gothic balustrades,
you saw the crowds of combatants. A sally of the defenders of the castle now driving out
their besiegers; anon a fierce rally beating back the troops of Macbeth; while forth from the
mêlée, with difficulty disentangling themselves from the fighting, rushing crowd – now
Macbeth, now Macduff, now Siward, would struggle forward for a more conspicuous place'
(*Lloyd's Weekly London News*, quoted in Phelps and Forbes-Robertson, *Phelps*, p. 100). In
Irving's staging, 'The fighting was not all in sight of the audience; it seemed to be raging as
fiercely off the stage in the distance. From every angle of sight the audience could see men
fighting off the stage as well as on it. The distant clash of arms, the cries and cheers, and the
rushing on and off the stage of fighting groups gave the illusion of a great battle' (Pitou,
Masters, p. 109). In his revival of 1888, the English troops sang off stage as they fought.
'Simulated distance made it a kind of hum, but there was a distinct tune to it' (Hughes,
Shakespearean, p. 113).

4   Edmund Kean, 'with a voice choked and stifled by the various and overwhelming feelings
which assailed him . . . rushed upon Macduff with terrible impetuosity – an impetuosity and
eagerness compounded of a determination to hold out to the last, and a desire to fly for
ever from the development of those supernatural mysteries which open one after the other
to distract and destroy him' (Hawkins, *Kean*, vol. I, p. 276). In Macready's production, 'the
gates are burst open with a tremendous shout, and Macduff rushes in . . . and throws

But get thee back, my soul is too much charged   5
With blood of thine already.
MACDUFF   I have no words;
My voice is in my sword, thou bloodier villain
Than terms can give thee out.
                    Fight. Alarum
MACBETH   Thou losest labour.
As easy mayst thou the intrenchant air
With thy keen sword impress as make me bleed.   10
Let fall thy blade on vulnerable crests;
I bear a charmèd life which must not yield
To one of woman born.
MACDUFF   Despair thy charm,
And let the angel whom thou still hast served
Tell thee, Macduff was from his mother's womb   15
Untimely ripped.
MACBETH Accursèd be that tongue that tells me so,
For it hath cowed my better part of man;
And be these juggling fiends no more believed
That palter with us in a double sense,   20
That keep the word of promise to our ear
And break it to our hope. I'll not fight with thee.
MACDUFF Then yield thee coward,
And live to be the show and gaze o'th'time.

himself on guard crying, "Turn, hellhound, turn!" Macbeth tries to warn him off, but Macduff advances against him with four blows to the head; they lock swords, reverse positions, and Macbeth flings him away with an expression of ineffable contempt.' When Macduff reveals that he was 'Untimely ripped' from his mother's womb, 'the effect upon Macbeth is wondrous. Struck with utter dismay, he stands gazing upon his enemy in breathless horror as if all the sinews of his frame had relaxed at one moment' (Downer, *Macready*, p. 337). Irving seemed a 'wild, haggard, anguish-stricken man battling for his miserable existence with the frenzy of despair. He was old now; with his grizzled hair and gaunt face, "he looked like a great famished wolf"' (Hughes, *Shakespearean*, p. 113). The Macbeth in Ayliff's 1928 modern-dress production 'emptied his revolver into the charmed Macduff at point blank range, and then took to his sword with an uncomfortable effect of farce' (Styan, *Revolution*, p. 150). In Glen Byam Shaw's production, the struggle carried Macbeth and Macduff up to the highest point of the battlements, and Macduff pushed Macbeth off the battlements to his death (Mullin, *Macbeth Onstage*, p. 157).

7b–8a ('thou bloodier . . . out') Cut by Nunn.
9–10   Cut by Nunn.

>   We'll have thee, as our rarer monsters are,   25
>   Painted upon a pole and underwrit,
>   'Here may you see the tyrant.'
> MACBETH   I will not yield
>   To kiss the ground before young Malcolm's feet
>   And to be baited with the rabble's curse.
>   Though Birnam Wood be come to Dunsinane   30
>   And thou opposed being of no woman born,
>   Yet I will try the last. Before my body,
>   I throw my warlike shield. Lay on, Macduff,
>   And damned be him that first cries, 'Hold, enough!'
>   *Exeunt[,] fighting. Alarums*
>   *Enter [Macbeth and Macduff,] fighting[,] and Macbeth slain*
>   *[Exit Macduff, with Macbeth's body]*

29 Cut by Nunn.

32b–3a ('Before . . . shield') Cut by Nunn.

34 SD *Exeunt . . .* The Folio stage directions are not entirely clear here: 'Exeunt fighting. Alarums. Enter fighting, and Macbeth slain'. Then, in the next scene, Macduff enters 'with Macbeth's head'. Presumably, having killed Macbeth in Scene 8, Macduff made an exit with Macbeth's body, and returned in Scene 9 with the head. Davenant kept Macbeth on the stage and gave him a dying line, 'Farewell vain World, and what's most vain in it, *Ambition*.' Garrick went further and wrote for Macbeth a dying speech:

> 'Tis done! The scene of life will quickly close.
> Ambition's vain, delusive dreams are fled,
> And now I wake to darkness, guilt and horror;
> I cannot bear it! Let me shake it off –
> It will not be; my soul is clogg'd with blood –
> I cannot rise! I dare not ask for mercy –
> It is too late, hell drags me down; I sink,
> I sink – Oh! – my soul is lost for ever!

> (*Macbeth*, 1773, p. 69)

'[Garrick composed] a pretty long speech for Macbeth, when dying, which, though suitable perhaps to the character, was unlike Shakespeare's manner, who was not prodigal of bestowing abundance of matter on characters in that situation. But Garrick excelled in the expression of convulsive throes and dying agonies, and would not lose any opportunity that offered to shew his skill in that part of his profession' (Davies, *Miscellanies*, vol. II, p. 118). Jean Georges Noverre describes Garrick's performance of 'a tyrant' who may have been Macbeth or, more probably, Richard III: 'The approach of death showed each instant on his face; his eyes became dim, his voice could not support the efforts he made to speak his thoughts. His gestures without losing their expression revealed the approach of the last moment; his legs gave way under him, his face lengthened, his pale and livid features bore the signs of suffering and repentance . . . His plight made the audience shudder, he clawed the ground and seemed to be digging his own grave, but the dread moment was nigh, one saw death in reality, everything expressed that instant which makes all equal. In the end he expired. The death rattle and convulsive movements of his features, arms, and breast gave the final touch to this terrible picture' (*Letters*, pp. 84–5). Kemble retained Garrick's dying speech. In 1794 Charles Kemble played Macduff to his older brother's Macbeth. Macready recalled how, as Macbeth died, Charles Kemble 'received him in his arms, and laid him gently on the ground, his physical powers being unequal to further effort' (*Reminiscences*, vol. 1, p. 148). '[Macready's] closing scenes could not have been surpassed. His physical energy was terrific, and he took grandeur from the desperate mind. He turned upon Fate and stood at bay' (Marston, *Actors*, vol. 1, p. 79). Macbeth and Macduff lunged at each other five times, 'and on the sixth lunge Macduff delivers the death stab. Macbeth staggers back, catches himself, and with a momentary suggestion of his regal stride, returns, only to fall on Macduff's sword in yielding weakness. The spirit fights, but the body sinks in mortal faintness. Thrusting his own sword into the ground, Macbeth raises himself by its help to his knees where he stares full in the face of his vanquisher with a resolute and defiant gaze of concentrated majesty, hate, and knowledge, and instantly falls dead' (Downer, *Macready*, p. 338). When Phelps played Macbeth, the final fight with Macduff, says Fontane, was 'as brilliant as ever. No beating of tin shields, no victory offstage, but real, visible hacking at each other, until to the jubilation of the gallery Macbeth is defeated and the curtain falls' (*London Theatre*, p. 87). Edmund Kean's acting of this episode was said to be 'very grand', 'full of that fine contrast between fierceness and feebleness, the spirit fighting, while the body was perishing under mortal faintness, which first attracted public fame to his *Richard*, and which leave him, in these efforts, almost without a competitor' (*Times*, 7 November 1814). 'As the expiring flame burnt up brightly at the last, [Kean] aimed a final blow at his antagonist, and then fell forward on his face, "as if to cover the shame of his defeat"' (Hawkins, *Kean*, vol. 1, p. 276). The dominant impression created by Irving during the fight was of 'a wild, haggard, anguish-stricken man, battling for his miserable existence with the frenzy of despair'. At his death, 'he fell on his face, and the soldiers gathered "to execrate the prostrate tyrant in shouts". Malcolm was raised shoulder-high to a general cry of "Hail, king of Scotland" and the curtain fell' (Hughes, *Shakespearean*, pp. 113–14). 'The last we saw of Macbeth [Richardson] was his being chased off-stage by a sword-brandishing Macduff. This was more ludicrous than tragic' (*New Statesman*, 21 June 1952). In Wolfit's 1945 production the Macduff finished off Macbeth by throttling him with his bare hands (Crosse, *Playgoing*, p. 148).

ACT 5, SCENE 9

Retreat, and flourish. Enter with drum and colours, MALCOLM,
SIWARD, ROSS, *Thanes, and Soldiers*

MALCOLM I would the friends we miss were safe arrived.
SIWARD Some must go off. And yet by these I see,
       So great a day as this is cheaply bought.
MALCOLM Macduff is missing and your noble son.
ROSS Your son, my lord, has paid a soldier's debt;   5
       He only lived but till he was a man,
       The which no sooner had his prowess confirmed
       In the unshrinking station where he fought,
       But like a man he died.
SIWARD   Then he is dead?
ROSS Ay, and brought off the field. Your cause of sorrow   10
       Must not be measured by his worth, for then
       It hath no end.
SIWARD   Had he his hurts before?
ROSS Ay, on the front.
SIWARD Why then, God's soldier be he;
       Had I as many sons as I have hairs,   15
       I would not wish them to a fairer death.
       And so his knell is knolled.
MALCOLM   He's worth more sorrow,
       And that I'll spend for him.
SIWARD   He's worth no more;

Cut by Charles Kean.
1–20   Cut by Kemble, Phelps, and Forbes-Robertson.
  2   Cut by Nunn. Nunn cut this scene considerably. His text consisted of
       ROSS Enter, Sir, the castle.
       MALCOLM I would the friends we miss were safe arrived.
           Enter Macduff
       MACDUFF Hail, king, for so thou art.
         The time is free. Hail, King of Scotland.

They say he parted well and paid his score,
And so God be with him. Here comes newer comfort.   20

Enter MACDUFF, *with Macbeth's head*

MACDUFF Hail, king, for so thou art. Behold where stands
Th'usurper's cursèd head. The time is free.
I see thee compassed with thy kingdom's pearl,
That speak my salutation in their minds;
Whose voices I desire aloud with mine.   25
Hail, King of Scotland.
ALL   Hail, King of Scotland.
Flourish
MALCOLM We shall not spend a large expense of time

19–20a   Cut by Garrick.
20 SD   *Enter . . .* In Davenant's alteration, Macduff entered with Macbeth's sword but not his head.
         Garrick, having died on the stage in the previous scene, presumably remained there, and
         Macduff entered alone. Macready died on the stage and 'Malcolm and the thanes enter
         with banners and accompanying trumpet flourishes. To the general cry of "Hail, King of
         Scotland," the curtain falls' (Downer, *Macready*, p. 338) At line 26, Phelps brought on 'All
         the Forces and Macbeth's Head on a Pole borne by an Officer. 6 Flags of England and
         Scotland surrounding the head – Troops fill the Stage. Characters down R & L – Macduff up
         stage Centre pointing to head – Malcolm in Front Centre back to audience' (Promptbook).
         In Charles Kean's Promptbook there is no dialogue after Macbeth's death: 'Macbeth was
         killed upon the stage, and the tragedy was there ended, the soldiers saluting Malcolm, "Hail,
         King of Scotland, hail!" as the curtain fell' (Bede, 'Macbeth on the Stage', p. 22) Glen Byam
         Shaw in 1955 had Macbeth killed off stage, but the head was merely pointed at on an
         unseen battlement (David, 'Tragic Curve', p. 130). The 'usurper's head' was not displayed in
         Nunn's 1976 production, but Macduff simply came on with his own and Macbeth's dagger in
         either hand (David, *Theatre*, p. 87).
21b–2a   ('Behold . . . head') Cut by Garrick and Forbes-Robertson.
22–42   Davenant largely rewrote these lines. Garrick incorporated some of Davenant but restored
         the final speech from Shakespeare.
26b   'Macduff's placing of the crown upon the head of Malcolm, lifted on the shoulders of the
         soldiery, forms the *dénouement* of the tragedy' as directed by Tree (*Boston Evening
         Transcript*, 15 September 1911).
27–42   Cut by Forbes-Robertson.
27–42   In Nunn's 1976 staging, the royal robe and crown were carried away, and 'the victors, utterly
         spent in their struggle against Evil incarnate, could only sit with their heads on their breasts

Before we reckon with your several loves
And make us even with you. My thanes and kinsmen,
Henceforth be earls, the first that ever Scotland   30
In such an honour named. What's more to do
Which would be planted newly with the time, –
As calling home our exiled friends abroad
That fled the snares of watchful tyranny,
Producing forth the cruel ministers   35
Of this dead butcher and his fiend-like queen,
Who, as 'tis thought, by self and violent hands
Took off her life, – this and what needful else
That calls upon us, by the grace of Grace
We will perform in measure, time, and place.   40
So, thanks to all at once and to each one,
Whom we invite to see us crowned at Scone.
                    Flourish
                                        Exeunt
        FINIS

and their swords slumped at their sides while Malcolm, shaken and trembling, announced
his impending coronation' (David, *Theatre*, pp. 90–1).

32–8   Cut by Kemble.

INDEX

BIBLIOGRAPHY

Promptbooks. Where available (as in the case of Peter Hall's and Trevor Nunn's productions) I have used the actual promptbooks themselves in the library of the Shakespeare Centre at Stratford-upon-Avon. Otherwise I have used the microfilms reproduced in *Shakespeare and the Stage*, Harvester Press Microform Publications, n.d., reels 41–6.

Unless otherwise stated the place of publication is London.

Addenbrooke, David, *The Royal Shakespeare Company: The Peter Hall Years*, 1974

Agate, James, *Brief Chronicles*, 1945

Allen, Shirley S., *Samuel Phelps and Sadler's Wells Theatre*, Middletown, CT, 1971

Appleton, William W., *Charles Macklin: An Actor's Life*, Cambridge, MA, 1961

Archer, William, *William Charles Macready*, 1890
    Henry Irving, Actor and Manager, 1885

Archer, William, and Lowe, Robert W., '*Macbeth* on the Stage', *English Illustrated Magazine*, no. LXIII, December 1888, pp. 233–52

Armstrong, W. A., 'Actors and Theatres', *Shakespeare Survey*, vol. XVII, Cambridge, 1964, pp. 191–204

Aston, Antony, *A Brief Supplement to Colley Cibber Esq.*, 1748

Aston, Elaine, *Sarah Bernhardt: A French Actress on the English Stage*, Oxford, 1989

Barroll, Leeds, *Politics, Plague and Shakespeare's Theater*, Ithaca and London, 1991

Bartholomeusz, Dennis, *Macbeth and the Players*, Cambridge, 1978

Beauman, Sally, *The Royal Shakespeare Company: A History of Ten Decades*, Oxford, 1982

Beaumont, Francis, *The Knight of the Burning Pestle*, ed. Sheldon P. Zitner, Manchester, 1984

Beckerman, Bernard, *Shakespeare at the Globe*, New York, 1962

Bede, Cuthbert, '*Macbeth* on the Stage', *Notes and Queries*, 7th series, vol. 8, 13 July 1889, pp. 21–2

Bell, G. J., 'Mrs Siddons as Lady Macbeth', in Jenkin, Fleeming, *Papers Literary, Scientific, &c.*, ed. Sidney Colvin and J. A. Ewing, 2 vols., 1887, vol. I, pp. 45–66

A Biographical Dictionary of Actors . . . 1660–1800, ed. Philip H. Highfill Jr, Kalman A. Burnim, and Edward A. Langhams, 16 vols., Carbondale, IL, 1973–93

Boaden, James, *Memoirs of John Philip Kemble*, 2 vols., 1825
   Memoirs of Mrs Siddons, 1827

Booth, Michael R., *Victorian Spectacular Theatre*, 1981

Boswell, James, *Life of Samuel Johnson*, ed. G. B. Hill and L. F. Powell, 6 vols., Oxford, 1934–40

Braunmuller, A. R., see Shakespeare, *Macbeth*

Brereton, Austin, *The Life of Henry Irving*, 2 vols., 1908

Bridges-Adams, W., *The Lost Leader*, 1954

Brooke, Nicholas, see Shakespeare, *Macbeth*

Brown, Ivor, *Shakespeare Memorial Theatre: 1954–1956*, 1956

Bullough, Geoffrey, *Narrative and Dramatic Sources of Shakespeare*, 8 vols., 1957–75, vol. VII

Burnim, Kalman A., *David Garrick, Director*, Pittsburg, PA, 1961

Byrne, Muriel St Clare, 'Fifty Years of Shakespearian Production', *Shakespeare Survey*, vol. II, 1949, pp. 1–20
   'The Stage Costuming of *Macbeth* in the Eighteenth Century', *Studies in English Theatre in Memory of Gabrielle Enthoven*, 1952, pp. 52–64

Campbell, Thomas, *The Life of Mrs Siddons*, 2 vols., 1834

Chambers, E. K., *The Elizabethan Stage*, 4 vols., Oxford, 1923
   William Shakespeare, 2 vols., Oxford, 1930

Cibber, Colley, *An Apology for the Life of Colley Cibber, Comedian* (1740), ed. B. R. S. Fone, Ann Arbor, MI, 1968

Cole, John William, *The Life and Theatrical Times of Charles Kean*, 2 vols. (1859), 1986

Coleman, John, 'Facts and Fancies about *Macbeth*', *Gentleman's Magazine*, March 1889, pp. 218–32
   Players and Playwrights I Have Known, 1888

Coleridge, Samuel Taylor, *Table Talk*, ed. Carl Woodring, 2 vols., Princeton, 1990

Cooke, William, *Memoirs of Charles Macklin, Comedian*, 1804

Cox, John D. (ed.), *Shakespeare in Production: Much Ado About Nothing*, Cambridge, 1997

Crosse, Gordon, *Shakespearean Playgoing 1890–1952*, 1953

Cumberland, Richard, *Memoirs of Richard Cumberland*, 1806

'Theatrical Retrospectives', *The Theatrical Inquisitor*, vol. II, February
    1813
Davenant, Sir William, *Salmacida Spolia, A Masque*, 1639
    Macbeth, 1674, See Shakespeare, *Macbeth*
David, Richard, 'The Tragic Curve', *Shakespeare Survey*, vol. IX, 1956,
    pp. 122–31
    Shakespeare in the Theatre, Cambridge, 1978
Davies, Thomas, *Dramatic Miscellanies*, 3 vols., Dublin, 1784
    Memoirs of the Life of David Garrick, Esq., 2 vols., 1780
Dent, Alan, *Mrs Patrick Campbell*, 1961
Dibdin, James C., *The Annals of the Edinburgh Stage*, Edinburgh, 1888
Donoghue, Joseph W., Jr, 'Kemble's Production of *Macbeth* (1794)',
    Theatre Notebook, vol. XXI, 1966–7, pp. 63–74
Donohue, Joseph W., 'Kemble and Mrs Siddons in *Macbeth*: the Romantic
    Approach to Tragic Character', *Theatre Notebook*, vol. 22, no. 2,
    Winter 1967–8, pp. 65–86
    Theatre in the Age of Kean, Oxford, 1975
Doran, John, *Their Majesties' Servants*, 3 vols., 1888
Downer, Alan, S., *William Charles Macready, The Eminent Tragedian*,
    Cambridge, MA, 1966
Downes, John, *Roscius Anglicanus*, 1708
Dryden, John, *Selected Criticism*, ed. James Kinsley and George Parfitt,
    Oxford, 1970
Evans, Gareth Lloyd, 'Shakespeare and the Actors', *Shakespeare Survey*,
    vol. XXI, 1968, pp. 115–25
Farington, Joseph, *The Farington Diary*, ed. James Greig, 8 vols., 1922–8
Faucit, Helen, *Some of Shakespeare's Female Characters*, 1891
Finlay, John, *Miscellanies*, Dublin, 1835
Flecknoe, Richard, *A Short Discourse of the English Stage* (1664), in
    Spingarn, J. E., ed., *Critical Essays of the Seventeenth Century*, 3 vols.,
    Oxford, 1908, vol. II, pp. 91–6
Fletcher, George, *Studies of Shakespeare*, 1847
Fontane, Theodore, *Shakespeare in the London Theatre 1855–58*, trans.
    Russell Jackson, 1999
Forman, Simon, 'Booke of Plaies', in Chambers, *William Shakespeare*,
    vol. II, pp. 337–8
Forster, John, 'Forrest as Macbeth', in Forster and Lewes, *Dramatic
    Essays*, ed. William Archer and Robert W. Lowe, 1896
Foulkes, Richard (ed.), *Shakespeare and the Victorian Stage*, Cambridge,
    1986
Furness, H. H., see Shakespeare, *Macbeth*

Garrick, David, *The Letters of David Garrick*, ed. David M. Little and
George M. Kahrl, 3 vols., 1963
The Private Correspondence of David Garrick, ed. James Boaden, 2 vols.,
1831
Genest, John, *Some Account of the English Stage from the Restoration to
1830*, 10 vols., Bath, 1832
Gentleman, Francis, *The Dramatic Censor*, 2 vols., 1770
Gildon, Charles, *The Life of Thomas Betterton*, 1710
Gilder, Rosamund, 'Shakespeare in New York 1947–1948', *Shakespeare
Survey*, vol. II, pp. 130–1
Griffin, Alice, Review of *Macbeth*, *Shakespeare Quarterly*, vol. VIII, 1957,
p. 516
Harbage, Alfred, *Sir William Davenant*, Philadelphia, 1935
Hawkins, F. W., *The Life of Edmund Kean*, 2 vols., 1869
Hazlitt, William, *Dramatic Essays*, ed. William Archer and Robert W.
Lowe, 1894
Works, ed. P. P. Howe, 21 vols., 1930–4
Heywood, Thomas, *An Apology for Actors* (1612); partially reprinted in
Chambers, *The Elizabethan Stage*, vol. IV, pp. 250–4
Hill, John, *The Actor: A Treatise on the Art of Playing*, 1750
Hillebrand, Harold Newcomb, *Edmund Kean*, New York, 1933
Hodges, C. Walter, *The Globe Restored*, 1968
Hortmann, Wilhelm, *Shakespeare on the German Stage*, Cambridge, 1998
Hughes, Alan, *Henry Irving, Shakespearean*, Cambridge, 1981
Hunt, Leigh, *Autobiography*, ed. J. E. Monpurgo, 1949
Dramatic Criticism 1808–1831, ed. L. H. and C. W. Houtchens, New
York, 1949
Dramatic Essays, ed. William Archer and Robert W. Lowe, 1894
Hunter, G. K., see Shakespeare, *Macbeth*
Irving, Laurence, *Henry Irving, the Actor and his World*, 1951
James, Henry, *The Scenic Art*, ed. Allan Wade, 1949
Jones, Emrys, see Shakespeare, *Antony and Cleopatra*
Jones, Marion, 'Stage Costume: Historical Verisimilitude and Stage
Convention', in Foulkes, *Shakespeare and the Victorian Stage*
Jonson, Ben, *Works*, ed. C. H. Herford and Percy and Evelyn Simpson,
11 vols., Oxford, 1925–51
Kelly, John Alexander, *German Visitors to English Theaters in the Eighteenth
Century*, Princeton, 1936
Kemble, Frances Anne, *Journal*, 2 vols., Philadelphia, 1835
Records of Later Life, 3 vols., 1882
Notes Upon Some of Shakespeare's Plays, 1882

Kemble, John Philip, *Macbeth and King Richard the Third, an Essay*, 1817

Kendal, Dame Madge, *Dame Madge Kendal by Herself*, 1933

Kennedy, Dennis, *Looking at Shakespeare: A Visual History of Twentieth-Century Performance*, Cambridge, 1993

Kernan, Alvin, *Shakespeare, the King's Playwright*, New Haven and London, 1995

Kirkman, James Thomas, *Memoirs of the Life of Charles Macklin Esq.*, 2 vols., 1799

Knowles, James Sheridan, *Lectures on Dramatic Literature*, 1873

Larner, Christina, *Witchcraft and Religion: The Politics of Popular Belief*, Oxford, 1984

Leach, Joseph, *Bright Particular Star: The Life and Times of Charlotte Cushman*, New Haven and London, 1970

Lewes, George Henry, *On Actors and the Art of Acting*, 1875
    Dramatic Essays, see Forster, John

Lichtenberg, Georg Christoph, *Briefe aus England, 1776–8*, trans. M. L. Mare and W. H. Quarrell as *Lichtenberg's Visits to England*, Oxford, 1938

The London Stage 1660–1800, ed. W. Van Lennep, E. L. Avery, A. H. Scouton, G. W. Stone, and C. B. Hogan, 11 vols., Carbondale, IL, 1963–8

Macklin, Charles, Manuscript notes written in preparation for his *Macbeth*, enclosed in a copy of Appleton's *Macklin* in the Harvard Theater Collection; partially printed by Appleton.

Macready, William Charles, *Macready's Reminiscences and Selections from his Diaries and Letters*, ed. Pollock, 2 vols., 1875

Magnin, Edward, *Piozziana*, 1833

Manvell, Roger, 'Ellen Terry's Lady Macbeth', *The Listener*, 2 February 1967, pp. 159–61

Marston, John Westland, *Our Recent Actors*, 2 vols., 1888

Martin, Sir Theodore, *Helena Faucit*, Edinburgh and London, 1900

McIntyre, Ian, *Garrick*, 1999

Morley, Henry, *Journal of a London Playgoer* (1866), Leicester, 1974

Mullin, Michael, 'Augures and Understood Relations: Theodore Komisarjevky's *Macbeth*', *Educational Theatre Journal*, vol. 26, no. 1, March 1974, pp. 20–30; reprinted in Tardiff, vol. xx, pp. 192–7
    'Strange Images of Death: Sir Herbert Beerbohm Tree's *Macbeth*, 1911', *Theatre Survey*, vol. 17, no. 2, November 1976; reprinted in Tardiff, *Shakespearean Criticism*, vol. xx
    '*Macbeth* at Stratford-upon-Avon, 1955', *Shakespeare Studies*, vol. ix, 1976, pp. 269–82

Macbeth Onstage: An Annotated Facsimile of Glen Byam Shaw's 1955 Promptbook, Columbia, MO, 1976

Murphy, Arthur, *The Life of David Garrick Esq.*, 2 vols., 1801

Nagler, A. M., *A Source Book in Theatrical History*, New York (1952), 1959

Nicholl, Allardyce, *A History of English Drama 1600–1900*, 6 vols., Cambridge, 1955–9

Noverre, Jean Georges, *Lettres sur la Danse et sur les Ballets*, 1783; trans. Cyril W. Beaumont as *Letters on Dancing and Ballet*, 1951

Nungezer, Edwin, *A Dictionary of Actors*, New Haven, CT, 1929

Odell, George C. D., *Shakespeare from Betterton to Irving*, 2 vols. (1920), 1963

Oulton, W. C., *The History of the Theatres of London*, 2 vols., 1796

Oxberry, W., *Oxberry's Dramatic Biography*, 3 vols., 1825

Paul, Henry N., *The Royal Play of Macbeth*, New York, 1950

Pearson, Hesketh, *The Last Actor-Managers*, 1950

Beerbohm Tree, 1956

Pepys, Samuel, *Diary*, ed. Robert Latham and William Matthews, 11 vols., 1970–83

Pitou, Augustus, *Masters of the Show*, New York, 1914

Pittock, Murray, *The Invention of Scotland*, 1991

Phelps, W. May and Forbes-Robertson, John, *The Life and Life-Work of Samuel Phelps*, 1886

Planché, J. R., *Recollections and Reflections*, 1901

Playfair, Giles, *Kean: The Life and Paradox of the Great Actor*, 1950

Poel, William, *Shakespeare in the Theatre*, 1913

Pollock, Lady, *Macready as I Knew Him*, 1884

Puckler-Muskau, Prince, 'In Praise of Macready's Macbeth', rptd in A. M. Nagler, *A Source Book in Theatrical History*, New York, 1952, pp. 473–5

Robinson, Henry Crabb, *Diary, Reminiscences and Correspondence*, ed. T. Sadler, 2 vols., 1872

Robson, William, *The Old Play-goer*, 1846

Rosen, Barbara, ed., *Witchcraft*, Stratford-upon-Avon Library, vol. VI, 1969

Rosenberg, Marvin, *The Masks of Macbeth*, Cranbury, NJ, and London, 1978

Rosenfeld, Sybil, *A Short History of Scene Design in Great Britain*, Oxford, 1973

Rothwell, Kenneth, and Melzer, Annabelle Henkin, *Shakespeare on Screen*, 1990

Rowe, Nicholas, see Shakespeare, *Works*

Russell, E. R., 'Mr Irving's Interpretations of Shakespeare', *Fortnightly Review*, 1 October 1883

Scott, Sir Walter, 'The Life of John Philip Kemble', *Quarterly Review*, vol. XXXIV, 1826, pp. 196–248

Shakespeare, William, *The Works of Mr William Shakespear*, ed. Nicholas Rowe, 6 vols., 1709

Antony and Cleopatra, ed. Emrys Jones, Harmondsworth, 1977

Macbeth, a Tragedy. With All the Alterations, Amendments, Additions and New Songs, 1674 [Davenant's alteration]

Macbeth, a Tragedy, as Performed at the Theatre Royal, Drury Lane, 1773 [Garrick's text]

Shakespeare's Macbeth . . . Revised by J. P. Kemble and now first published as it is acted at the Theatre Royal in Covent Garden, 1803

Macbeth, as Performed . . . at the Royal Princess's Theatre, 1853 [Charles Kean's text]

Macbeth, as arranged for the stage by Henry Irving, 1888

Macbeth . . . as Arranged for the Stage by Forbes Robertson and Presented at the Lyceum Theatre on Saturday September 17, 1898, 1898

Macbeth, ed. H. H. Furness (New Variorum), Philadelphia, 1903

Macbeth, ed. G. K. Hunter, Harmondsworth, 1967

Macbeth, ed. Nicholas Brooke, Oxford, 1990

Macbeth, ed. A. R. Braunmuller, Cambridge, 1997

Shattuck, Charles H., *The Shakespeare Promptbooks*, Urbana, IL, and London, 1965

Shakespeare on the American Stage, 2 vols., Washington, DC, 1976–87

Shaw, George Bernard, *Our Theatre in the Nineties*, 3 vols., 1931

Siddons, J. H., *Memoirs of a Journalist*, 1873

Siddons, Sarah, *Reminiscences*, ed. William Van Lennep, Cambridge, MA, 1942

Smollett, Tobias, *Peregrine Pickle* (1751), ed. James L. Clifford, Oxford, 1964

Speaight, Robert, *William Poel and the Elizabethan Revival*, 1954

Review of *Macbeth*, *Shakespeare Quarterly*, Winter 1976, pp. 16–17

Spencer, Christopher, *Davenant's 'Macbeth' from the Yale Manuscript*, New Haven, CT, 1961

Spencer, Hazelton, *Shakespeare Improved*, Cambridge, MA, 1927

Sprague, A. C., *Shakespeare and the Actors: The Stage Business in his Plays (1660–1905)*, Boston, MA, 1945

Shakespearean Players and Performances, 1954

Stevenson, Robert Louis, 'Salvini's Macbeth', *The Academy*, 15 April 1876, pp. 366–7

Stone, George Winchester, 'Garrick's Handling of *Macbeth*', *Studies in Philology*, vol. 38, October 1941, pp. 609–28

Stone, George Winchester, and Kahrl, George M., *David Garrick, a Critical Biography*, Carbondale, IL, 1956

Styan, J. L., *The Shakespeare Revolution*, Cambridge, 1977

Tannenbaum, Samuel A., *Shakespearian Scraps and Other Elizabethan Fragments*, New York, 1933

Tardiff, Joseph C. (ed.), *Shakespearean Criticism*, Detroit, 1984–, vol. xx, 1993

Thomas, David, and Hare, Arnold, *Theatre in Europe: A Documentary History: Restoration and Georgian England, 1660–1788*, Cambridge, 1989

Thomson, Leslie, 'The Meaning of *Thunder and lightning*: Stage Directions and Audience Expectations', *Early Theatre*, vol. ii, 1999, pp. 11–24

Traister, Barbara Howard, *The Notorious Astrological Physician of London: Works and Days of Simon Forman*, Chicago, 2001

Trevor-Roper, Hugh, 'The Invention of Tradition: the Highland Tradition of Scotland', in *The Invention of Tradition*, ed. Eric Hobsbawm and Terence Ranger, Cambridge, 1983, pp. 15–41

Weiner, Albert B., 'Samuel Phelps' Staging of *Macbeth*', *Educational Theatre Journal*, vol. 16, no. 2, May 1964, pp. 122–33

Williams, Gordon, *Macbeth: Text and Performance*, 1985

Williams, Simon, *Shakespeare on the German Stage, Vol. I: 1586–1914*, Cambridge, 1990

Williamson, Audrey, *Old Vic Drama 2: 1947–1957*, 1957, pp. 163–89

Wills, Garry, *Witches and Jesuits*, New York and Oxford, 1995

Willson, D., *King James VI and I*, New York, 1956

Winter, William, *Shakespeare on the Stage*, 1st series, New York, 1911

Wood, Anthony, *The Life and Times of Anthony Wood*, ed. A. Clark, 5 vols., Oxford, 1891–1900

CPSIA information can be obtained at www.ICGtesting.com
Printed in the USA
LVOW04s1019210914

405124LV00017B/949/P